NO JOB FOR A WOMAN

Sandra Mara

POOLBEG

Published 2008
by Poolbeg Press Ltd
123 Grange Hill, Baldoyle
Dublin 13, Ireland
E-mail: poolbeg@poolbeg.com
www.poolbeg.com

1 3 5 7 9 10 8 6 4 2

A catalogue record for this book is available from the British Library.

ISBN 978-1-84223-337-5

Typeset by Patricia Hope in Sabon 10.75/15

Printed and bound in the UK by
CPI Mackays, Chatham ME5 8TD

About the Author

Sandra Mara was Ireland's first female private investigator, following in the footsteps of her father, Bill Kavanagh, who started Ireland's first detective agency in 1947. An international investigator for over twenty-five years, she acted for government agencies, multinationals, professional bodies and media outlets around the world. She was on the board of the International Security Investigation Service (ISIS), the Swiss based PI equivalent to Interpol, and was a founder member and former President of the Institute of Investigators.

Sandra was a member of numerous international organisations, including the Forensic Science Society, the World Association of Detectives (WAD), the Association of British Investigators and the Council of International Investigators. She was the recipient of several awards and was voted International Investigator of the Year by the World Association of Detectives, travelling to Singapore to accept her Award. She also won the Irish Security Association "Innovation Award" for "outstanding work in raising the standards in her specialised area".

Sandra holds a master's degree in journalism from DCU and was investigative journalist with *Magill* magazine for four years, exposing political and other scandals, such as the Donegal gardaí story. Sandra was a journalist with the *Sunday Tribune* and a contributor to *The Examiner* and *The Dubliner*, as well as numerous radio and television programmes both in Ireland and abroad. She is a regular panellist on Newstalk's *Late Night Live*.

Acknowledgements

This book would probably never have been written but for the constant nagging of family and friends who persuaded me to write about my "war stories". These stories were picked at random from my case files and are just a sample of the thousands of cases I investigated over twenty-five years of international investigation. In some instances, the names and certain details have been changed to protect the innocent – or, occasionally, the guilty. If it wasn't for those people, innocent and guilty alike, there would have been no story.

Over the years I have had the pleasure of working with some wonderful international investigators, particularly my early mentors such as my Dad, Bill Kavanagh, New York detective Irving Shumbord (my second dad), Ed Blaney (my Irish "minder" and teacher) and the many fellow investigators world-wide who imparted their knowledge and experience over the years. I particularly want to thank the members, past and present, of the World Association of Detectives (WAD) who unselfishly share their expertise with other investigators at their seminars each year. I recommend WAD most highly to investigators and their clients alike.

To my publishers, Poolbeg Press and all the team, my grateful thanks, especially my editor, Brian Langan, a true professional who made life easy for me. It was a real pleasure to work with you, not forgetting Paula Campbell and of course Kieran Devlin, who first contacted me and signed the cheque!

Finally, to my husband John – the man's a saint, as I abandoned him time and again to dig through case files, losing all track of time. Honey, I'm home! Also my daughters Sandra and Trina, and my sons Damien and Kevin, who as children occasionally unwittingly "helped me" in my investigations, as well as the very special Katie, Elissa and Daniel, who make everything worthwhile. Thanks for all your support.

This book is dedicated to the memory of my parents, who inspired me with a thirst for knowledge and the determination to find it. Despite their best efforts to discourage me from becoming a private investigator, I ignored their advice to opt for a "safe" career and did it anyway, with no regrets.

I would especially like to dedicate it to the constants in my life – my husband John, sons Kevin and Damien and my daughters Trina and Sandra, and the lights of my life, Katie, Daniel and Elissa.

Contents

1

Private Investigations – It's a Mystery to Me

As the song says, it's a mystery to me that the life of a private investigator appears glamorous to other people. What seems interesting and exciting to others was just a way of life to me. I'd been brought up with the job and knew nothing else. As I got older, I began to appreciate that something I took for granted really *was* different and, with hindsight, at times exciting, although back then I didn't give it a second thought. It was certainly very challenging and rewarding, both financially and in the satisfaction gained through resolving people's problems, whether business or personal.

Although I eventually came around to the idea of writing a book on the life and files of a female "private eye", life got in the way, as it does. To my surprise, writing this book was a mixture of hard work, enjoyment, reflection and revelation, as I revisited long-forgotten memories, picking through case files and dusting off photographs. It brought laughter and tears for all the funny, sad, happy and gratifying moments given to me by the vast array of people who passed through my life on the way to this book.

As a child growing up, I often heard my father say he would write a book about his career as Ireland's first-ever private eye – he started the first detective agency in Ireland back in 1947. I always believed that he should, as his stories were really interesting, exciting and very glamorous. He was both innovative and adventurous, working world-wide as a PI, based in an Ireland of a very different era, at a time when most people wouldn't have believed such a profession even existed. This was a great advantage to him in his work.

He thought time was on his side to write his memoirs – he'd do it "someday", he used to say. Sadly "someday" never came. He died from lung cancer in his early sixties. Like all the best movie detectives, he always had a cigarette between his lips – even at the end. His stories are, for the most part, lost in the mists of time, although I still have a lot of his files and a great deal of memories. He had some fascinating tales to tell – those that could be told, that is, as I learned from my own experiences, having had many cases of "truth being stranger than fiction".

Although I have been writing professionally for over ten years, I never got around to writing my own "war stories". I finally succumbed to friends, family and on occasion, even foe, telling me to "write that book". I hope it will give you an insight into a very different side of Irish life. I've included one or two from my father's files. I can't take the credit (or blame) for it all; I'm sure the old man did a bit of "ghost writing" while I burned the midnight oil – he always did have a wry sense of humour!

For me, the job of being a PI was very rewarding in so many ways, though there were times when I asked myself,

"Why the hell am I doing this?" The times spent on surveillance in the freezing cold in the middle of nowhere, stuck on what turned out to be an eighteen-hour surveillance without a chance of relief . . . of *any* kind. Thank God, I had a well-trained bladder. All part of the glamour of being a PI!

Writing this book has answered that "why am I doing this?" question time and time again. For one thing, without it, I probably wouldn't have had the opportunity to travel the world at other people's expense! Now, even with hindsight, I know I wouldn't have swapped my job then with anyone. The adrenaline when a difficult case is solved, and the frustration when things don't come together, are all part of a day's work; but then I suppose that could apply to most jobs.

My children also grew up with the investigation business, just as I had, and knew no better. It is only now, when I recall certain events, that I think I must have been mad! Take the time I was about to go into a bank on routine business and found an armed robbery in progress. I'd left my daughter Trina, who was only about five or six at the time, in the car outside, something you couldn't do today. As the raiders pushed past me on their way out, I recognised one as Mario Felloni, the son of the notorious Tony Felloni, a career criminal, and his wife Anne Flynn, both of whom have numerous convictions – not all religious. Tony Felloni had done time in jail for drug and other serious offences and is currently serving a twenty-year sentence.

Racing the short distance back to the car, I was amazed to find that my daughter had noticed a "suspicious" red car parked nearby and had written down the number. She'd even drawn a "sketch" – in her own childish way – of the driver, who was wearing a black wig! I stupidly (with hindsight) gave chase and spotted the gang as they abandoned the car in a laneway. I called the police and gave them the details. They were caught, convicted and spent time in Mountjoy Jail for their trouble. I thought nothing of it, nor did my daughter. It was only years later, when I looked back at those times, that I realised it wasn't a "normal" response of a mother to the experience – but for me, back then, it was exactly that.

Tony Felloni and other members of his family came to media attention again later on, following numerous convictions for drug trafficking. A quarter of a million pounds was seized from the unemployed Felloni, who was one of Ireland's biggest heroin dealers for over two decades and no stranger to jail. Two of his children, Regina and Luigi, also got jail sentences. The Fellonis held substantial sums in banks, building societies and post offices, north and south of the border, as well as over £250,000 in cash and £19,000 in sterling bank drafts found at their home, at a time when Felloni owed Dublin Corporation rent arrears of £8,000.

Felloni, known as King Scum, received the longest-ever drug-related sentence at the time and had his appeal turned down by the judge, who said that the then fifty-six-year-old gangster was a career criminal who had continued to deal in heroin while on bail. The judge ordered that property, cars and other assets seized were to go to the State.

The judge was right; crime *was* a way of life for him and his family. I recall my mother, who worked in the business, telling me that Anne Flynn, Felloni's wife, had stopped her in Dublin city centre years previously. Pushing a pram, she pointed to her new baby and said: "Take a good look at him; he's your next customer!" Obviously she was planning a family crime empire even then!

That encounter with the Fellonis wasn't the only time my children were involved in my job, through no fault of their own. On more than one occasion, I had twenty-four-hour police protection at home as a result of serious threats to my life, following successful investigations and prosecutions. My children took it in their stride and even joked about it – it was just "Mam's job". On some occasions, they came to "work" with me, just as I had done with my dad. They gave me "cover" for certain types of routine investigations and were at no risk. Who would think a woman out with her kids was a PI on the job? A case of history repeating itself.

Unlike me, they never had any desire to go into the business. By the time they had grown up, they wanted "normal lives" and, I have to say, I agreed with them. I only realised it when one day I phoned home from Nassau Street, in Dublin. It was a bad line and my eldest daughter caught the word "Nassau". She immediately assumed I was in the Bahamas, because I was always away somewhere on a case! It was then that it hit me: perhaps my father had been right after all – it was no job for a woman, at least not one with a young family!

Surrounded by the world of private investigation, the intrigue, the mysteries, the heartache of many clients – whether it was a missing family member, a family law issue, organised crime, major fraud, drugs, danger and deception, not to mention threats to my life – I was always busy with new challenges. I was never afraid – possibly foolishly so, particularly in the times in which we live – but I truly never believed I would come to any serious harm. It is only since I left the business for journalism that I can look back and see that it was anything but a normal lifestyle.

2

My First Case . . . Kind of

My first memory of being directly involved in an investigation was when I was just nine years old. It happened by accident.

We lived in Dublin, but my father's work took him all over Ireland and abroad. Sometimes he would take me with him on country jobs, probably as a cover – who would suspect that a man out with his young daughter was actually investigating something, especially in those days? PIs were only on television and *they* were all in America. Ireland didn't *have* any private detectives, did it?

My dad had a lot of business around the country in relation to his security contracts with companies such as Waterford Crystal or Shannon Diamond and Carbide and other international businesses operating in the Shannon Free Zone. On one particular trip to Limerick, he took me with him and we stayed, as always, in the National Hotel, now long since gone. I remember with great fondness Jimmy, the head porter, who always looked after me, keeping an eye on me in case I got up to mischief.

I had a friend in Limerick, Mamie, with whom I spent many happy hours playing. Mamie was the granddaughter of a former Lady Mayoress of Limerick and she lived with her parents and grandmother in their pub next door to the National Hotel. The bar was unique in Limerick and probably anywhere else. It had neither a licence nor beer and served only tea or spirits – despite which, it was always busy. For the locals who dropped in for a chat and a jar, it was the centre of information on the "goings-on" in Limerick at the time.

One evening as Mamie and I played, I overheard my dad say he was looking for an old lady from Limerick, who was unknowingly an heiress to a fortune. Unnoticed, I listened with great interest, taking in every word. I knew my father was a private detective but I'd never thought about what exactly it was that he did. I was too young to be interested in the articles about him in magazines and newspapers and never listened to him on radio or television. He was just my dad. But listening to that conversation was the first time that I ever remember being conscious of his job and, suddenly, it sounded exciting – like something from a television show. I didn't realise that, for him, it was just run-of-the-mill.

I was consumed with the desire to find this heiress before my father did. How innocent and naïve I was! I had absolutely no idea how to go about it, and I didn't know Limerick very well, never having strayed too far from the hotel on previous visits. I knew, from what I'd overheard, that he had very little information about the woman other than her name and the fact that she'd been born in Limerick. If she was still alive, she'd have been a very old lady by then. The only other thing I remember overhearing was that her father had been in the Boer War – not that I knew what that was –

and that she was known as Ladysmith, a pet name given to her by her father after the siege of Ladysmith in South Africa.

It all seemed like a great adventure to me, especially as I was becoming bored in Limerick, which had little to entertain a nine-year-old compared to the delights of Dublin at the time. While my father was at a meeting, I slipped away from the hotel in search of the heiress, hell-bent on finding her before he realised I was missing. I obviously thought that cases like this were solved in half-an-hour, just like on television! It never occurred to me that I didn't even know her real name – just Ladysmith – and I had no idea of her surname.

I wasn't sure where to start, but from the clues I'd picked up from my dad's conversation, I headed across the city, asking any old person I came across if they'd heard of anyone called Ladysmith.

After what seemed an age, tired, footsore and very hungry, I was getting nowhere. It felt like I'd been walking for hours but, of course, at nine, I had no real sense of time. I remember eventually stopping yet another old man and asking if he'd ever heard of a woman called Ladysmith, expecting the usual answer. When he actually said "Yes", I couldn't believe it. He seemed surprised and said he hadn't heard that name in years. He told me about a young girl he'd known called "Ladysmith" Gleeson, saying he'd "courted" her many years before. Everyone knew her as "Ladysmith", he said, and even *he* had never used her real name. He talked on and on, recalling the old days and reminiscing about their time together, saying he remembered her as if it were yesterday. They'd never married because he'd thought she was "far too good" for him. They'd long ago lost touch and he didn't know if she'd ever married or had a family. After they parted, he never saw her again and, though Limerick was a relatively small place then, he had never run into her in all the years. He didn't know if she was still alive or in the area, but he did remember where she had lived over sixty years before and he wrote down the address for me.

With the innocence of a child I made my way there, asking directions along the way. I was sure that if I could find the address, she would be there waiting for me and I could give her the wonderful news of her inheritance. I finally reached the place, only to find that most of the street had been demolished. I was devastated.

Even to my childish eyes, it seemed a very poor area. The only building still standing was the local church. I was delighted to find the parish priest inside and I told him that I was looking for an old lady who used to live across the street. Without knowing why, I took care not to tell him the *real* reason I wanted to find her. I doubt if he would have believed or helped me; most likely he would have put it down to a child's over-active imagination. The kindly old priest brought me into the sacristy, took out the parish records from an old wooden cupboard and painstakingly went through them, until he found the information I was looking for. I couldn't believe my luck; he remembered the old lady as having been a life-long parishioner. The house she'd lived in had been knocked down and she'd moved to another part of Limerick, not far away.

Clutching the address, I ran all the way, stopping only to ask directions as I got nearer the street. When I finally reached the house, I banged excitedly on the door of the old tenement building. A young woman holding a baby answered the door and I asked for the old lady. Annoyed at having been disturbed by a child, she said there was an old lady living at the top of the house, but she didn't know her name. I raced up the rickety stairs two at a time, hoping it was "Ladysmith".

When I finally reached the top, out of breath, I knocked on a small garret door not much bigger than I was. An old white-haired lady opened the door. With a black shawl around her shoulders and her hair in a bun, she looked every inch the picture of the old grandmother in every fairytale. I told her my story and she looked at me with a mixture of bewilderment and amusement, not quite believing what I was saying.

Still, she invited me in and as I looked around, I noticed how small the room was. I still remember that room vividly. The single bed, a small chest of drawers, a table and a well-worn armchair seemed to be all she had. An old rug took pride of place in the centre of the room. Though sparsely furnished, it was clean as a new pin and it was clear even to a child like me that the old lady was desperately poor.

There was no sign of any luxuries, not a book nor a radio to keep her company. I hoped with all my heart, as only a child could, that she was the heiress to the fortune. I repeated my story to her and, when she realised that I was telling the truth, she sat me down and told me her story. Her father had been in the British Army and had gone off to the war. She said she barely remembered him, as he had been killed when she was just a young child. Years later, when she was older, she learned that her father's family hadn't approved of his marriage. Unlike her mother, he came from a wealthy background. After his death, his family cut off all contact with their daughter-in-law and their grandchild, "Ladysmith". Her mother was in greatly reduced circumstances after her husband's death, but she was a proud woman and never let her in-laws know that she was virtually destitute. They had no other relatives that "Ladysmith" knew of and, when her mother died, she was taken in by her mother's friend and neighbour who, despite having a large family herself, brought her up as her own daughter. But for her kindness, "Ladysmith" said she would have been sent to an orphanage. She had never married – she had been "walking out", as she put it, with a local young man but it didn't work out. She never understood why. She had lived alone and, from all appearances, in abject poverty ever since.

From what she'd told me, I was convinced I'd found my heiress. I couldn't wait to get back and break my exciting news to my Dad. I'd forgotten just how long I'd been away; time had just slipped by and I'd never given a thought to the trouble I'd be in when I got back, so enthralled was I in following the trail of the missing heiress. Stuff straight out of the *Famous Five*!

I raced all the way back to the National Hotel, stopping only now and then to ask the way. As I rushed up the steps of the hotel, I was stopped by Jimmy the porter, who said my father was "going frantic" looking for me. Jimmy broke the news to him that I was back, safe and well, and that I seemed to have had a little adventure.

When I told my father that I'd found the heiress and that her name was "Ladysmith" Gleeson, he realised I was telling the truth and that I was on to something. The person he was looking for *was* called Ladysmith Gleeson, but I didn't know that at the time. In my excitement, anxious to find her, I hadn't even heard her surname. It was remarkable good luck that I had found someone who had known her, Between my father's relief at my return and his disbelief at what I had been doing – and, more to the point, successfully doing – I got away with just a good telling-off for going missing.

11

My father was highly amused that I appeared to have actually found the missing heiress before he'd even gotten a chance to look for her, although I think he was still very sceptical at that point. He drove back to Ladysmith's house with me in tow and, following a more detailed conversation, she produced her birth certificate and other papers, which confirmed that I was right. She *was* the daughter of the dead soldier.

I was delighted that this gentle old lady could, at last, have some of the nice things in life. The legacy ensured that at least the rest of her days could be lived out in comfortable surroundings and she could indulge herself in the little pleasures so long denied her.

A successful end to "my first case", even if I didn't get a share of the fee! Little did I know that that first taste of success was to set me on a road to adventure which would last for many years to come.

3

Escape Route with a Catch

After my first foray into the world of investigations, I didn't have to wait too long before finding myself back in the middle of things yet again, but this time through no fault of my own. It happened when my parents took me to the AGM of the Association of British Investigators in the Great Western Hotel, near Paddington in London. The hotel was what was then known as a railway hotel, so called because it had a connecting staircase leading directly to Paddington Railway Station. The Great Western was one of the main hubs for the mail train, which carried mail-bags full of money orders, cheques and even cash. It was made famous when Ronnie Biggs and his gang carried out the Great Train Robbery, described as one of the most infamous British robberies of all time.

Back at the Great Western, a group of about a dozen private eyes – part of the larger group of private detectives who had gathered for the AGM – were sitting around the

13

hotel foyer, shooting the breeze. I was sitting on the arm of my father's chair as he chatted to his friends and colleagues. Relaxing over a quiet drink, they were discussing the day's business, when suddenly, without warning, the armchair overturned and I was thrown to the ground. Shocked, I looked on in amazement as my father raced up the hotel staircase, followed by other members of the group. I heard him shout out, "Seal all the exits", but I had no idea what was going on. I realised something was up when several British Railway policemen burst into the hotel, shouting and gesturing. They quickly followed the private detectives up the staircase in hot pursuit – but of what, I still didn't know. It soon became clear there'd been a robbery on the railway.

In the excitement, everyone had forgotten about me as I hung around the foyer, while my mother and the other wives talked excitedly about what was happening, their eyes firmly pinned on the staircase. As I looked around, I noticed a man acting strangely. He seemed to be trying to hide behind a large column in the hotel lobby and I was curious. I noticed an open door that led out onto the street and it looked like he was slowly edging towards it. He saw me but didn't pay me too much attention – I was only a kid. I was certain it was the man everyone was looking for, but I had no time to tell anyone as he would have been gone by then. I took my chance and casually walked towards the door. I closed it and stood firmly in front of it.

The thief obviously felt no threat from a young child walking towards him. In fact, he probably thought I'd be a good "cover" for him. He casually walked towards the exit, trying to bluff it out by asking me what all the noise was about. Before he could make his getaway, I shouted out – I can't remember what exactly, but it was loud enough to draw attention and rattle him. In one swift movement he ran away from where I was standing, up a back staircase and out of my view. My shouts and agitated pointing towards the stairs led the chase to divert back up the staircase, much to my amusement. It was like something out of a *Carry On* film as the thief ran in and out of various rooms and corridors looking for a way out, but in vain.

At one point, he tried to get out onto a window ledge, but was spotted by a policeman keeping watch outside. The terrified thief quickly retreated and tried to find another escape route in the rabbit warren of a hotel. On and on the chase continued, with my father, Bill Kavanagh, and a Scottish detective, John Grant, chasing the man through the kitchens, out onto a flat roof and from there to a fire escape, where he managed to gain access to another area of the hotel.

As he tried to make his getaway, my father and John Grant finally caught up with the thief who put up a determined fight, to no avail. They recovered the stolen mailbag, packed with money in registered letters, cheques, postal orders and bank drafts, which he'd hidden in the hotel. Not quite the £10 million Ronnie Biggs had managed but nonetheless a substantial sum at the time.

The daring duo of Kavanagh and Grant PIs brought the hapless thief back downstairs and handed him into the custody of the waiting police. Surrounded by admiring hotel guests and staff, they got a round of applause and a great fuss was made of them. It certainly gave everyone something to talk about for the rest of the conference.

The bungling robber later pleaded guilty at Marylebone Magistrates Court. He didn't have much choice really, did he? Talk about being caught red-handed! Convicted, he was sentenced to a jail term, having had a long and, up to then, relatively successful criminal career behind him. His luck had run out when he picked the wrong day to rob a train and attempt an escape via the only hotel in England that was hosting a Private Detectives' Convention. A case of the not-so-great train robbery!

Inspector Lee of the British Railway Police wrote to my father thanking him for his assistance and he made a special mention of the help I'd given in spotting the thief before he made his getaway through the forgotten open door. I'd only had a very small role in this adventure, but I felt very important at the time, as would any youngster. My father wasn't quite so happy, however, and although proud of me, he firmly barred me from getting involved in any more escapades. I was sternly warned of what might have happened had the man attempted to take me hostage. I never saw it that way and although I listened, I didn't let it get in the way of any future chances for excitement that might come my way, growing up as I did with a father who was a PI. Next time, if there was a next time, I'd keep quiet about it.

Not surprisingly, as a child I didn't appreciate the real risk I had been exposed to and it wasn't until many years later, when I had my own children and my daughter *was* taken hostage by twelve armed men during a robbery on a cash and carry warehouse on Richmond Road in Dublin (which you can read about in Chapter 7), that I realised just how he'd felt that day.

4

In God I Trust . . . All Others Pay Cash!

From the files of Bill Kavanagh, Ireland's first Private Eye

Inevitably, life's experiences, even at such a tender age, had an effect on me and helped to form my judgements, opinions and overall attitude to life, but I wasn't aware of that until I was a lot older. Because of the confidential nature of my father's job, I had no idea of his day-to-day work, nor was I terribly interested as a child, despite my earlier enthusiasm. Initially for me it was a game – a childish adventure – more than anything else. He seldom spoke about it at home, although I would see some of the high-profile stuff in the papers from time to time.

One case I do remember him talking about, albeit many years after it had happened, was one which changed his attitude to the Catholic Church. Brought up a Catholic by devout parents, his father still went to Mass and communion daily, even when in his nineties and totally blind. My father, however, was always an independent thinker, being very close to his maternal grandfather, who taught him that God was everywhere and brought him to synagogue, chapel and church, regardless of the Catholic teachings of the time, much to the displeasure of his father.

Having said that, my father's mother was a determined redhead, who stood up to the then Archbishop of Dublin, Edward Joseph Byrne, when she was told she couldn't send her son to the school of her choice. Although a primary school, it was innovative and taught science, and she wanted the best for her "bright lad". Despite her best efforts, the local parish priest refused him a place without explanation. In anger and frustration, she marched up to the Archbishop's Palace in Drumcondra and refused to leave until the Archbishop saw her – a brave act back in the Ireland of the late 1920s. Granting her a few moments of his precious time, he perfunctorily refused her request. Outraged, she drew herself up to her full four-foot-ten-inches and informed him that she was moving all her children to the nearest Protestant school with immediate effect. Funnily enough, her beloved started in her school of choice the following week!

Many years later, another Archbishop also had an effect on my father's life in a somewhat different way, when he undertook a case at the request of John Charles McQuaid, the then Archbishop of Dublin. He had several meetings with McQuaid at the Archbishop's Palace in Drumcondra, where the Archbishop outlined his requirements. As was standard practice, my father asked for confirmation of his instructions in writing, but McQuaid declined, saying he preferred not to put it in writing for fear it leaked out, making his quarry aware of his interest. He reminded my father that he was a "man of God" and said that his word should be good enough. Fees were discussed and agreed upon and McQuaid paid him a "retainer". The account would be paid in full on completion of the investigation. With a blue-chip client like the Church, there was nothing to worry about.

The Archbishop was concerned at the growing strength of the Communist Party of Ireland (CPI) and particularly the influence they appeared to be having on the young people of the country. McQuaid said he was planning to set up a diploma course for youth leaders in order to counteract the influence of the CPI. It was very much the "reds under the bed" syndrome that was then prevalent with McCarthyism in America, and the Irish Church were getting in on the act. They weren't about to allow their authority to be questioned by anyone, the attitude being, "what they have they hold".

Today, it would seem an intrusion into people's privacy and right of association, not to mention an outrage for the Church to hire private investigators to look into any organisation – but in those days the Catholic Church in Ireland had a stranglehold on the country. They were virtually the dominant "political" as well as religious organisation, dictating to the State what could be legislated for, despite Article 42.2 of the Constitution which separates Church and State, a practice constantly ignored in Ireland at the time.

The Archbishop's instructions to my father were very clear. McQuaid wanted him to minutely investigate the Communist Party of Ireland. He wanted to know everything about them, their names and addresses, their strength and numbers, their modus operandi, where, when and how they were recruiting and influencing the young and sometimes not-so-young workers of the country, where they were getting their funds and why, in particular, they appeared to be gaining support in Dublin. What he wanted was an intelligence report at a level usually done by governments. But then the Church *was* the government in all but name. McQuaid saw himself with a battle on his hands, a battle for the hearts and minds of a growing number of disaffected young Irish men and women. He feared that the Catholic Church would lose its grip if the communists were allowed to develop and promulgate their message unhindered.

Nothing was put in writing, but my father took the word of a man of the cloth, particularly such a high-profile one, and agreed to investigate the matter on his behalf. As the investigation progressed and ongoing reports were made to Dr McQuaid, he would give further instructions as to how he wanted things to move on.

Not unusually, the CPI started to feel the backlash of the Church, who were acting on the information they now had. The CPI became uneasy. They were all too aware of the might and power of the Catholic Church in Ireland at that time, the same Church that had their special position written into the Constitution and were undoubtedly a force to be reckoned with. In order to protect and preserve their position, they attempted to fight back, and the fight was a dirty one by any standards.

By then the case had been ongoing for almost two years, during which time my father received many threats to his own safety and that of others. One of his men was thrown into the river Liffey in Dublin and a seventeen-year-old lad who called to our house with a message from his father was shot in the leg. On yet another occasion, four men called to our house in the early hours of the morning, while my father was away. They banged the door down and, when my mother rushed downstairs and opened the door, thinking it was an emergency, they threatened her that her baby would be kidnapped if my father didn't back off. They left in a waiting taxi. My mother clearly identified one of these men as Dominic Behan, brother of playwright Brendan Behan.

When my father heard what had happened he was, unsurprisingly, angry. Never being a man to bow to threats, he met a fight head on. Having been a paratrooper in the Second World War, he was used to battle. This time was no different but now it was personal. He "borrowed" a hand grenade from an old friend (now long since dead), a member of the Detective Unit of An Garda Síochána, the Irish police force, who had "borrowed" it from HQ. The police had confiscated grenades and other weapons from political activists, such as IRA members, and the explosives and guns were kept under lock-and-key at Garda HQ, awaiting disposal. With the grenade in his pocket, my father made his way to the city-centre headquarters of the group behind the threats. Casually walking into their premises, he produced the hand grenade, his finger firmly gripping the pin. I can only imagine the "conversation" that ensued, but it apparently had the desired effect. They were left in no doubt as to the consequences if there were any further threats or attempts at intimidation. It ended there – no more threats were received, nor were there any further attacks on personnel or family members. The grenade was quickly returned to the Garda HQ and no one was ever the wiser . . . until now!

Throughout this time, John Charles was kept informed of these developments, and he was well aware of the dangers to which my father, his family, his men and indeed *their* families were exposed. Eventually, after more than two years, during which time McQuaid continuously sought more and more information, the investigation was finally complete. The account was drawn up and presented for payment to the Archbishop. On being handed the bill for what had been a dirty, dangerous and lengthy investigation, John Charles McQuaid, Catholic Archbishop of Dublin and self-proclaimed "man of God", promptly denied ever having instructed my father to undertake *any* investigation on his behalf. He simply refused to pay the bill!

There was little that could be done in the Ireland of the time, especially with no written instructions. Had this been his intention all along? My father, an honourable man, had taken his word, but he learned a very expensive lesson. Litigation would have been pointless then, as no solicitor or lawyer would have been prepared to go up against the might of the Church and few would have believed that the Archbishop of Dublin would tell blatant lies about the matter. Ireland in those days was in the grip of the religious mafia and only a fool would have pursued such a course of action.

My father never forgot that hard-learned lesson and, though a very Christian man, he never again held any respect for a Church fronted in Ireland by such an unprincipled representative. His life-long motto thereafter was the advice passed onto him by a long-time friend, an eminent Senior Counsel and later High Court Judge, who told him, "Get the money while the tears are in their eyes" – a very definite case of eaten bread being soon forgotten.

Of course, history has taught us that there were many ruthless, unprincipled and indeed even evil men in the Church and Ireland appears to have had more than its fair share, but today we're no longer shocked at the human frailty of priests or politicians. With revelations of Catholic bishops and priests fathering children, misappropriating church funds or abusing children in their care, Ireland has grown up quickly. Today, such an action by a prominent Church leader would not surprise even the most trusting. Our childish innocence and trust in the Church is gone forever.

5

Undercover in the Glasgow Gorbals

From the files of Bill Kavanagh, Ireland's first Private Eye

The Gorbals, Glasgow's hell on earth, always had a reputation for being a rough place by any standards and the 1960s were no different. With huge tracts of tenements, high unemployment and all the usual social problems, crime was rife and virtually a way of life for most of its residents.

Everything from petty theft to major gang warfare was commonplace and it was described as one of the darkest, most dangerous places in Europe at the time, making Ireland's infamous "animal gang" look like pussycat territory. Notorious for murders, stabbings and open-razor fights, the rat-infested tenements, which oozed poverty, disease and hardship, were home to over 90,000 people at the time. The Gorbals were notorious, as the heavy-drinking, hard-living, scar-faced "bampots" put the fear of God into friend and foe alike. They thought nothing of flashing a cut-throat razor – and using it – at some perceived slight. Even the "polis" – the Scottish police force – considered it a no-go area. It was the wild-west of Glasgow and the hard men had to be meaner and more ruthless than anyone else to survive. They ruled by fear and nothing was out of bounds. They'd slit your throat for a few bob, or just because they didn't like the look of you. Living amongst these throngs of humanity were many "ordinary decent people" trying to keep their heads down, just scratching a living and trying to survive their lot.

It was into this den of vice, deprivation, gangland turf wars, stabbings and murders, that my father Bill Kavanagh found himself in the early 1960s. With the close connections between Ireland and Scotland, there were always investigation cases going back and forth and he'd worked with a few close Scottish colleagues, including John Grant of Grant and McMurtrie (who featured in the "not-so-great" train robbery at the detectives' convention in London), Sid Miller's Scottish Bureau of Investigation and a number of other Scottish investigators – many of whom were ex-coppers.

It all started out when one of his Scottish colleagues asked him to help with an investigation. They needed a very experienced investigator who wasn't afraid to go undercover in a difficult and dangerous case. Their problem was that the Scottish investigators were well-known locally as ex-coppers or PIs and, at best, would get nowhere, their cover blown, or at worst, they'd be found at the bottom of the Clyde. Never one to turn down a challenging job after his paratrooper adventures, my father readily agreed, knowing that if he managed to infiltrate the gang, he would be away for several weeks. If found out, he'd either be spending a long time in hospital – if he was lucky – or shipped home in a box. Naturally, he didn't tell my mother what he'd agreed to, just that he was doing a job in Scotland. There was no point in worrying her over something that might never happen!

His cover was that he was an Irish criminal on the run, part of a gang that had carried out a big heist in Ireland, and he needed to lie low for a while. It was easy enough in those days to move between Ireland and Scotland and he had plenty of experience in "handling" cons, fraudsters, thieves and hard men in his own town. He knew how they operated and the approach to take. He turned up in a local pub frequented by the gang but made no approach to them. He never looked in their direction or tried to engage them in conversation. Their curiosity eventually got the better of them and they joined him, trying to "suss" him out. During the conversation, he dropped the name of a well-known "hard man", one of their own then "doing time". They warmed to him and they all had "a few jars" together.

He took things slowly, not asking any questions or prying into "their business", cracking jokes and generally integrating into their company over the following days. Eventually he said he had to move on as things were getting "a bit hot" for him; he was afraid the Irish cops would be on to him if he hung around for too long. It didn't take much persuasion for them to get him to lie low at their place. "Their place" was a dingy Gorbals tenement; the entrance stairway stank of human excrement that pervaded the entire block and sometimes even ran down the stairwell, but it was a "safe house" – a no-go area for the cops.

After a couple of weeks, he had the inside track on the recent big job they'd pulled, as they boasted how they'd gotten away with a jewellery heist worth thousands of pounds, which they planned to fence as soon as things cooled down. They even let him in on the fact that the local pub, a well-known dive that was the haunt of prostitutes, pimps and hard-men, kept their "stash" in the cellar and gave them drink on the slate against their future "earnings". While he was "lying low", they pulled another job. It was a wages snatch from a large industrial employer and they even "invited" him along, but he made his excuses and declined. After the "job", they brazenly returned to the tenements to count "their" money, in the belief they were safe there.

Meanwhile, information on their activities was being passed back to the Scottish agents in hurried phone calls from telephone boxes scattered across the city. Surveillance was also maintained on the gang's activities, to ensure that direct evidence was obtained. Within hours of the wages snatch, their no-go area was raided by Scotland's finest. As they broke down the door of the flat, there was a mad scramble to get rid of the money, aided and abetted by my father, who had to maintain his cover. The gang rushed in all directions, throwing it on to the fire and getting rid of it any way they could. It was no use – they were all arrested, my father amongst them by prior arrangement so as not to blow his cover and to ensure that he stayed alive and in one piece. They were all taken to the local "polis" station and later to court, where my father was "rearrested" before the case was heard, supposedly on foot of a warrant from the Irish police.

That was the last time the Gorbals gang saw him. As far as they were concerned, he had been taken back to Dublin to serve his time. The only "time" he served was at the party held in Glasgow to celebrate the successful "sting" operation.

After a month or so "on the run", my dad came home safe and sound. My mother was none the wiser as to what he'd been up to and it was a long time before he eventually told her. The boys all dined out on that story at every PI convention for many years.

6

Bing, Burton, Brynner . . .

From the files of Bill Kavanagh, Ireland's first Private Eye

Despite being kept at arm's length from the action, I still got to travel with my parents from time to time and indeed my dad was often happy to use me as "cover" for the usual reasons.

Over the years, I got to see all parts of Ireland and very many other countries, and on the way I met many famous people. Sometimes they were clients of my father or on occasion he was hired by their lawyers, a film studio or an agent to look after their interests, undertake an investigation or provide personal security for them. I met stars and entertainers from all walks of life – people like Bing Crosby, Joan Crawford, Pele, George Best, Robert Mitchum, Yul Brynner and Princess Grace, who visited Ireland from time to time in a private capacity, as her family were from Mayo.

Princess Grace and her husband Prince Rainier came to Ireland in July 1965 to attend the Bal de Petit Lit Blanc. The biggest and most glamorous event ever seen in Ireland, it was a private function held over three days in Powerscourt. The

Gardaí were responsible for their personal security, while my father provided security for the ball, having a huge number of uniformed and plainclothes male and female staff on duty.

Monaco's Consular General in Ireland, Lord Killanin (Michael Morris) was worried that the 600 wealthy guests would attract international criminals to the rich pickings. Killanin wasn't wrong, as my father's staff caught a number of would-be thieves attempting to steal valuable silver and other items from Powerscourt, not to mention some of the many mink coats on show on the night. The Princess thanked my father personally for his attention to detail and later sent him and my mother a piece of Waterford Crystal for his efforts.

Ironically, in 1982 I was in Monaco on a case and was actually outside the Palace on 14 September when the news came through that Princess Grace had been killed in a car accident. There was an air of total disbelief and shock, not unlike the death of Princess Diana in 1997.

I wasn't in awe meeting these people; I took it in my stride, as would most young children, not realising they were famous stars. To me they were just ordinary people and it never even occurred to me to get their autograph, although many years later my own young daughter *did* ask George Best for his autograph!

Liz Taylor and Richard Burton

I met Liz Taylor and Richard Burton when he was making *The Spy Who Came in from the Cold* in Dublin, based on the novel by John le Carré. Le Carré was actually a former spy, David Cornwell, who was writing from personal experience. His book was so successful that he gave up spying and became a writer.

I remember my father saying how upset Liz was during her time here, not only because of her apparent insecurity but because she suffered a number of misfortunes in Dublin. Her chauffeur-driven car knocked down and killed a woman, which left Liz in a state of shock, added to which over £17,000 (€125,000 today) worth of jewellery was stolen from her city centre hotel room while she was on the film set. It was a fortune at the time, particularly in Ireland which was not exactly a wealthy country back then, but it still paled against Burton's fee for the film – a cool $750,000! Following investigations, my dad managed to recover some of the smaller pieces for her, which had been stolen by a small-time gang who "got lucky" knowing the hotel room she was in; but most of the items were never found.

My dad took me along to see the film being shot on location in Smithfield, Donabate, the North Strand and Dublin Zoo, as well as at Ardmore Studios, as his company provided security both on the set and for the stars. Liz Taylor was visiting the set at the time – probably to keep an eye on the womanising Burton as, despite still being newly-weds, she was reputed to be very jealous. When I was introduced to her, she was very nice to me and raved about my long red hair, as only an actress could. Before I left, she called me over and gave me a beautiful small gold "yellow rose" brooch which I treasured for many years. I didn't think about it at the time, but later I wondered if it was because my father had managed to recover some of her jewellery.

Bing Crosby

Bing Crosby was another of my dad's clients. They first met back in 1949 when Crosby was working on the film *Top o' the Morning*, a comedy set around the theft of the Blarney

Stone. Crosby was cast in the lead role as Joe Mulqueen, a "singing" insurance investigator. Bill and Bing seemingly hit it off and remained friends, with the real investigator providing security and investigations services for him whenever he needed them.

I met Bing Crosby several times as a child and remember being allowed to join his party at the races, when he was a guest of the American Ambassador, Grant Stockdale, and his wife. It was my first time at a race meeting and my dad introduced me to Bing, who was very nice to me and even gave me a tip for a horse he fancied called Santiago. With all the confidence of the young, I put all my pocket money on it and was thrilled when it came in at five to one. I overheard them talking about a party that night and although quite a young child I automatically assumed I'd be invited. I wasn't disappointed as, accompanied by my parents, we attended a small gathering at the American Ambassador's residence in the Phoenix Park. I spent most of the time "playing" with Sally Stockdale, the Ambassador's daughter. Although she was much older than me and unlikely to be interested in a kid, she got the short straw and had to look after me that night. It wasn't until years later that I realised how kind they'd been in allowing me to be there at all.

Stockdale later allegedly committed suicide by jumping from a fourteenth-floor window. There were grave doubts that he'd killed himself – his death was believed to have been a mafia "hit" made to look like suicide. In an innocent Ireland, I'm sure people had no idea about the seedy side of American life, but in his short time in Ireland as American Ambassador, he brought it all that little bit closer to a green – in every sense of the word – Ireland. Little did I know then, as a child, the darker side of the American Ambassador, who allowed a little girl to be part of the party.

Joan Crawford

Joan Crawford also brings back memories for an entirely different reason. My father was retained by her and had to meet her every day during her stay in Dublin. I remember meeting her somewhere with my father and when he introduced me to her, she made a huge fuss of my dog, while barely acknowledging my existence. It didn't bother me; I just assumed she loved dogs. She was staying in the Gresham Hotel in Dublin and after one or two meetings with her, my father began to take me along with him. I never thought anything of it at the time, but I have memories of her "floating" out of the bedroom in a negligee, giving him a big hug and a kiss. On one occasion, she appeared in a black dress, open at the back, and asked him to zip her up. My father obliged.

Years later, as a cynical adult, I wondered if I'd been brought along as "protection" for my father – a handsome man – either from potential advances from the star or to avoid the risk of allegations against him, as she had a reputation for "collecting" men.

Given the allegations in her adopted daughter Christina's book, *Mommy Dearest*, which suggested that she had no maternal feelings and only adopted children as a publicity stunt, I could understand why she was more interested in the dog than in some strange child. Once I began to tag along, Ms Crawford insisted that Shane, a big German Shepherd, be brought to her suite every morning. When Shane arrived each day, she would order a full Irish breakfast to be sent up to her room, which she hand-fed to the dog. There was never a sadder dog when Ms Crawford left Ireland and Shane reverted to his normal diet.

Yul Brynner

Yul Brynner and my dad first met in New York in the 1960s at a function. Yul told him that his son Rock was going to Dublin to study for his master's degree at Trinity College. When he realised my dad was a private detective, he said he was a bit concerned about Rock and asked my dad to keep on eye on him from time to time and to let him know if he got up to anything untoward. I don't know if he thought Dublin was wild in those heady times, or if he had some specific reason for his concern, but it was an official assignment. Perhaps it related to the fact that Rock was friendly with many socialites, rock stars and "in" people; he even took a job as a "roadie" for the Rolling Stones at one point.

I'm not sure if he ever had anything to report but I don't doubt that there were a few good parties to be had at Rock's flat in Pembroke Lane in Dublin, where some of the Guinness set spent time.

Coincidentally, as often happens, while dealing with a family law and child custody case on behalf of a client, Tara Browne, the then heir to the Guinness fortune, who was divorcing his wife of three years and wanted custody of their children, the case paths crossed. During the course of observation on her, she was seen to be socialising with various people, including, coincidently, Rock Brynner. She was a frequent visitor at the Old Stand pub in Andrew Street, the Quo Vadis restaurant and the Shelbourne Hotel. Mr Browne eventually changed his will, cutting out his wife and leaving everything in trust for his two infant children, Dorian and Julian. A month later, he was killed in a car crash in London. He was twenty-one.

As for Rock Brynner . . . I'm still looking for *that* file, but as Rock went on to become a respected doctor of philosophy, it couldn't have been anything of great consequence, but perhaps it was a good indication of the love and concern his father had for him. Yul kept in contact with my Dad, infrequent though it was, as both men were travelling the world in pursuit of different aims. They had many interests in common, were born within a month of each other and both died of lung cancer in the mid-1980s.

7

Just A Job

Over the years, people have asked me what it is like being a PI – is it exciting, glamorous, dangerous? Everyone has their own impression of just what's involved. A surprising number think it really *is* a mixture of Raymond Chandler's Philip Marlowe, Sam Spade or Miss Marple. Funny how the men were always "interesting", while female detectives were depicted as frumpy "amateur" sleuths! Sherlock Holmes is another fictional detective that comes to the public mind, as I found out when an old friend and tailor to the stars, Louis Copeland gave me a magnifying glass and deer-stalker as a joke many years ago.

To me, I never really thought about it; it was just a job – my job. Undoubtedly it had its moments, some good, others not so good. There was a lot of international travel to exotic places, which was great if it was for a professional investigators' conference – they always picked great locations. One year we had the conference on Oahu in Hawaii, on the estate used to film *Magnum PI*. It was a beautiful place and it would have been great to have really worked from there. But that was just television, after all, and real-life PIs never get to solve the case in half-an-hour! When you're working, you don't really get to see these exotic places through a tourist's eyes. There's no chance of nipping out to take in the sights or visit the beach. A client has paid you serious money to get the job done, not for sightseeing. Even a brief trip away from the job could mean you miss something going down – Murphy's Law always applies. Of course, there are many times you wouldn't want to take a "tour". The job could be in some awful place, miles from anywhere interesting, so you just want to get it done and get home.

As for glamour . . . sometimes, but at a price. With the long hours, it's not a job for clock-watchers, as there *are* no "working hours". You stay with the job until you finish or the person under surveillance goes home – and even then it might not be over, depending on the case. Not an ideal job if you have a family. As for a social life, it depends on the cases under investigation at any given time.

Exciting? It had its moments. When things start to come together, there's a great sense of satisfaction, that "eureka" moment when you've joined all the dots and it all makes sense or you get the evidence your client needs to win their case. It doesn't always work that way, however. Sometimes a client has gotten it wrong and there may be no evidence or an innocent explanation may emerge. Perhaps it's just a matter of economics, when the cost of doing the investigation is beyond a client's pocket, although I found that when it came to business matters, money was never an issue if it meant solving their problems.

Dangerous? I suppose, with hindsight, there were risky moments. Adding up all the incidents, you may well think it

35

was dangerous, particularly when I got death threats, of which there were several. On one occasion, I even got a threat from a garda who was stupid enough to leave the threatening message on my office answering machine! Given that the incidents were spread over a long period of time, I suppose it wasn't too bad. I never really considered it as being dangerous; in fact, I never gave it a second thought. Foolish, perhaps, but I think I was so used to the job, having grown up with it, that I took it for granted.

Years before I ever became involved in the business, while still in school, I went to meet a friend in Arnotts department store in Henry Street, one of the many stores my father's store-detectives operated in. As I stood waiting for my friend, I was confronted by two well-known female criminals – one was Anne Flynn, married to the notorious Tony Felloni, currently doing twenty years in Mountjoy for drug trafficking. Flynn herself had numerous convictions for shoplifting, pick-pocketing and other offences, including vicious assaults. Well known to the police, she often went "undercover", dressed as a nun or wearing a wig to disguise herself. In court she usually claimed to have a metal plate in her head and "didn't know" what she was doing. I knew them both to see and they apparently knew me, having seen my photograph in a newspaper the previous week.

To my surprise, without any warning, Flynn pulled a knife and threatened she'd "slit" my throat, as both women shouted abuse. Perhaps she resented the fact that my father's staff were constantly hauling her into court for theft and other crimes. I was just the easy target. I was probably too naïve to be afraid. Although annoyed, I acted calmly, reaching for the phone on the reception desk and dialling the police.

Before I could finish, Flynn ripped the phone from the wall, threw it on the ground and ran away.

Now I really *was* angry, being a fiery red-head I suppose. I called the cops from another phone. Gardaí from the nearby Store Street station arrived at Arnotts and together we went in a squad car to the flats in Summerhill where Anne Flynn, aka Mrs Tony Felloni, lived. I formally identified her and her friend. They were taken into custody and ended up with another assault charge on their record – not that that bothered them; it was almost a badge of honour. That was the first and last time I had any trouble from them. My father wasn't too impressed with me when he found out what I'd done; it wasn't my fight after all.

Another incident I recall involved my mother. She was on a bus with her elderly father when she was attacked from behind by a woman – another well-known female criminal. As this nasty piece of work boarded the bus, she recognised my mother, who was sitting with her back to her. My mother worked in the family business and had had previous encounters with the woman, having had her charged on numerous occasions for pickpocketing and theft. This feral female repeatedly hit my mother on the head with a six-inch stiletto-heeled shoe, leaving her unconscious and pouring blood. Nobody, including the bus conductor, intervened to help as the attacker jumped off the bus. My mother's clothes were saturated in blood – never to be worn again. An ambulance took her to the Mater Hospital and it was many months before she fully recovered.

My mother caught sight of her attacker before she lost consciousness and was brave enough to eventually give evidence against her in court but then, as now, sentencing for such offences, particularly for women, was derisory and no deterrent.

On yet another occasion, a male detective working for my father was attacked by a well-known inner-city thug. It was Christmas Eve and the man was shopping for last-minute gifts for his family when the thug attacked him with an open razor, slashing his face from ear to ear. He spent Christmas in the operating theatre, hovering between life and death.

Thankfully, he recovered but he carried the horrendous scars of his ordeal for the rest of his life. He was identified his attacker, who had numerous convictions. He was charged but, once again, he got off lightly, having "signed himself in" to a psychiatric hospital after the attack. He claimed he was "ill" at the time and didn't know what he was doing – all part of the game they play with the Gardaí and the courts, which ensure that, for some, crime does pay, and there are virtually no serious consequences to their actions.

Long after I'd given up private investigation, my grown-up children reminded me of certain incidents they recalled, such as arriving home from school to find we had twenty-four-hour police protection at the house. It was only then that I remembered it probably was somewhat dangerous on occasion and I understood why my father used to say it was "no job for a woman". After many years, he gave up trying to persuade me to be a barrister, something I was interested in but never had the time to pursue, being so busy with the PI work.

I think Dad finally accepted the fact that I could handle the job when I was voted International Detective of the Year by the World Association of Detectives. I was both shocked and delighted, as I had no idea that I'd been nominated. Apparently my name had been put forward by several detectives, including a Chief Superintendent of the Yorkshire Police, and some

American, Australian and European investigators I'd worked with, members of ISIS, an international security and investigation organisation – the PI equivalent to Interpol with its HQ in Switzerland. I had worked with ISIS for a number of years, having been appointed as a member of its governing council, the only woman on the board at the time. It was a great honour to be voted International Detective of the Year, given the number of investigators world-wide who were nominated. The award was presented to me at the World Association of Detectives Convention in Singapore, which was attended by hundreds of detectives from every continent.

The PI world is an increasingly difficult field to work in, despite the technological developments, which can make life somewhat easier for the investigator. In today's society, life is cheap and it is all too easy to stumble across the path of the burgeoning gangs of crime lords, who let nothing get in the way of making a fast buck. I've no doubt that if an "attempted hit" on me in a family law case – which you can read about later in the book – had happened today the outcome would have been very different and I wouldn't have lived to write this book.

The ready availability of guns and assault weapons today and the total disregard for life makes the PI business a less attractive job option, regardless of the high earnings. Even on a practical basis, surveillance work in a gridlocked city makes life difficult for a professional investigator, despite the availability of satellite technology to help track a target. Unfortunately, we don't have the benefit of street "grid systems", which make it easier to tail a car in places like the US.

When I think of what my children grew up with, I can understand why they had no interest in going into the business.

It probably wasn't a normal life. It was certainly different from what their friends' parents were doing, whether for good or bad, and to be honest, I'm glad they've chosen different paths. I'd probably be the one lying awake at night, worrying about their safety. I guess everything comes full circle.

Unlucky for Some

If it wasn't enough that I worked as a private investigator, I seemed to have the knack of being in the "wrong" place at the right (or sometimes the wrong) time. Over the years I have come upon more than one bank robbery or spotted something suspicious going down.

Sitting at a red traffic light outside Ballybough flats one day, I noticed three men emerge from the flats, apparently in a hurry. As they ran towards a car that had pulled in ahead of me, I noticed one of them shove the leg of a kitchen table up his sleeve. As soon as the lights changed, the car took off in the direction of Clontarf – where I was headed.

I took note of the descriptions of the guys, including the driver, certain that they were on their way to do a "job". I stopped a patrolling garda and gave him details of the car, the registration and what I'd seen, but he didn't seem very interested. Further on, I flagged down a motorcycle cop and again told him the story and he radioed the station with the details.

That evening I heard there had been an attempted robbery on Bank of Ireland in Clontarf, but before the gang made their getaway, the gardaí turned up and arrested them. The detective unit later asked me to recount my observations. When I did, they told me that I had described the men and the table leg exactly – the boys I'd seen coming from the flats had been caught red-handed robbing the bank, armed with more than the table leg. The new car had been stolen just minutes before I'd spotted it. Timing is everything, they say – guess they were just unlucky that day.

The Hostage

On another occasion I dropped into my offices one Saturday morning with my daughter, then aged three or four, before going to a cash-and-carry across the road before it closed at midday.

The narrow entrance was having work done and was badly lit but as we walked in I saw a man ahead of me and I noticed a gun sticking out of his trouser pocket. I immediately turned to walk back out but before I could, another man appeared, blocking our exit. He had a sawn-off shotgun in his hand and there was no arguing with that.

He ushered us into the large warehouse, where there were dozens of shoppers, including several nuns. Most were lying on the floor, as up to twelve gunmen shouted orders at us. I was worried about my little girl – though obviously frightened, she never cried. We were forced to the floor at gunpoint, close to a large open ice-cream cabinet and I covered her as best I could with my body.

The place was in chaos as the nuns prayed aloud and were told to "shut up" by the armed men, one of whom let off a warning shot into the roof. Using the distraction, I manoeuvred a nearby floor polisher and a timber pallet closer, to hide my daughter. I still clearly remember her saying – "If we just keep quiet we'll be all right mammy."

I could hear the robbers telling people to empty their wallets and one man close to me threw hundreds of pounds under the ice-cream freezer, in an effort to hide his cash. The men alternatively shouted, "We're the IRA" and later, "We're not the IRA" – either way it didn't matter, as we were in no position to argue with the heavily armed gang.

After a couple of hours the men ordered us to move to the back of the warehouse, shouting "this is to show we mean business" as they viciously clubbed a middle-aged man to the ground. Another gang member hit a young lad with the butt of his gun, and blood flowed down his face. They dragged several other hostages to an upstairs office. They had previously cut the telephone lines, but unknown to the raiders and us at the time, they'd missed one independent line. A staff member who'd heard them shouting at people to get down, had dialled 999 and had managed to keep the open line hidden. The gardaí heard everything that was going on.

Waving guns in our faces, they dragged us up and forced us into a walk-in meat freezer, one gunman said, "I'm holding an automatic and the trigger is cocked", but before they could lock us in, all hell broke loose as more gunfire was heard.

We had no idea that the place was surrounded by over three hundred gardaí, including Special Branch men armed with Uzi submachine guns, backed up by helicopters and hundreds of troops from the Irish army, as well as several marksmen. The gang began firing at the gardaí who were closing in and a Special Branch man was shot, his hand burst open and he lost a lot of blood.

A number of hostages were pistol-whipped by the angry gangsters and they hit a woman across the face, refusing to surrender to the gardaí. After a stand-off lasting several hours, the gang demanded food, a priest and a solicitor. A spokesman for the gunmen said through a mediator, "Everyone is fine. There are no children in here, everybody is being treated okay and as far as we're concerned no-one has been hurt. We don't want to shoot or kill anyone, we won't open fire provided the [Special] Branch don't rush us. We have to protect our own lives."

When the gardaí burst in, the gangsters in their panic had left the freezer open. As we escaped from the freezer and took refuge anywhere we could at the back of the warehouse, I could see men everywhere. All were armed and in civilian clothes. I couldn't tell which were gang members or which were gardaí.

Suddenly a tall dark-haired man wearing a long black leather coat grabbed my little girl and ran. As I ran after him, screaming for him to let her go, I was held back by two men. She made no sound, struck dumb with terror. It seemed an age before I found out that she was alive and well. The man who grabbed her was a Special Branch man, rescuing her from the gang – the gardaí had taken her to safety in a squad car. In the heat of the moment, her safety was paramount – they hadn't time to ask questions or find out who her mother was.

Finally reunited with her, I didn't dare let her out of my sight for a very long time. She was very traumatised by the ordeal, and for several years afterwards she suffered from nightmares. Even in daylight she would "freeze up" if she saw any man running in her direction – however innocently.

The gang, one of whom worked as a porter in the Mater Hospital, were convicted and got lengthy prison sentences in Mountjoy. They neither knew nor cared about the devastation and trauma they'd left behind that day – all for the sake of a few quid.

8

Backing Up the Journalists in Bandit Country: Slab Murphy

It was quite a common occurrence to be instructed by newspaper editors or their lawyers when a writ for libel hit their desk. My job was to investigate the parties suing the paper, collate the information and present my findings. This was particularly crucial with regard to any information detrimental to the claimant's case, which the other side would not like to emerge in court. It was a bargaining tool and the case could be resolved without incurring the major costs of court proceedings. Basically, they wanted me to be able to back up their story to show it had not been libellous or at least was fair comment. Sometimes it was a straightforward case of mistaken identity or someone trying to pull a scam on the newspapers in the hope of getting a big payout; others were more sinister.

The case of Thomas "Slab" Murphy versus *The Sunday Times* was one such. Murphy operated a farm at Cornonagh, Crossmaglen, County Armagh, and at Ballybinaby,

Hackballscross, Dundalk, County Louth, colloquially known as "bandit country" at the time. *The Sunday Times* had published an article in June 1985 under the headline "Portrait of a Check-in Terrorist" which said that British police had discovered an IRA plan to plant bombs in twelve seaside resorts. They'd arrested over twenty people and seized documents listing specific targets. *The Sunday Times* said police "appeared to have destroyed one of the Provisional IRA's active service units . . . in Ireland itself the planning of mainland campaigns is surrounded now by a more tightly-knit security . . . last February the IRA's Army Council appointed a farmer in the Republic, called Slab Murphy to be its 'Operations Commander' for the whole of Northern Ireland . . . Murphy is likely to have had to sanction certain key Provisionals travelling to Britain to take part in this summer's planned bombing campaign."

Slab Murphy sued, as did his brother Patrick. Murphy's counsel sought the highest damages in Irish legal history at the time for his client, saying the article meant he was "a prominent figure in the Provisional IRA, an unlawful organisation and an organisation associated in the public mind with unlawful violence, brutality and murder". Slab Murphy said his reputation was injured and his life endangered by the article. His farm straddles the border between the Republic of Ireland and the North. Aerial photographs taken by the *Sunday Times* and produced in evidence showed oil and petrol tanks on either side of a hedge which straddled the border.

Slab Murphy had extensive business interests. Investigations showed that four of his companies alone had a turnover of £1.475 million sterling over a four-month period of 1985, at a time when Ireland's economy was in recession and people were leaving the country in droves in search of jobs. Our investigation found that Michael McKevitt, then a member of the PIRA, who would later hit the headlines in connection with the Omagh bombing, worked as a tanker driver for one of the Murphy-owned oil companies.

It was a difficult investigation, given both the terrain and the location – two different things when it comes to Republican enclaves, particularly those that straddle the border – but in this instance, given what we were dealing with, it was doubly so, as later evidence in court would confirm. Brigadier Morton, a British Army officer, said in evidence at the subsequent court case: "we knew radio-controlled bombs had been detonated from the Murphy homestead and believed that Thomas Murphy had taken part in several terrorists attacks . . . gathering enough evidence to convict him in court for murder and other crimes proved impossible."

Informers weren't tolerated in bandit country and the Gardaí weren't treated much better. If our agents were even *suspected* of meddling in IRA business, they'd be lucky to get away with a beating. They could even end up "missing in action". It was a case of "tread softly and carry a big stick". One particularly dedicated garda attached to Hackballscross station had been targeted. The house he was building was torched to the ground just as it neared completion, injuring him in the process. Forensic reports proved the fire was started deliberately but no-one was ever charged in connection with the arson. The policeman remained in the force but transferred to another station.

We were making sporadic "forays" into the area while undertaking background investigations, liaising with solid contacts and establishing sources likely to be of assistance to the defence case. Thomas "Slab" Murphy was a big businessman, the "main man" in the area, and he controlled his empire with an iron fist. Getting hard evidence was difficult, as no-one was willing to testify, afraid of the consequences to them and their families. *Omerta* was the golden rule, rigidly enforced.

In 1988, during my investigation, three years after the article appeared and while still waiting for a court date for the libel action, the *Sunday Times* got a lucky break. Gardaí found an ammunition dump stockpiled with mortar rocket-fins and ammunition in undergrowth close to Thomas "Slab" Murphy's home.

At the time, Operation Scorpion, an Irish customs investigation, was also ongoing and Slab was its main target. In April 1989, oil tankers belonging to Murphy's operation were seized by Irish customs. Evidence was later given in court that, following the first seizure on 6 April, two Customs Officers, Denis Beirne and Seamus Colgan, who were parked on the public road, were attacked. Beirne gave evidence of having been attacked with a concrete block by Slab Murphy, while Colgan told the court that Slab's brother, Patrick Murphy, smashed their car window while another man ripped out their two-way radio, cutting off all contact with customs HQ. Colgan was told he'd be taken to "Cross" (Crossmaglen, Country Armagh, an IRA stronghold) to get him "fixed" and said he believed he was about to be killed.

Two months later the Garda Special Task Force raided Slab's "estate" to arrest him but he escaped, jumping out of a window in his house that opened onto Northern Ireland territory. The raid wasn't a complete failure. Gardaí found three passports, including one in the name of a Jim Faughey, which bore Slab's photograph. He used it to travel to Greece and Yugoslavia several times between 1986 and 1989. It was hardly a holiday, as he usually stayed just forty-eight hours. The Irish passport was one of a hundred blank passports that had been stolen from the Department of Foreign Affairs in Dublin five years earlier. "Slab's" luck was running out. It was a crucial piece of evidence linking Thomas "Slab" Murphy to a number of IRA operations. In 1985, passports from the same batch had been found in a "safe house" in Glasgow, along with detailed plans for a bombing campaign in British holiday resorts. Two years later, the arms ship the *Eksund* was intercepted off the French coast and IRA men on board were found in possession of false passports, also from the same batch as those stolen from the Department of Foreign Affairs. Slab presented himself to gardaí in Dundalk for questioning but in the grand tradition of "whatever you say, say nothing", he remained silent throughout his forty-eight hours' detention.

When the case against the *Sunday Times* eventually came to court in 1990, Justice Kevin Lynch set a legal precedent in allowing the newspaper to cross-examine witnesses about Murphy's reputation, saying, "What's sauce for the goose, is sauce for the gander". Senior gardaí, five specialising in National Security and Intelligence, and Customs Officers involved in the incident outside Slab's home, all gave evidence of their belief that Slab was involved with subversives. British military gave evidence of being fired on by eight men in the vicinity of Murphy's farm, one of whom they believed, but couldn't prove, had been Thomas Murphy himself. Fine Gael TD Brendan McGahon, from Louth, Murphy's stronghold, also gave evidence against Slab.

The jury retired, returning three hours later with their verdict. They found that Thomas "Slab" Murphy was a prominent figure in the PIRA and had planned murder and bombings and was therefore a man of worthless character and was awarded nothing. In the case of Patrick Murphy, the jury found that it was untrue to say he was a prominent member of the PIRA and planned murder and bombing of property but found that the brothers were actively supportive of the IRA and were men of worthless character. They found that while Thomas Murphy was a man of violence, Patrick Murphy was not and they awarded him £14,800 in damages.

A furious "Slab" rushed from the court surrounded by his "supporters". His efforts to make easy money had exposed him to a wider audience – not what he had intended. He had originally demanded a £500,000 out-of-court settlement in the knowledge that he had recently obtained £120,000 and £15,000 from other publications in the recent past. *The Sunday Times* decided to take their chances and it paid off, not only financially but in vindicating their journalists.

The witnesses showed uncommon courage in appearing in the case. Brendan McGahon TD, in particular, had a lot to lose for his courageous stand. After the case, McGahon said, "it did take some courage to go into the witness box, but I remember the words of John F. Kennedy; all that is necessary for evil to triumph is that good men should keep silent. I believe that I spoke for the silent majority in County Louth who are opposed to IRA gangsterism."

Since then, Thomas "Slab" Murphy has been in the public eye on several occasions. The Assets Recovery Agency located major assets in Manchester in a £15 million tax probe. They seized ten properties. Slab managed to sell off six others before they swooped. Working closely with CAB, the Irish Criminal Assets Bureau, they raided the Murphy home at Ballybinaby in 2006 and found colour-coded records showing his assets. It was also found that additional assets were held in Dublin, Scotland, London and Kent. "Slab" denied any knowledge of these properties, saying "I do not own any property and in fact had to sell my own home some years ago to cover legal fees following an unsuccessful libel case . . . I make a living from farming."

At the time of writing, "Slab" still hadn't paid the *Sunday Times* legal fees of £600,000 awarded against him. In recent times, he has again hit the headlines and has been remanded on continuing bail to the Special Criminal Court, a high-security court, to answer claims on alleged revenue offences. It looks like this particular saga is set to run for some time to come.

Most of my investigations into this case remain confidential for obvious reasons.

9

Behind Enemy Lines:
The Northern Ireland Objective

Insurance claim investigation is usually straightforward but during the late 1980s and early 1990s I acted for a major UK insurer concerned about the large number of claims from Northern Ireland. It was at the height of the troubles and bombs were going off all over the North as well as in the UK. The clients were very aware of the risks of working in Northern Ireland and the dangers faced by agents working on investigations and surveillance operations in bandit territory, whether they were Loyalist or Republican areas.

Most insurance investigations elsewhere in the world, although sometimes difficult, are not usually a threat to personal safety. Northern Ireland presented a clear and present danger. If caught, at best our agents could get a beating, more likely tar and feathering, torture or even death – especially if our actions were seen as a threat to the paramilitary "livelihood" and fund-raising enterprises. It was a shoot first, ask questions later situation and it was happening just a couple of hours away from my Dublin offices.

As I'd worked with this company for some time in relation to other "safer" cases I agreed to take on the job of investigating claims made in the North. The company had only recently entered the Northern Ireland market and were very pleased with the large number of people taking out policies with them. They soon found out why.

Not every claim is false but it's not unusual to have false or exaggerated claims made by individuals or "professional claimants". My clients arranged to meet me in their UK offices, where a strategy to investigate and deal with spurious claims was discussed. They were extremely concerned about the serious political situation in the North. As investigators, we would be in real danger, given that we'd have to carry out covert surveillance in the North on both sides of the political and religious divide at a time when it was most volatile. It was potentially a lose-lose situation as, if caught, no matter which side it was, we would be viewed as spies and informers. No quarter would be given for the fact that we were just private investigators checking out insurance frauds.

The clients made it very clear that under no circumstances were we to risk life and limb investigating these claims in Northern Ireland. They felt exposed and vulnerable and were at a loss as to how to deal with a situation entirely outside of their experience. Used to dealing with the UK market and the "normal" fraudulent claims, they now found themselves insuring people in what was, to their mind, a battle ground.

The initial cases related to a health insurance product which provided a fixed income if a claimant was unable to work for a specific period due to ill health or injury. Payments were made on a weekly basis up to age sixty-five. Not every case is investigated. Obviously, those giving rise to suspicion are put under close scrutiny but random cases are selected and checked out on an ongoing basis. Around 60 per cent of random checks show up some discrepancies, misleading information, untruths and, on occasion, fraudulent claims.

The first three cases were in staunch Unionist enclaves in rural areas of Northern Ireland. The terrain was difficult and undertaking any observation and surveillance was at best, extremely dangerous. In themselves, the cases were straightforward but investigators from the South would be under immediate suspicion, so I had to put in a team that consisted of people who knew the ground, being originally from the North but no longer part of the Northern Ireland community. I spearheaded this team, taking a chance that a woman would be underestimated and seen as less of a threat. To the surprise of the insurance company, who really had little hope of finding anything, we got lucky.

The first case related to a self-employed courier who had taken out a permanent health policy. Within three months he'd made a claim, saying he was unfit to work for the foreseeable future. His claim was backed by a medical report. The man's house was on an isolated country road which gave us no cover. It was very difficult to keep observation without drawing attention and any strangers in the area would be readily identified. The only thing we could do was to maintain surveillance from a dugout close by and settle down to wait.

For the first day there was little activity, other than a woman, identified as the subject's wife, and child, who were seen coming and going, but there was no sign of the subject. Day two was more of the same. Surveillance is not easy and is never glamorous. Most times it is boring, until something happens and the adrenaline rushes in, but in such dangerous territory, at all times we had to be constantly on high alert, which can be exhausting, knowing that at any time we could be rumbled, with God knows what consequences.

There *are* times when you are ensconced in a comfortable hotel or at least a warm car, but more often than not it is less than comfortable. In this case, long cold hard hours went by without being able to change position, move about or even stretch our legs for fear of being seen. As it was summertime, the days were long and cover of darkness was slow in coming.

On day three we had a breakthrough, as the target's vehicle suddenly appeared and pulled into the driveway of his house. He jumped from the high-bodied truck and let himself in with a key. A double-check on the truck's registration confirmed that our man was the owner. As a bonus, the truck was emblazoned with the name of a well-known courier company, giving us yet another lead. This information led to further investigations, which confirmed that the man had been employed by the courier company for some time as an overnight driver, using his own truck. His routine was to travel to the depot, load up and head off to various parts of Northern Ireland and Britain on overnight deliveries. He was often away for days at a time, which explained why he'd made no appearance during the first two days' surveillance. Once we'd confirmed this pattern, we "accompanied" him on his rounds and videoed his energetic activities in the course of his job.

A full report accompanied by photographic and video evidence was sent to the UK. I arranged to meet the insurers' head of claims in Belfast the following week to discuss the case. I parked the car and as I walked toward the meeting point ten minutes ahead of my appointment time, I heard a massive explosion. I could see smoke rising and the area was quickly surrounded by the RUC and military. Needless to say, we never had that meeting in the Europa Hotel, once described as the most bombed building in Europe. The head of claims hurriedly returned to the UK, convinced he'd just escaped certain death. A teleconference was held between Dublin and London and it was decided not to pull the plug on this claim until the other claims were examined. This is rather unusual, as each case is normally dealt with individually but instinct and gut reaction told me something was not quite right about this whole scenario. My sense was that it was another "scam" being run by a certain paramilitary organisation to "fund" their agenda.

The next case concerned yet another difficult observation location in similar terrain. Residents in the area were particularly "jumpy" as a local man who was said to have "stepped out of line" had been murdered less than half-a-mile from our target house two weeks earlier. In this case the forty-year-old claimant had taken the policy out eleven months previously. Within a short time he "fell ill" and by the time I got the case, the insurers had been paying out for five months. He claimed to be suffering from a damaged hand and an arthritic back and knee. A local medical examination corroborated his complaints. He said he could no longer work as a mechanic and had difficulty even dressing himself. He couldn't drive anymore due to the pain and found it impossible to bend over to inspect an engine or even tie his laces. If genuine, the company would have to make these index-linked payments for a further twenty-five years. Nice work if you can get it.

The man's house was kept under observation, with all the usual difficulties expected in Northern Ireland. The recent murder made for further problems, as locals were on alert for any unusual activities in the area. Common to the Northern countryside, the man lived in a large bungalow set on about two acres, with a big workshop at the back. Judging from the number of cars coming and going over a period of a few days, it was obvious that he was operating a business from home. Again, a very simple, straightforward case but for the location and the volatile political situation. Observation was almost impossible and the idea of embedding ourselves was a non-runner due to the nature of the tight-knit community, where strangers were viewed with suspicion. Even the best vantage point was dead ground, giving us no line of sight view, and we were left with no option but to take the bull by the horns.

Having first "tinkered" with our car, accompanied by a male agent I drove in on the pretext that I had an overheating problem, saying the local postmistress had sent me to him. To cover my tracks, I had called to the post office, telling them I was having trouble with my car and asking if there were any mechanics in the area, knowing I'd probably be directed to our man. If he checked, my cover story would be accepted.

The workshop doors were open about three feet and a man fitting the description of the subject emerged from under a car and asked our business. He was wearing overalls and had very oily hands and it was obvious he had been working on the car. I told him I'd a problem with the car and he agreed to take a look. He bent down, popped open the bonnet, got in and out of the car several times and spent about twenty minutes checking out the thermostat and fan without any obvious difficulty – all captured on covert video. While we were there, several other customers came in and either left their cars for repair or made arrangements to book them in. The garage was well stocked and fully fitted out and there were a number of cars being worked on. There were no other mechanics around and later investigations confirmed that the man was self-employed and worked alone. The man "fixed" the car and I paid him what he asked. It was more than evident that this was another fraudulent claim.

The next case we investigated was again situated in wide-open countryside, giving us very little cover, no better than the previous two cases. The man lived in a bungalow set on a three-acre site. A large barn was clearly visible at the back of the house, with his nearest neighbour being more than a mile away. Both because of the terrain and the political situation, the location was a real nightmare to keep under close observation. The man was an agricultural contractor in the local area but claimed he was unable to work due to an accident involving a JCB and that he was more or less confined to the house. The claim was being paid on a monthly basis and he'd been receiving a cheque for months and was getting used to it.

On day one we saw the man – identified from a description we had – leave his house and jump into a transit van parked in his driveway. He drove several miles, picked up two other men and drove to a farm in the heart of a Loyalist area. During the course of observation, all three men were seen working. The subject was operating a JCB, digging trenches and laying drainage pipes. He continued all day until after six o'clock when he packed up and drove home. From around six o'clock the following morning, there was a lot of activity in and around his house, with several vans arriving, loading materials from the barn and driving away. The man himself was seen hitching a trailer to his van and loading building materials. Accompanied by a couple of men he drove ten miles to a building site, where they dug out and fitted a septic tank. On the third morning he left with a load of piping sticking out of the back of the van.

Having established that not only was he fit to work but was extremely agile and active, evidence of which we had recorded, we decided to cut short our observation. My colleague, who was originally from the North and knew the general area, "kicking with the right foot" being a non-Catholic, volunteered to call at the house under a pretext of wanting a job done. Later that evening, just as the man arrived home, he called to the house and asked him to price a job in a nearby village. The man was very anxious to do the job and went to great lengths to tell him the extensive work he was doing in the area, all of which was recorded.

From our observations and investigations we found he employed ten local men and was operating a thriving business in which he was personally very active. A check on the vehicles in the barn revealed that he owned a number of vans, trucks, plant and machinery and was doing "very nicely thank you". This thirty-nine-year-old's monthly claim had been made just four months after he took out the policy. He thought he was sitting on a gold-mine that wouldn't run out for another twenty-six years!

Taking an overview of these three claims and a number of similar additional claims investigated over the following months, there was one theme running through it all. They all lived within a thirty-mile radius of each other and were all from the same political background. Obviously it was an organised scam but how much went to the individual and how much went to the organisation we didn't know.

Our job was to establish if the claims were fraudulent and of that there was no doubt. We had kept the insurance company informed of the ongoing situation and they decided to hold off cutting any payments until we'd completed the last case and the agents were out of the area. Once they had my final report, the insurance company immediately stopped the payments and brought charges for conspiracy to defraud them.

The case was due to be heard in Belfast. The UK company executives were expected to give evidence, as was I. They agreed to travel to Belfast but only if they were picked up at the airport by helicopter and whisked back again as soon as the case was heard. They were scared stiff of becoming the target of a "hit" during their short visit, such was their fear of the Northern Ireland situation. This was all agreed and arranged. A few days before the case was due to be heard, the UK offices of the insurance company got a phone call. The message was simple: "Don't mess with UDA business." That there was a paramilitary organisation behind the "scam" was in no doubt but of course proving exactly which one was another matter.

Having given the matter some brief consideration, the company made an executive decision to drop the case but they cut off all payments to the fraudulent cases and, despite threats, they refused to re-instate them. The company stopped taking any new business from Northern Ireland, a market they had just entered less than a year previously, relieved to be rid of their personal "Beirut".

10

The Stripper, The Man U Footballer and the IRA

A former Manchester United football player, whom I will call B, contacted me about what he described as an embarrassing problem. Now, I'm no doctor, so what could it possibly be? He said that while he was in Dublin he'd been introduced to what was described as a "good investment" by a footballing associate. The man, "Charlie" said he'd been making a killing on the exchange rates, getting stg£1,000 for an investment of IR£1,000 through a contact. He offered to cut the Man U player in on the deal. B trusted "Charlie" and jumped at the opportunity.

A meeting was arranged with "Charlie's" contact, Patricia – he wasn't told her second name and he never thought to ask. He agreed initially to invest IR£1,000 and over the following weeks he collected stg£1,000, re-investing another IR£1,000, always getting the sterling return weeks later. Patricia took her cut and everyone was happy. Whenever he met Patricia to exchange the cash, she gave no any indication that she knew anything about football or that she recognised him.

As time went on, B, happy with the return he was getting, continued to trust Patricia, who strung him along, convincing him to part with ever-increasing sums – first IR£3,000, then IR£20,000 and IR£25,000, rising to a "one-off investment" of IR£250,000 with the promise to double it. Not surprisingly, after the initial small profits, none of his bigger pay-outs materialised. I asked if he ever got a receipt – already knowing the answer.

He began to worry what he'd got into and, for the first time, asked questions. Was the money being used to finance drug deals or paramilitary activities? What exactly was going on? Patricia feigned outrage at the suggestion. "Absolutely no way," she assured him. She had a private arrangement, she claimed, saying her contact was in the "money markets" and could get large amounts of sterling during the summer. She said she was "only a small part of the scheme", which involved "big players", including a woman who was "running the highly confidential scheme", assuring him his investment was "rock solid".

B wanted to know exactly who was behind the scheme and how he could be guaranteed the promised return. To "prove the investment was blue chip guaranteed" she offered to set up a meeting with the principals, who were "well-known financiers and business people". Strangely, that meeting took place in a car-park in Leixlip, when Patricia produced a notebook purporting to show large "investments" attributed to well-known people. He never met any "principals". This was "proof", she claimed, as she "confided" the names of the "top brass" supposedly backing the scheme. Despite the big hitters in Patricia's book, he was far from reassured and pushed her for the repayment of his investments, seriously worried it really was seed money for drug deals.

He always met Patricia in obscure locations, car parks or shopping centres. He had no address for her and although he knew she drove a blue van, incredibly, he'd never thought to get the registration. He could see no way out other than walking away and taking the loss. He continued to pressure her, hoping to get his money back; the profits no longer mattered.

In a cloak-and-dagger scenario, Patricia said she was meeting the "principal" (who'd be driving a silver Mercedes) to collect the cash outside a Dublin bank. He could watch from there but was not to approach her or she'd be in trouble for divulging her boss's identity. He watched and waited as every silver Merc approached but didn't stop and with no sign of Patricia, his worst fears seemed to have been realised.

Just as he was about to leave, Patricia phoned, saying the "drop" couldn't be made due to snow in the north. She claimed that the woman who was running the scheme had a very wealthy boyfriend, whom I will call Mr F, who was guaranteeing the money. Coincidentally, or perhaps not, when he first met Patricia he'd mentioned he knew a Mr F, a prominent player in the investment business. He'd asked if it was the same man and she confirmed it was. His fears allayed, he said, "He'll be okay for the money."

It was over eighteen months since B first parted with his money and Patricia was still talking her way out of trouble. There was little B could do, reluctant to go to the police. The last thing he wanted was to have it all over the newspapers. Under constant pressure, Patricia began to make some payments, all small amounts of stg£3,000 or stg£5,000 at a time before the new deadline. She gave him a cheque made out to "cash", signed by someone called Kelly. He didn't know who it was and at that point probably didn't care – he just wanted his money back. Not surprisingly, it turned out "Kelly" was another "investor" stung by Patricia.

Under pressure, she finally gave him a contact number of a "friend". When he rang the number, it turned out to be a hair salon. B was worried Patricia had "done a runner" with his cash. He phoned the salon several times but got no joy. Convinced the bird had flown, he racked his brain for anything Patricia had told him about herself over the past eighteen months, though he doubted any of it was true.

He remembered that she'd mentioned a publican who'd invested money with her but when he contacted the man, he denied knowing her. B rang him again. This time the publican agreed to meet him but when he turned up, he had another man with him. No introductions were made, the publican just said, "He's involved in the movement" – meaning the IRA. B didn't know what to think; they weren't exactly on the same side of the fence. He just nodded and said nothing. The man sat, just listening, as the publican admitted knowing Patricia, saying he only had "a few bob invested with her". He said he knew very little about her but he'd had a letter from her a few days previously, which simply read: "Dear X, I have been set up. I promise I will pay back all your money personally, will be in touch in a few weeks." That was the last he heard from her.

The publican thought Patricia's husband played in a band. Then again, he said he couldn't be sure of anything, she'd told so many lies. When the IRA man eventually spoke, he said his only interest in the matter was that he'd "invested money on behalf of a friend, now it was personal". He'd checked out the phone number for Patricia – a hairdressers, as B already knew – and he'd found out where the owner lived, and called to the house and "questioned him". The "meeting" between

B, the publican and the IRA man ended abruptly when the IRA man told B to go, saying he'd be in touch.

B was later contacted and told to be in a city centre park the following Wednesday. He was to bring "Charlie", the man who'd introduced him to Patricia. They were to watch the "summer seat" to identify a woman they believed was the woman running the scheme. B showed up. "Charlie" didn't. He claimed he arrived an hour later. When B got there, he saw a man and a woman talking to two people and was given "the nod" to come over, by the man "from the movement". There was a woman and the hairdresser's boyfriend there. The boyfriend had nothing to say but the woman answered the IRA man's questions, denying any knowledge of Patricia's "business transactions".

When B met the publican, the "heavy" from the "movement" said he'd called to the salon and spoken to the owner and later "visited" him at home. Unknown to all concerned, the man reported this "visit" to the police, saying a gun had been pulled on him and two passports and £150 in cash taken. When gardaí investigated, they discovered that his "visitor" was a well-known member of the Provisional IRA. B knew nothing about this turn of events but after his meeting with the IRA man and the publican, he'd told a friend what he'd heard about the man and where he lived. Armed with the address, the friend, trying to help, innocently called to see the man to find out if he knew anything about Patricia.

At this point, all hell broke loose as they were suddenly surrounded by a group of heavily armed men. B said he was afraid for his life, thinking he'd been caught between different political and criminal factions. He couldn't have been further from the truth. The "gunmen" were an armed response unit from the Gardaí, who'd been monitoring the "Provo" and his paramilitary connections. B, his friend, the "man from the movement" and everyone else were arrested and brought to various police stations. Some were held overnight and subsequently charged under Section 30 of the Offences Against the State Act. B was questioned, while his friend was held in custody for two nights, despite having no political, criminal or paramilitary connections. This was supposedly due to B's Northern origins and the fact that Patricia's scam had also been perpetrated on members of both the IRA and Loyalist groups in the North. The hairdresser's boyfriend was an innocent, caught up in the mess.

Following the Garda raid on the city centre park and the arrest of the men, the man from the IRA was charged with armed robbery. B's friend was held in custody for two nights and then charged. When he was brought before Justice Gillian Hussey at Kilmainham District Court the next day, the case was struck out. He was free to go, the Gardaí having established that he was an innocent victim.

Patricia, however, was still nowhere to be found. It seemed she'd disappeared off the face of the earth. The police could offer no assistance in finding her and not too many people were willing to admit having been taken in by a pretty face. In desperation, B contacted me. He'd explored all avenues and had run into a brick wall. He wanted me to find Patricia and, hopefully, recover his money. Despite the best efforts of several businessmen, the police and even the Provos, Patricia had vanished and B didn't even know her surname.

I got my first lead when I interviewed "Charlie". He recalled that Patricia once mentioned that her husband Tommy had been made redundant from a particular company – it may have been a line but I had to check out every detail. Our company had a long association as security advisors to his former employers, a highly respected company with strict policies of propriety, who were happy to help. Many of Patricia's "investors" were small-time, hard-working families under financial pressure who'd put in small amounts – £20, £50 or £100 – in the hope of clearing other debts; some of them may have even worked there. Patricia wasn't fussy where she got the money; they were all mugs to her.

Luckily, for once Patricia had told the truth, but the only address they had for "Tommy" and his next-of-kin, Patricia, was an old one – but it was a start. Investigation showed they'd moved a few years previously. Now, at last we had her full name: Mrs Patricia McDermott. But there was no guarantee she was still with Tommy or using that name. A check on the Registry of Birth, Marriages and Deaths gave me her maiden name and address at the time of her marriage. I compiled a description of her from B, his friend, and from old neighbours. Described as being 5'5" with long dark hair, mid-thirties, attractive, very friendly and a good talker, the description could have fitted anyone.

Having tracked her down to another rented property, it seemed the family had disappeared overnight, owing rent and unpaid bills. There were a lot of unhappy people looking for them and they didn't even know about her scam. Investigations at the local schools proved equally unhelpful. The children hadn't been to school for weeks and there'd been no contact from the parents. They'd just disappeared, but with four children in tow ranging from two to seventeen, she might prove a little easier to track down.

Having checked out all flight and ferry departures for a group like the McDermotts, a few possibilities arose. There was no guarantee they'd all travelled together or indeed at all. They could still have been in Ireland but, given the long trail of fraud, with sorry punters still being located all over the country, it would have taken a very brave woman to stay around, especially when she'd conned and humiliated the Provos.

Stories abounded about the money she'd "conned" from people fronting various business interests for the IRA. No doubt they too wanted their money back. People caught in Patricia's sting included small builders, who "invested" various amounts valued at between €116,000 to €200,000 today. Publicans invested anything from the equivalent of €30,000 to one who was believed to have put in over €540,000.

The Chinese mafia, the Triads, were also actively looking for her through their own sources. At the time, two groups in particular, the Shui Fong and the Wo Shin Wo Triads, were active in Dublin. It was believed they'd "invested" large amounts of money from their activities, which included restaurants, gambling, enforcement and other areas, and were laundering money through Patricia. Whether she realised this or not is not clear. Was she really that brave or that stupid? Who knows. What *is* certain is that she never planned to get caught – hence her plans for a new life abroad.

The scam appeared to have operated from one end of the country to another. Patricia "collected boyfriends" who invested money or innocently introduced friends – wealthy new targets – to her scheme. Well, they *were* wealthy before she got her hands on their money. The case became known in the office as "Patricia the Stripper", not because she took her clothes off but because she'd fleeced so many people, completely stripping them of any cash they had and coming back for more!

The hard slog went on for some time and after extensive investigation and a lot of leg work, it was eventually confirmed that Patricia and her family had taken a ferry to Wales and, from there, a coach to London. It was a cheap and inconspicuous way of travelling to the UK with a large family. Patricia wasn't stupid; no flashing cash on air fares for herself and her large brood. It was commonplace for entire families to migrate to England in search of work and they just blended in with all the rest.

By now, I knew her husband Tommy played traditional Irish music. There was a strong possibility he would look for work in some of the many Irish pubs and clubs around Cricklewood and Camden Town in London. They didn't need the money, but he was a keen musician and if my information was right, he wouldn't venture too far from his love of music. In the best gumshoe tradition, it meant an old-fashioned foot-slog around London Irish pubs and clubs to try and track them down.

After several days and nights of pub and club crawling – a difficult task as you can imagine – I finally got a break. Tommy McDermott had been playing locally with a traditional Irish band and the family had been staying at the Irish Club in Russell Square since their arrival in London. But like the pimpernel, they had left just days before, with Patricia paying their bill in hard cash. As expected, they left no forwarding address, not even with their new-found but short-lived friends in the band.

The hunt continued, as it emerged that Patricia had collected a new passport weeks prior to her hurried departure. With no passport then required to travel to the UK, it seemed that her long-term plans were destined for foreign fields. London was just her first stop-off on the road to a new life. As neither Patricia nor her husband had any qualifications or languages, it was unlikely they'd head for Europe. They could stay in

Britain but with Tommy's penchant for Irish music, I suspected it'd only be a matter of time before their whereabouts would filter back to some very unhappy people. If those people happened to be the boys in the IRA, life could become very uncomfortable for them.

On balance, my guess was that they'd have to go much further afield, perhaps to America or Australia. Narrowing the options down led me to check out flights to the US, Australia or New Zealand – all far enough away from the long arm of the IRA and the raggle-taggle band of ordinary people who'd fallen for her scams. The US seemed unlikely for various reasons so, following my instinct, I directed my attention to Australia and New Zealand.

It seemed that my suspicions were right when investigations confirmed that, a few months before their disappearance, Patricia had sought a "Police Certificate of Character", then required for a visa to New Zealand, from Ireland. The application was made before her scam came to police attention and the required certificate had been sent to her then address in Leixlip, County Kildare. By the time the certificate arrived, things had got too hot for Patricia and she'd already taken flight. She never got the certificate. It was strange that she was ever issued with it in the first place as, with a bit of digging, the police would have found out that Patricia was no stranger to controversy and had had a number of close shaves in the past. She'd conned a number of well-known criminals out of £100,000 in the Ballyfermot area of Dublin a couple of years earlier, much to the embarrassment of her brother, a member of the Gardaí.

Meanwhile, the police were still on her trail but they weren't having much luck tracking her down and had contacted Interpol for assistance. Before I found out that

Patricia had applied for a visa to New Zealand, I'd already contacted a colleague in Auckland, fellow private investigator Dan Thompson, who ran down two possibles. Both Irish, recently arrived with families and in the same age bracket, it sounded promising. One was a Patricia Chambers, the other a Patricia Owens. Owens was Patricia's maiden name. I thought I'd gotten lucky but, on investigation, it was clear that these were two totally unconnected innocent people, proving coincidences do happen. Still convinced that she was headed for the Oz-NZ region, the investigation moved to Australia.

Over the years I'd had a great working relationship with an old friend and colleague, Rod Bevan of Brisbane Investigations in Queensland. Rod was a great investigator who could be relied on to come up with the goods every time. Rather than travelling to Australia on a hunch, I contacted Rod and gave him the details of Patricia's movements to date and a recent photograph I'd managed to get my hands on, to ensure positive identification. I was still convinced she'd try to get into Australia via the back door of New Zealand, then a soft touch for many "tourists" wanting to "visit" Australia. Rod, as always, didn't fail the task. Within two weeks of my request, he'd pinned her down to an address in Glendalough, Western Australia, over four thousand miles from his Brisbane base. Tommy's penchant for all things Irish had tripped them up again! Patricia and her husband had rented a house at Harborne Street in Glendalough. With the huge distances involved, it was time to get another colleague on board to keep the McDermotts under surveillance until we got a team out there.

I phoned Trevor Bailey, from Donald Floyd and Co, another great firm in Western Australia, and asked him to take up surveillance. Trevor confirmed the McDermott's were still in place in rented accommodation in Glendalough. The problem was, they had a fortnightly tenancy and could up and go at any time, something Patricia was proficient at. With this information, we confirmed the McDermotts had entered Australia on 17 May, arriving in Perth. It was now late August. I wanted my client to be the first in what was now a very long line, to recover the money Patricia had stolen. One interesting piece of news was that Patricia appeared to be pregnant. She was a heavily built woman, so perhaps she just looked pregnant. With four children already in tow, a pregnancy was likely to slow her down, giving us enough time to get out to Australia, but there was nothing to confirm the agent's suspicions just yet.

Meanwhile, our investigations continued and it seemed Trevor had been right on the money. Planning on staying in Australia and not wanting to be deported if they were ever found, Patricia and her husband hatched a plan they believed would copper-fasten their residency in Australia. She got pregnant. The plan was to get around the system by having a child in Australia. She was wrongly convinced that if she had a child born there, it would automatically be an Australian citizen and would guarantee the family the right to stay in the country permanently. Having first flown to New Zealand, where they stayed for a couple of weeks, they picked up a tourist visa to enter Australia by the back door. A short time later, Patricia applied for an extension to stay on in Australia, on the grounds of diminished health as a result of her "unexpected" pregnancy, which made it inadvisable for her to travel.

The McDermotts then applied for a work permit for Tommy, claiming they were running short of funds due to her "unexpected situation". They claimed to have only Aus$900 left to provide for all six McDermotts. While Australian Federal Police were still conducting enquiries in relation to these applications, we made them aware that Patricia was wanted in Ireland for fraudulent activities and that the Irish police has sought the assistance of Interpol in locating her – unsuccessfully up to that time. At the beginning of September, the family were granted a temporary extension and a work permit on humanitarian grounds – for the time being at least.

At the same time, we discovered that on 3 September Tommy traded in the car he'd been driving and handed over Aus$6,000 in cash for a newer Mazda van. It was another factor that would come back to haunt them, as they had now made a false declaration, claiming to have had only Aus$900 left to support the family. Information indicated they had not opened a bank account and all their dealings in Australia had been in cash.

Armed with this information, it was time to pay Patricia a visit. I'd already booked my flight to Australia when I was subpoenaed in a High Court case I was required to give evidence in and had to cancel my visit to Patricia, so I sent a couple of my investigators instead.

On arrival in Australia they discovered that Patricia and her family had been true to form and had done a moonlight flit from their accommodation. The chase started all over again but this time it didn't last long and we were right behind her. The family were tracked down to an address in Heathridge, Perth, where they were staying at the home of new friends, the Fagans, who knew nothing of their background. Patricia had been refused a further extension of her visa and had instructed a lawyer in Perth to take her case to the Australian High Court based on her mitigating circumstances. It wasn't expected to succeed as, unknown to Patricia, Interpol had become actively involved, at the request of the Gardaí.

The McDermotts were getting quite comfortable and decided to get their own place. Moving on from Heathridge, the happy gang were safely ensconced in a small rented house in a remote area in Perth, in Western Australia. Knowing nobody in the area became a bit of a strain and Patricia and her husband decided to find the nearest Irish club to socialise and have a few drinks. They quickly became firm friends with the local Australian members and the Aussies were delighted to have a traditional Irish musician in their midst.

The investigators called on Patricia at her newly rented home. She was speechless with shock and not exactly welcoming to her fellow-countrymen. She couldn't understand how we'd found her. They explained her predicament and told her they were investigators representing a client she'd defrauded of a large sum of money and they wanted it back. They didn't mention the client's name and Patricia, having had many successful hits, didn't ask any questions. Having first denied any knowledge of what they were talking about, she eventually admitted it but claimed the money was all gone, blown on hotels, flights and good times. In a dramatic gesture, she hysterically took off her wedding and engagement rings, screaming, "That's all I have, take them!" Used to being the actress, given the amount of people she took in, she was apparently worthy of an Oscar on this occasion. The investigators gave her twenty-four hours to get the money and arranged to meet her at the Irish club the following night. She was warned not to make a run for it, as she was under surveillance.

The investigators set up base in the Irish club and got to know the locals. The Aussies' general conversation was centred on the political troubles "back home"; it was obvious where their support and sympathies lay. Deciding to play this political card, though nothing was actually said, reading between the lines the Aussies assumed that "the boys" were connected with the "struggle for freedom" back home. The investigators left them to their assumptions and neither confirmed nor denied anything, but they did say they were in the area to "see" the McDermotts about some "missing money", letting them know Patricia had pulled off a major financial scam back home.

By the time Patricia and her husband arrived at the club the following night, the investigators were already "mates" with the Aussies but the McDermotts weren't to know that. They tried to brazen it out now they were amongst their "new friends", telling them that the guys were "just bad debt collectors" trying to hustle them. It didn't take long for the locals to let the McDermotts know they knew "the boys' real connections" and the scam she'd pulled on the "boys" back home, high-tailing it to Australia with the money raised for "the cause". The Aussies wanted no part of it and were quick to tell the McDermotts to give the money back, pronto. The McDermotts were not sure if the lads were investigators, as they'd said, or had been sent by "the boys". Seizing their opportunity, the lads said nothing to clarify the situation. The end result was that they quickly agreed to return what money was left from their scam after the "expenses" they'd already blown on high living on the road to Australia.

The Australian police were notified and kept informed of the situation and they issued the McDermotts with deportation notices.

There was one very relieved and happy Man U footballer when I called him to tell him that not only had I found

Patricia in Australia, but I'd also managed to recover all his money. The footballer was happy to pay my not insubstantial fee and he even added a generous tip to say thanks!

I don't know if "the boys" from the IRA ever got their money; somehow, I don't think so. Perhaps they should have hired a private investigator!

11

The Politician Versus
The Private Detective

Some time ago I was consulted by a distraught wife, exhausted by her husband's philandering. It had been going on for years, she said, much to her embarrassment – but her husband always denied it, telling her she was neurotic. A well-known politician, he also had business interests which allowed him to be frequently away from home, giving him both time and opportunity to cover his tracks.

The wife alleged that she had suffered domestic violence, which was reported to her GP. The marriage had broken down. At this point she decided to ask me to try to find evidence that her husband was having an affair and I agreed to take the case.

The politician was kept under surveillance. On the day of the All-Ireland final, he was expected to go to Croke Park to watch the match. Having checked all the likely hotels, I was surprised to find a reservation had been made for two nights in the name of the politician and his wife at a city centre hotel.

Unfortunately, he'd neglected to tell his wife about the trip. It was a strange move to book into a city centre hotel likely to be occupied by some of his constituents, who would surely know that the lady sharing his bedroom was not his wife.

The hotel was kept under surveillance and the politician arrived with a younger woman, who signed the register in the name of the man and his wife. Having established which room they were in, accompanied by another agent, I took up observation close by and we could clearly hear the man's distinctive voice talking to the woman from inside room 56. After a few minutes, the politician left and went down to the bar, where he was joined minutes later by the woman, now wearing a low-cut dress. After a quick drink they left the hotel, stopping to talk to two gardaí on the street. I noted the guards' ID numbers, signified by a letter and numbers on their epaulettes, which identifies their station, in case they were needed later to corroborate my evidence and confirm they'd spoken to the politician and the woman on the date and time in question.

The couple went to the Gresham Hotel, drinking until the bar closed to non-residents, when they left their friends and walked up O'Connell Street. As they walked, an argument erupted and they could be heard shouting loudly at each other, stopping from time to time as the argument became even more heated. The politician shouted, "I did not fucking kiss anyone," to which the woman responded, "You fucking did kiss her – three times! I'm going home." At one point the politician violently pushed the woman against the plate-glass window of a well-known department store. I was left in no doubt that his wife's allegations of brutality were true.

The couple returned to their hotel and went to their room, where the argument continued and could be heard at the other end of the corridor. They made no attempt to lower their voices or moderate their foul language. The politician shouted, "Get away from that fucking door! How do you think you can get home? There are no buses or trains. I spent a lot of money to bring you here and, by Jesus, I'm going to get my money's worth." It got increasingly violent, as things were thrown around the room and something heavy hit the door. The politician continued to shout abuse, calling her a "fucking whore" and a lot more besides. A screaming match ensued with both parties hurling obscenities at each other.

It was clear from the argument that it was an ongoing relationship and that the "lady" was married, as she shouted: "My husband is a decent man. He never gave me the life you give me, you pig . . . You are always threatening me. You can strangle me, but if you touch me again, I'll jump out of that fucking window and you can explain that to the guards." The politician retorted: "I always suspected you were obliging the guards, you whore. Do you think I'm a blind fucking eejit?" . . . and so it went on until three in the morning. Another man came out of his room and complained that he couldn't sleep, saying he had phoned reception several times to complain about the row. Eventually, shortly after three o'clock, things calmed down and no further exchanges were heard.

Surveillance was maintained until the following morning, when the couple had breakfast delivered to the room before eventually heading to Croke Park. Ironically, to add to the politician's woes, the couple were clearly shown together on camera during RTÉ's coverage of the game. Funnily enough, it never appeared to impede his political career.

12

Céad Míle Fáilte: A Welcome too Hot to Handle

A few years ago, a major publishing house contacted me with a problem. It appeared that an entry in one of their travel guides suggested that a certain hostel in Ireland was giving a welcome even warmer than the traditional Irish *céad míle fáilte*. The owner wasn't happy and was suing the publication for libel. The female writer had stayed at the small remote unlicensed hostel earlier in the year, while gathering information on the local amenities. She later wrote about her experience, in which she described the "would-be" extra friendly services of the owner if he'd had his way. In her review she claimed that when she'd asked if there were any other guests, the owner had said she was the only one, but added, "If you get scared, you can come into my bed." She said she *had* been "very scared – but of him".

As an experienced researcher for international travel guides, she had found Ireland to be very safe and said in her review that she felt this behaviour "unusual" and "out of character for the country". Soon after the publication of the guide, the owner of the hostel sent a solicitor's letter threatening to sue for damages. My instructions were to investigate the background to the hostel and its owner, with specific instructions that I was to check into the hostel to see if the man "might live up to the reputation as ascribed to him in the book". In other words, they wanted me to be the bait.

The hostel was in a remote part of Ireland. The only way to get to it was down a long lonely country lane, with no lighting and far removed from any neighbours – not the most pleasant of tasks for a lone woman, given the suggested background to the case. Background investigations indicated that the hostel was operated by a single middle-aged man. Locals described the hostel owner as being "not the full shilling".

It was not without some trepidation that I went in search of this hostel, advertised only by a broken piece of timber, nailed to a tree, with the word "hostel" roughly scrawled in blue paint. It was certainly in the backwoods all right and I really wasn't looking forward to the night ahead. As I approached the building, I saw a sign outside which said: "To stay – walk in." I knocked and shouted out a couple of times, but there seemed to be no-one around. The place seemed a little eerie, although it was the height of summer and the nearest town some miles away was bustling with tourists.

I'd already checked around to see what accommodation was available locally and found that every hotel and B&B was booked up. There was no shortage of tourists around, while the hostel was empty. I asked taxi drivers and checked around the local pubs, asking if they thought I'd get a room at the hostel, mentioning it by name to see their response. It was the same everywhere. Without exception, everyone said it wasn't a good idea for a lone woman to go out there. But I did anyway. That was the job.

I hung around outside the empty hostel for a while and eventually a man turned up and asked if I wanted a room. He seemed a little strange, although courteous and friendly, but not overly so. He looked dirty and shabbily dressed and he constantly called me "love" and "pet" during the course of our conversation. I put this down to just being a "mannerism" – at least, I hoped that's what it was! He showed me around the accommodation, all of which was located in the small bungalow adjoining the owner's own bedroom. I knew this, because he insisted on showing me *his* room.

The other rooms consisted of two or three bunk-beds to a room and a couple of single and double rooms. It was rough-and-ready with no mod cons; to say it was basic would have been a compliment. He said there was no-one else staying there, so I could pick any room I liked. The room farthest away from his looked good to me. I paid up-front for the room, which looked as if it had never been cleaned. Not an encouraging start to my "weekend away"! I definitely wasn't looking forward to the night ahead.

Later that evening, he knocked on my door and asked if I would like a cup of tea, saying I was free to have the run of the house. A later offer of joining him for a few drinks was also politely declined. I spent most of the night lying fully clothed, with one eye open, on a rock-hard single bed. Thankfully, nothing happened.

The following morning I was taken aback when the hostel owner knocked on my "locked" door and walked in before I had time to answer him. He said he'd be going out for a minute but he'd see me when he got back and we'd have breakfast together. Not likely, I thought, and decided I'd already had enough. I left before he had a chance to come back. He hadn't "tried anything on", but experience and my gut feeling left me very uncomfortable and I wasn't about to hang around to see if anything untoward happened! With no other guests and with no-one else around in this remote woodland setting, I was already pushing my luck.

Within minutes of his departure, I left the hostel and headed for the town, where I made further enquiries in the locality about the background to the place, which was well-known to the locals. People told me about two French girls who'd stayed at the hostel only weeks beforehand. They had become afraid of the owner's persistent approaches and had left, as they felt he was inappropriately "over-friendly" towards them.

Others told of an American guest who had left the hostel in a hurry and arrived at the local hotel in a state of panic. She had been staying in an en-suite room and decided to take a shower. As soon as she got into the shower, she heard a knock on the shower-room door and a man shouting, "Have a good wash now!" As the only guest staying there that night, she was very frightened. She got dressed immediately but was too scared to leave through the main exit, so she made her escape through the bathroom window as quickly and quietly as she could. Distraught, she checked into the local hotel in a state of shock and told the staff what had happened. They were apparently not overly surprised, as it wasn't the first time they'd heard such rumours. Now they had it first-hand.

No wonder the locals had warned me about staying there. My investigation indicated that, far from the travel guide article causing a fall in business, the owner's own actions were undoubtedly responsible for it. The man was well known around the town, hawking for business from incoming tourists. If a tourist refused to accept his offer of accommodation, he would scream and shout abuse at them, cursing their kith and kin for generations to come. He'd follow them around the town, cursing and swearing at them. Not exactly the behaviour destined to win him any tourist awards. He was also known to have a serious gambling problem as well as being a very heavy drinker, which possibly explained his uninhibited venture into the American girl's bedroom.

Investigations showed he'd also caused a lot of grief for a local businesswoman, imagining he was romantically involved with her, despite the fact that she was in a relationship. They'd never had any contact, social or otherwise, but whenever he saw her with her boyfriend, he'd shout abuse at her. He stalked her day and night and telephoned her constantly, until she was forced to get a restraining order against him. He had numerous criminal convictions over a period of years, for various offences – not exactly a good recommendation for someone in the tourist business. Given his reputation and background, as one local put it, "with him, anything could happen". They were probably right but I wasn't about to stay around to find out!

Needless to say, as a result of my findings, all threats of a court action against my clients were dropped. Just another "glamorous" PI job!

13

The CIA and the Bats in the Belfry

This is definitely a Chapter 13 story – the true story of how perfectly sane and rational people, often in high-powered positions, can lose touch with reality, living in fear of their lives because of what can best be described as an illness. Over the years, I've had a number of such clients approach me to take on their "case". One story worse than the next, it seemed they were beset by demons, aliens wanting to abduct them and psychos out to kill them.

You might think the obvious thing to do was to steer them gently towards the medical profession. Believe me, I tried. The tables turned on me and I was plagued day and night. They virtually camped in my offices and accused me of being "in league with *them*", whoever "they" were. Most of these people had already been to the police, who in turn would recommend that they contact me. I naturally would suggest that they go back to the police and demand to see the Superintendent, who had batted them my way in the first place.

All this was very unsatisfactory and time-consuming, so I eventually spoke at length to a psychiatrist who suggested a way out. I gave it a try and, frankly, it worked. Let me tell you about a couple of these cases and you'll see what I mean.

One case concerned a very highly educated lady who, just months previously, had held a high-profile position. I was aware of her high profile in the media over the years and she seemed very much in charge and on top of her game. No brief was too detailed or complicated for her and she excelled at her job. When she first made an appointment, I presumed that it was a problem within her company.

The truth, however, was far removed from that. She believed she'd been targeted by the CIA. Not beyond the bounds of possibility – they target all sorts of people for all sorts of reasons. This was different. Because of the connections with her company, she believed that the CIA had sent a hit man to "take her out". She originally thought she herself was the sole target but said she then realised that the CIA were also "after" the boss of the company. She was convinced there had been a "mole" in her company, planted by the CIA. The "mole" targeted the boss because, she said, "the CIA saw him as a conduit to other things through his wide-ranging connections with US government agencies".

She said she herself had suffered "covert torture" and "radiation attacks designed to shut down my immune system". This "torture" consisted of a "bug" placed in her ear to "pick up auditory nerve traffic"; "puncture pimples" on her throat to "focus the blood pressure on the carotid artery"; "targeting the cough reflex in the throat" as a harassment tactic; "fingernail torture, focusing on the nerve at the base of the nail"; as well as bamboo torture, causing spurting of nail growth, which she claimed was also done to Howard Hughes and to her mother. She said electric currents were being passed through her legs and spinal cord, "puncture marks" at the base of her ears and "two-inch burns across the skull" as well as "attacks on the brain via the electricity" in her home. These were just some of a three-page-long list of torture tactics employed against her, she claimed, "all because I tried to protect the Chairman of my company from the CIA and FBI".

No amount of reasoning or discussion would work with this type of client. Telling her I was unable to take on her case proved equally ineffective and joined me in the US government conspiracy against her. No matter what I tried, she wouldn't go away, as time and again I'd find her sitting in reception, awaiting my return to the office.

On the advice of the consultant psychiatrist, I agreed, at no fee, to examine her house with electronic equipment usually used to de-bug premises and phone lines. After several hours, she was completely reassured that she was finally free of the CIA's monitoring and interference, as they would now "know" we were on to them and be afraid of exposure.

I advised her to contact her doctor for a "check-up" to ensure that she was free from all these gremlins and I offered to send a "report" to him on her behalf, which she agreed I could do. This, I felt, was the only way to ensure that she got the proper medical help she really required. Hopefully, she had a more peaceful life in the belief that her tormentors were gone, at least until she got medical help.

She was not alone in her delusions. On a regular basis I had people from all walks of life – businessmen, academics and others suffering from similar problems – contacting me seeking a solution.

A prominent and successful businessman came in with similar problems. Not the CIA this time but nonetheless he was plagued with delusions that the walls of his home and offices were bugged by competitors. Industrial espionage is commonplace in business and I have often been asked to "sweep" premises for bugs. All too frequently, I found them. Business, like politics, can be dirty work. This time was different, however, and it was apparent that he was very ill. Nothing would placate him until I agreed to scan both premises and "clear" the problem – again, at no charge. To charge a fee would, in my opinion, be tantamount to fraud.

The businessman was relieved and his family were happy to have their father and husband back. Today, he continues to be a successful businessman and to my knowledge no longer suffers from such delusions.

I encountered numerous similar cases over the years and in all these cases, the client was suffering from psychosis – a mental health problem that causes the person to have delusional beliefs and lose touch with reality. Anyone suggesting they were ill were seen as part of the "conspiracy", even their own family members, and in most instances, they refused to get the medical help they really needed, which is the only real solution. After my intervention the problem was, to their mind, resolved and they then usually agreed to see a doctor. Paranoid psychosis is not uncommon but in recent years it seems to have increased. Dabbling in drugs, cocaine in particular, is believed to be responsible for the many young people currently suffering from psychosis, as mental health practitioners can testify.

14

Sleuths, Gumshoes, Private Eyes . . .

Despite the incident in Arnotts involving the Fellonis, I was still not deterred from going into the business. Seeing my determination, my father thought up another scheme to persuade me to change my mind. I guess he thought I'd either find out what the PI world was really like and run a mile or, at worst, I'd get a taste for the business in a busy city and know just what I was letting myself in for.

I was sent to stay with PI friends of his in New York. I first stayed with Irving Shumbord, the ex-FBI investigator who ran the ABC Detective Agency at 132 West 43rd Street in New York City. Irving employed ex-federal agents and NYC detectives, so I was thrown in at the deep end with hard-bitten PIs.

From there, I went upstate New York to Albany, where I spent time working with Ed Blaney and his family. Ed was originally from Monaghan, having served with De Valera in Boland's Mills – the last bastion to fall during the 1916 Easter

Rising – though he was then only a kid himself. He left for America soon after the Rising and joined the New York Police Department, the NYPD. When Dev and Frank Aiken were fundraising in America, Ed accompanied them around on a fund-raising tour of New York and raised funds through his NYPD colleagues, many of whom had Irish connections. Ed later became a detective, working with the murder squad until his retirement, when he set up his own detective agency with his son Kevin and wife Margaret in upstate New York. Their agency covered a wide area, including Utica, Syracuse, Rochester and Buffalo. My time spent in New York City and upstate was a highlight of my life at the time and I loved every second of it – much to my father's despair!

Ed Blaney later returned to Ireland in 1973 for the first time since he'd emigrated and my father arranged for him to meet his old comrade Eamon de Valera, then President of Ireland, in Áras an Uachtaráin in the Phoenix Park. It was a memory he treasured until the day he died. Being Americanised, Ed was amazed at my father's ability to arrange a meeting with the President. Back then it wasn't such a big deal, especially for an old comrade who'd stood shoulder to shoulder with Dev, his former Commandant of the Third Dublin Battalion of Volunteers. Besides, Dev was just about to retire!

Both Irving and Ed treated me like family during my stay. They went out of their way to show me the ropes, as I tagged along with them when they were working their cases. One of the first cases I remember was an accident and insurance claim with Irving. The case was several years old and had been back and forth between the insurance company and several investigation agencies, who couldn't get to grips with it. It seemed straightforward enough, but when we drove outside the city to the rural area where the accident had occurred, the maps and sketches of the scene made at the time of the accident didn't make sense.

We asked around to see if anyone remembered the accident, which had left one man dead, but eight years had passed and the victim was from out of town, so the locals didn't remember it. When the accident happened, one car had careered on, crashing into a metal advertising hoarding, which collapsed onto the car, causing the fatality. The only hoarding we could see was located at the far end of town, on a small rural road. It didn't match the sketch of the accident in any way.

The local police department couldn't throw any light on the case – or at least, they didn't. All I could think of was, had the advertising sign been moved to a different site since the time of the accident? It seemed almost too obvious to suggest. I thought Irving would probably think I was stupid, but I said it anyway, expecting him to laugh at me. Instead he said, "You know, maybe you've got something there." We got onto the company responsible for erecting the signs and found out that the sign *had* been relocated five years beforehand, which was why our sketches didn't make sense. With this new information, Irving was finally able to sort out the case. To this day, I'm still not sure if he was just testing me out and already knew that the sign had been moved! Years later, that little case came back to me when I got an investigation into an old accident case that hadn't been settled by the insurance company – but more about that later.

Life in Albany was laid back even by Irish standards and the PI work consisted mainly of insurance investigations, skip trace (an American term for missing debtors and criminals on the run), civil cases covering business or family law, surveillance and personnel investigations. No real James Bond stuff there.

Many of the other PI agencies did a bit of "bounty-hunting" – tracking felons, which included anything from prisoners on the run to people with outstanding arrest warrants for anything, even motoring offences. I remember one PI from California, Sue Sarkis, a glamorous Barbara Streisand lookalike who was a bounty hunter. Twenty-five years ago, before it became popular, she had false fingernails with diamonds encrusted into them. I remember jokingly asking her how she managed to catch these guys without breaking her nails. She said she usually waited until they went into a bar and after a minute she'd join them on the high stool. When the guy got "comfortable" with her, she'd cuff him and call the cops. Job done, bounty collected. Not my idea of PI work, though!

I got to see other investigators at work in New York, as Irving introduced me to friends and colleagues of my father – people like Miriam Oslar, a larger-than-life blonde with a Barbara Streisand accent. Together with her husband, George, they had an office on Normandy Drive, Miami Beach, Florida, but *she* worked from her apartment in Brooklyn, which in itself was something to see. We had to take off our shoes before we went in and I wondered if she expected her clients to do the same. It was a vast apartment and everything, from the carpets and curtains to the walls and couches, was pure white – to match her hair. Everything, and I mean *everything*, was covered in heavy-duty plastic. I was afraid to sit down; it felt like I was in a museum. She was very warm and welcoming but, somehow, I didn't fancy "working" in that environment, so I stuck with Irving for a while longer. I found out that one of her specialties was the repossession of airplanes; perhaps I should have stuck closer to her, as little did I know then that, years later, I'd be asked to find a missing jumbo jet!

I was sorry to leave New York when the time came to go back to school. I'd spent three months "working" with Irving and Ed and had met many other NY detectives during my time there. I was determined to go back the following year, if they'd have me, and that's what I did.

This time I had a better idea of what to expect and I knew my way around New York City. One of the main things I did on this "secondment" to New York was to learn about the relatively new field of polygraphs, better known as lie detectors. Irving had great contacts with Victor Kaufman and the ex-FBI guys who had set up the New York Lie Detection Laboratory (NYLDL). With Irving's persuasiveness, they agreed to put me through the course.

They had a wide range of polygraph equipment, ranging from small portable lie detectors to others built into what looked like normal office desks. The NYLDL had numerous clients, from government agencies to corporate bodies. They did polygraph testing and analysis and provided "expert witness" evidence in court cases.

My "initiation" into the area of polygraphs was excruciating. They "wired" me up and asked me questions like "Do you have a boyfriend?" and others designed to embarrass a teenager, particularly when you knew that *they'd* know if you were lying. Worse still, they waited to do this "test" at a time when my father was in New York on a case and "just happened" to stop by the offices of the New York Lie Detection Laboratory! Was I set up or what?

I suppose it came with the territory. My father was pretty strict on me, an only child and a girl at that. He took no nonsense and although at the time, being a teenager, I thought it was very harsh, in later life I realised it was for my own protection. In fact, I think my own kids had it as hard, if not harder than I did. I made sure they knew where the line was and not to cross it, but kids, being kids, will push their luck sometimes and mine were no exception – well, the boys anyway. In hindsight, I feel for them in some of the things I did to keep them "in line" as teenagers, probably much to their embarrassment, but I'd do the same again in a heartbeat. I am lucky in that I now have four wonderful adult children, all well-rounded and successful in their own right by their own efforts, and I'm proud of them all.

I'll probably embarrass them one more time if I tell some of the stories of how being a PI worked to my advantage in bringing up teenage boys . . . but I'll do it anyway – there had to be some perks to the job!

Now and again, given that I worked erratic hours, I would already have left for work by the time the kids went to school. The boys were under orders not to take their bikes to school, as a neighbour's child had recently been killed on his way to school on his bike. I gave them the bus fare and got all the usual promises. However, I knew that one son in particular would probably do it anyway, so I made a point of keeping him under surveillance. As soon as he thought the coast was clear, he headed off in traffic, riding his bike the three miles to school, oblivious to the fact that I was tailing him.

When he arrived home from school that evening, I said nothing – I didn't have to. He was greeted with a series of photos pinned around the house, all tracking his every move that day. For the first time in his life, he was speechless, as I told him never to try it on again, adding: "You never know who might be following you." I never told him who *had* followed him. Until now, he assumed it was one of my agents, as he hadn't spotted them, but just to let you know, son – it was me! Hopefully, he's still talking to me.

After a few more "incidents" like that, they virtually gave up trying to pull the wool over my eyes – although once or twice the same lad did get away with it. For instance, he was a good footballer and mad about the game, so I agreed to let him off school to go to an Ireland international match. It was months later that I found out the match was an away game! On another occasion, he was sent to the headmaster's office for some minor incursion at school. He knew that, whatever it was, I'd be notified and he'd be in trouble. Finding no-one around, he checked out the chapel and found the headmaster, who was also a priest, hearing confessions. Never one to miss an opportunity, he went in and "confessed" whatever he'd done in the knowledge that the headmaster could never tell me, as it was then under the seal of the confessional. Years later when he eventually told me that story, I had to laugh. Perhaps he had learned a bit of lateral thinking from me after all.

I suppose it was tough for kids to have a mother who could check out their every move and keep them under surveillance if the need arose. But really, that was probably only occasionally; the threat was more than enough, although I don't doubt there are a few more "stories" I've yet to hear. Sorry, guys!

Growing up, I probably met more real-life "private eyes" than most people see in a lifetime on television. Some, like Hal Lipset from San Francisco, were larger than life and well known throughout America. Hal brought the darker and more clandestine side of private investigation – bugging and wire-tapping – into the public arena when he bugged a US

Senate meeting to show how effective and insidious bugging devices could be. While it made his name, it also backfired somewhat, as draconian laws were introduced to outlaw bugging.

There was always a way around such matters, as proved by the Watergate scandal, which revolved around Nixon and the campaign to re-elect him as President (a project aptly known as CREEP – Campaign to Re-Elect the President). Five men were charged with burglary and illegal wire-tapping. *Washington Post* reporters Bob Woodward and Carl Bernstein's investigative journalism blew the plot wide open, leading to Nixon's resignation. Their source, "Deep Throat", was former FBI Director Bill Felt Sr.

During the trial it was revealed that government investigators were involved in the cover-up. So when the Senate Watergate Committee were looking for a Chief Investigator, Philadelphia Attorney Sam Dash, head of the Senate Rackets Committee, recommended Hal Lipset, as they didn't trust their own government investigators. Dash had worked with Lipset, defending the Teamster Union's imprisoned President, Jimmy Hoffa, who was appealing a conviction for jury tampering, as his conviction had hinged on illegal bugging by the government. Now that Dash was on the other side, he wanted an honest, unimpeachable investigator working with him. Everyone was looking over their shoulder, not knowing who to trust, and the stakes were high.

Years later, Hal told me that Bob Woodward ironically became his "own deep throat". Lipset was appointed Chief Investigator at a time when Woodward and Bernstein began to hit brick walls. It was a mutually beneficial arrangement; they met regularly and exchanged information, with Woodward pointing Hal in the direction of people ready to talk. After months of tough and dangerous investigation, someone powerful wanted Hal off the case. As he said himself: "In the political cauldron that was Washington, I was out as fast as I was in." He was just too good at his job. At the end of the day, the Watergate Committee got what they wanted and brought about the resignation of the President of the United States.

Lipset, or Lipshit as he was affectionately called by his friends, loved the tranquillity and peace of Ireland. Though he visited occasionally, he was never here long enough to see the real underbelly of Irish politics. He probably would have recognised some of the players. I knew Hal very well, both from my childhood and later when I joined the business myself. We would meet in Dublin, the US or some far-flung place at World Association of Detectives Conventions, or WSSA, the World Secret Service Association, or simply when our paths crossed on investigations and he'd call me from time to time just to chat.

One or two of the PIs I encountered were eccentric to say the least. One guy in particular comes to mind, and I always thought a PI series based on him would make "interesting" viewing. I first met him at a World Association of Detectives meeting in Singapore, where he made his "entrance" dressed in black from head to toe. His six-feet-plus frame was topped off by a black wide-brimmed hat which covered his eyes. All you could see was a thick jet-black moustache that made Magnum PI look like he was clean-shaven.

Jack Torrance was his name. He operated a detective agency called Baskerville Detectives International (he must have been thinking of Sherlock Holmes) in San Pedro California. Once you'd met him, you never forgot him – not always a good characteristic in a PI. Throughout our week-long convention he appeared at every function, every dinner, seminar or opening of an envelope, always dressed in the same black outfit, complete with hat, which never left his head, day or night. On one trip to Sentosa Island, I watched in amazement as he took out a shoe-polish kit and lovingly began to "black-up" his luxuriant moustache with boot polish. We never saw him in the hotel for breakfast and wondered if he ate elsewhere, until late one night he let us into a little secret. He claimed he was actually staying in the local equivalent of a bed and breakfast, as it was a lot cheaper than the convention hotel, the Pavilion Intercontinental, which was one of the best hotels in Singapore at the time and extremely expensive. When the convention was over and it was time to return home, Jack, then three sheets to the wind as a result of the neat whiskeys everyone was buying him, told us he'd run out of money and had "done a bunk" out of the B&B's window! Whether it was the drink or an effort to wind us up, I never found out, but by the look of his (by then) shiny black suit – incredibly, he was still wearing it – it was a distinct possibility. He was just one of many eccentric characters I came across in the PI business over the years.

Another legendary PI and good family friend was David Almog, from Tel Aviv. David was also a Colonel in the Mossad, the Israeli Secret Service, and during the Yom Kippur War he spent time in the Sinai Desert on special missions. It was strongly rumoured that the Mossad had an undercover office in Dublin but, because of the nature of the intelligence business, this was never proved but was and probably is highly likely.

15

What's Bugging You?

Bugging is big business. It was big even back in the 1960s and 1970s, when people like Hal Lipset and Manny Mittleman were rolling out the latest bugging devices, and it has been a feature of both international business and Irish life ever since.

As a schoolgirl, I was a frequent visitor to New York with my parents and on one occasion, my dad brought me to meet Manny Mittleman, who like Hal Lipset was a Jewish technological genius who made bugging devices for international agencies, private investigators and government bodies. My dad's friend Irving Shumbord had a close working relationship with Mittleman, both as a PI and former FBI agent, and he took us to meet him in his workshop in New York City, to show us what he could do. I still have a clear memory of that visit; it was like something out of a mad professor's laboratory, with tangles of wires, contraptions and half-finished projects lying around his workshop. I wondered how he could ever find anything. But Shumbord was right, Mittleman was a genius.

No matter how difficult an assignment, he could come up with some sophisticated but unobtrusive device to do the job.

Manny put bugs in lightbulbs, torches, pens, wrist-watches, shirt buttons, briefcases, three-pin sockets, tie-pins, cuff-links, desk sets, cigarette packets and just about anything else you could name, light years before they were in commercial production, as they are now. He showed off his cigarette pack bug, offering my father a cigarette from an almost full pack. Shuffling them so that two cigarettes were higher than the rest, my dad, a heavy smoker, accepted his offer. Seconds later, Manny played back their entire conversation, recorded by a miniature mike hidden in the cigarette pack.

Today, you can buy virtually any kind of bug off the shelf or have something special made to order but, back then, Manny was a rare find. He showed us the olive in the martini bug – it was fantastic. A real olive, it contained a miniature mike, while the cocktail stick acted as the antenna. He tried it out for us and it came across loud and clear, and that was long before the James Bond movie. He claimed *he* had invented it, but Hal Lipset's man Bersche also laid claim to the "martini" bug, as you'll see below. I can't say either way – perhaps they both did!

Hal Lipset, whom you will already have met in the previous chapter, was a member of the World Association of Detectives and former commander of a US Army Criminal Investigation Division (CID), tasked with investigating crimes committed by American military personnel following the Battle of the Bulge in the Second World War. After the war he set up a private detective agency in San Francisco in 1947 – the same year my father started out – and he made his name handling defence investigations for the notorious mafia-controlled

Longshoremen's Union – made famous by Marlon Brando's *On the Waterfront* movie.

Hal became one of America's experts on electronic surveillance. He found fame when the *New York Times* reported that he'd taped his own testimony to the Senate Judiciary hearings with a bug hidden in a martini. It was a simple device – as long as you didn't try to eat the olive. He also planted bugs in the flower arrangements in the "hearings" room. It was dramatic and different enough in those days to bring both Lipset and his bugs to national attention.

Lipset was a legend, a larger-than-life character, not only for his martini bug; he also worked with Francis Ford Coppola as the technical consultant on the film *The Conversation*. Set in San Francisco, the film opens with a scene showing a woman and her lover plotting to evade her husband and his private detective, not realising their every word is being bugged. Hal's expertise was again called upon in *The French Connection*, when he acted as a technical advisor to the filmmakers.

No one spoke openly about bugging in Ireland but big organisations were conscious of their vulnerability in areas such as industrial espionage and insider trading. It wasn't just big business, as suspicious husbands, business partners, trade unions and government agencies were concerned about everything from affairs to the leakage of confidential information to the media. Nothing was sacred.

I undertook counter-surveillance for a wide range of clients. Sometimes they'd hear a news bulletin carrying details of a confidential meeting they'd just had or read about it in the paper hours later; naturally, they were worried if they had a "leak". Irish legislation was covered by the Wireless Telegraphy Act of 1926 and subsequent later SIs (Statutory Instruments) and Acts of 1972 and 1988 but, like any old legislation it was still a "grey" area. Most companies offering their services weren't even aware of the existence of legislation, as time and again other agencies expressed surprise and disbelief when I spoke on the subject and said these services were illegal under Irish law, if the intention was to "bug" some third party.

My father recognised the potential development of electronic surveillance early on – then, as now, we followed American trends in many things. Seeing the way things were going, in 1961 he introduced the first radio-equipped cars into his business, although it took the Department of Post and Telegraphs almost a year to agree to issue a licence for them.

In 1967 he went to the US and bought a large amount of state-of-the-art investigative equipment, bugging and de-bugging devices, counter-surveillance and scanning equipment from Manny Mittleman – his own personal "Q". For many Irish businessmen, it might have seemed a bizarre, Walter Mittyish investment, but by the 1960s, the US Federal Government were spending over $20 million a year on bugging equipment and the CIA were spending even more. It was big business for everyone.

Always pro-active, my father had a life-long thirst for innovation and development. His faith in the future of technology was proved right but he had a few hoops to jump before he actually got his hands on his shipment of expensive "toys" when they arrived at Dublin Airport in the summer of 1967. He imported twelve cases of equipment, including all the latest Japanese and American technology for crime-fighting and investigations, from portable ultra-violet lights, fingerprinting equipment, chemicals for showing up evidence, bugging devices, counter-surveillance equipment and even a portable lie detector. The shipment was stopped by customs, who'd never seen anything like it before. There was no legislation preventing its importation, but Revenue quickly stepped in to impose impossible duties at a rate far in excess of its purchase price.

After some negotiation, a deal was done. Charlie Haughey, then Minister for Finance, arranged to allow the equipment in duty-free – on one condition. In an informal arrangement, it was to be made available to Garda HQ at the Phoenix Park free of charge whenever they needed it. It seemed they "needed it" quite a lot, as my father had to trek up to HQ time and time again whenever he needed his own equipment for a case. No sooner had he gotten it back than they found another excuse to "need" it, as the boys in blue used it to fight crime on the mean streets of Dublin at his expense! And so it went on for many years, until eventually the equipment was replaced with more up-to-date technology and the Gardaí actually began to buy their own! I wonder if the "arrangement" backfired on Haughey, as perhaps the "forces of the State" used the equipment he'd "requisitioned" for them two years later, when he found himself in the hot waters of the Arms Trial.

I still have some of that original equipment today – more from nostalgia than anything else – and I am still amazed at how advanced it was in its day and how forward-thinking my Dad was in importing it in those less-than-booming economic times. Despite a certain level of scepticism and naivety, big organisations were extremely conscious of their vulnerability in areas from industrial espionage to insider trading. Whether it was suspicious husbands and wives, business partners, trade union meetings, or even "official" investigations, be they gardaí or the bugging of the media by certain politicians – nothing was out of bounds. Jack Lynch, speaking in the Dáil in 1970, said: "There is, in all states, a security system, whereby telephones and other communications are intercepted. It applies in this country as well as others." He wasn't joking, but that was only half the story.

However, many high-profile cases didn't come to public attention until much later, when journalists Geraldine Kennedy (now *Irish Times* editor) and Bruce Arnold became victims of State bugging on the orders of C.J. Haughey. Bugging had been raised in the Dáil in 1980 and again in 1982, when Kennedy and Arnold's phones were tapped over a long period by the then Minister for Justice Sean Doherty, on the explicit instructions of Haughey, who was determined to find the source of media leaks revealing the Fianna Fáil dissidents' heave against his leadership. In answer to the outcry over the political bugging of phones, Fianna Fáil claimed that Fine Gael and Labour had been active in tapping phones themselves. When Haughey ordered the bugging of the journalists' phones, he'd obviously forgotten his 1964 statement, when, as Fianna Fáil Minister for Justice, referring to a *Sunday Telegraph* revelation of the State bugging of Labour TD's phones, he said: "We are only dealing with criminals . . . law abiding citizens are outside the scope of this debate."

In later years, companies openly advertised bugging services, often illegally, for all purposes. Bugging was used for all sorts of reasons, mainly cited as "national security". Who knows, perhaps some of this "official" bugging was being done by government agents using my father's equipment?

It must be said that monitoring of communications is an essential part of national security operations and has been for generations. Due to modern technology, communication can be both the key and the "weak link" in subversive organisations, making them easier to track by police and government agencies tasked with the protection of its citizens and territory. The Auditor and Comptroller General's report only refers to a monetary sum for the Secret Service – no details are ever given and it doesn't specify what percentage of the financial budget is used for bugging equipment.

One of the early on-going jobs my father undertook was the routine de-bugging of trade union offices as well as the homes of at least one or two Labour Party members, including that of the late Dr David Thornley, a television journalist and Labour TD. Both Mickey Mullen and David Thornley became great friends of his and were often in our house as, ironically, were Brian Lenihan Sr and Charlie Haughey.

Bugging has always gone on, from the time the first telephone exchange opened, and "operators" were instructed to pass on any information believed to be of a subversive nature, down to the "local country exchange", who listened in on party-lines to glean the local gossip.

I recall the Moyna/Mallon bugging in October 1983. Seamus Mallon, then deputy leader of the SDLP, made regular visits to Dublin to meetings at the New Ireland Forum, a discussion platform on the Northern Ireland conflict. Mallon usually stayed at the home of an old friend, Michael Moyna, on Dublin's northside. Over the bank holiday weekend in October 1983, Moyna's phone went out of order, a common occurrence in those days; it could often take weeks for repairs. Knowing this, they reported the fault immediately and were surprised to find it was repaired within the hour.

It was known in certain circles that telephone lines went "out of order" to facilitate their "repair", complete with a new wire-tap. However, the Moynas weren't suspicious. An hour after it had been repaired, a van of the type then used by Post & Telegraphs arrived with three men, who said they were there to fix the phone. When told it was already fixed, they claimed they had to put in a new line, which they insisted on bringing in through the back of the house, out of view of the neighbours. Mrs Moyna, her son and his wife were present when the men called. They fed a line under the carpet, through the kitchen and out an open window to an electricity pole and from there across a lane, over a roof and down a weed-covered drain.

When Moyna got home he couldn't believe they'd fed a wire through an open window – how were they supposed to close it? He lifted the carpet to re-route the clumsy job and found that the wire wasn't connected to the phone but led directly to a microphone hidden under the carpet. Following the lead back, it led to a small container, which turned out to be a radio transmitter. The phone company denied having sent anyone to fit a new line.

Suspicious that the bugging was connected to his friendship with Seamus Mallon, Moyna contacted him and together they contacted Garret FitzGerald, the Fine Gael Taoiseach. Gardaí were notified and after two months of "investigations" – which consisted of talking to the phone company and the Moynas – the Gardaí decided, somewhat bizarrely, that the bug had been planted by criminals planning to rob the house. The Taoiseach, Garret FitzGerald, claimed to be completely satisfied with the Garda findings. The matter, as far as the government and the Gardaí were concerned, was at an end.

It might have been, but for the *Sunday Tribune*, who headlined the story. Fianna Fáil's Brian Lenihan Sr claimed he'd received important information about the bugging and named four people who might "be of assistance into any investigation into the bugging affair". Subsequently, two Republicans, arrested and questioned about the bugging, claimed gardaí had attempted to plant bugging equipment on them. An identity parade was arranged but the Moynas said that none of these men "even remotely resembled" the men who had called to the house.

From there on it became an even bigger farce, as Moyna's cousin was arrested on a charge of possessing explosives. When the case came to court it was thrown out, as independent technical experts testified that the so-called "evidence was laughable". In a classic conspiracy theorist's dream, during the trial, Mr Moyna's son claimed to have recognised a garda involved in the case as being one of the three men who had called to his father's house to fit the new phone line. The garda was one of the men named by Brian Lenihan. Following a sworn statement by the Moynas, a meeting was held with Taoiseach Garret FitzGerald, Justice Minister Michael Noonan, Garda Commissioner Larry Wren and other officials. Amazingly, Noonan issued a statement saying the Moynas were mistaken, claiming that the officer concerned was "elsewhere at the time". Moyna Junior was quite clear in his recollection and identification, as was his wife, both having spoken to the "engineers" while they were working on the line.

The Department of Posts and Telegraphs then sent someone to the Moynas to collect the bugging equipment "for examination". Feeling justifiably cautious, the Moynas refused to part with the evidence, not knowing who to trust, given the history of State "prying" and the government's "denial" of Garda involvement. Charles Haughey, who wasn't above bugging people himself, blamed the British, while Fine Gael pinned the blame on the IRA. The media pointed to the Gardaí as being the main suspects – and so it went round and round.

Confused by the controversy, Seamus Mallon phoned me at home to see if I could shed any light on it. I had been giving lectures and media interviews on wire-tapping long before the story broke and he wanted to know if I could help in pinpointing the culprits. I was acutely aware, during that call, that it too was probably bugged, so I wasn't likely to discuss the matter to any degree over the phone. While I couldn't tell him much, it seemed obvious it was the work of amateurs – a botched job at best. The equipment they used was primitive in the extreme and their method of "planting" a bug naïve, with no chance of it going undetected. They'd used a microphone which they "planted" under a carpet – probably the last place you'd want to put it. Not only was it likely to be discovered as a result of the uneven lump in the carpet, but the sound quality, if any, from the less-than-sensitive microphone would have been muffled – much like putting your hand over your mouth while talking.

There was little to go on. It could have been any one of several players. If there was Garda involvement as believed, they were certainly not going to identify those involved. Perhaps it was an incompetent private investigator – and God knows there are many, but I didn't think that was the case. There appeared to have been no great effort to investigate the case and the Garda "investigation" – if you could call it that – was restricted to talking to P & T personnel and the Moynas – without any apparent "follow-up" on the information they gave them. Even the most inexperienced garda could do better than that.

My gut instinct was that it was the forces of the State acting illegally, probably using Garda personnel to do this "undercover" job. Obviously, they were inadequately trained and ill-equipped to plant the bug in an efficient and unobtrusive manner – which suggested, to their ultimate benefit, that it was the work of amateurs. Normally it would have been a job for the Intelligence and Security Branch of the Garda, but it would appear that they were not involved in this instance. The Special Support Unit of the Special Task Force had the technical equipment needed to monitor individuals or organisations they believed to be involved with subversive or left-wing activities, or potential "security risks". The most likely situation is that it was done in co-operation with an agreed "security policy" between Ireland and the UK, in the light of the then on-going negotiations relating to the North. Perhaps one day we might learn from State documents the true story of who was behind the bugging. The ham-fisted job merely drew public attention to the ease with which people's conversations and movements could be monitored.

More recently, in the case of certain gardaí in the Donegal division, the issue of bugging also reared its head. This time allegations of phone-tapping were made to the Bar Council and the Law Society by Senior Counsel Martin Giblin and the solicitor then acting for the McBreartys. Prior to a hearing of one of the hundreds of licensing summonses served on the McBreartys, in a private phone conversation, Giblin and the solicitor discussed the appointment of a Donegal barrister to assist them in the case and agreed to approach him on their next visit to Donegal.

At the next court appearance, before they'd contacted Nolan, Martin Giblin told the court he hadn't received any documentation in the case from the Gardaí. Gardaí strongly denied this and said that the papers had been delivered to Peter Nolan the night before. Giblin was astounded. No-one knew about Nolan, they'd made no contact with him and the only discussion about him was in that one phone conversation they'd had, just days before. The President of the Law Society wrote asking the then Garda Commissioner Pat Byrne to investigate the matter. The Gardaí denied the lawyers phoned had been tapped. Telepathy maybe?

16

Blackmailed . . . By the Cops!

Business was good; in fact, it was very good. The appointment book was booked solid for three months, with a long waiting list for cancellations. So when I got an urgent call one morning asking if I'd see a new client immediately, my first reaction was "impossible". The caller was well known to me – the principal of a firm of accountants, he already knew my workload. Between consultations, court attendance and case work – which often meant travelling abroad, writing up reports and overseeing investigators' case files – there was no way I could fit in his client until the summer, at the earliest. He asked me as a favour to him, as a personal friend, to hear him out. As he quickly outlined the story, I realised the urgency of his client's predicament and agreed to meet him immediately. It meant somebody had to be bumped off the list, but if what he said was true, it was a real emergency.

The client, S, was a big businessman. He arrived shortly after three in the afternoon accompanied by his accountant and outlined the circumstances surrounding his problem. While driving his Mercedes just outside Dublin, he had stopped at what he thought was a routine Garda checkpoint. Accused of drink driving by the Gardaí, he was not breathalysed but was taken to the police station for the alleged offence. His passenger, a young blind girl, was frightened and didn't know what was happening. The man was surprised that the policeman, Garda Jim Keogh, then serving in Swords Garda Station, seemed to know a lot about him. He referred to S's business and the fact that he'd lost his driving licence once before, which had cost him dearly in business terms. Keogh asked where he'd been and he admitted he'd been to dinner with his female passenger.

The cop kept needling him about the woman in his car, saying, "I'm sure your wife would like to know about that. That must be worth £10,000." At the station, he asked S to provide a blood or urine sample. Despite electing to provide a urine sample, S was unable to comply. He was released without having provided any sample – either blood or urine.

Subsequently, I learned that when he got home, S contacted a sergeant he knew and asked him if he could do anything to help him. The sergeant said, "leave it with me", phoning him back later to say he'd spoken to the arresting officer, Jim Keogh, who had said he'd think about it. On the advice of his "garda friend", phoned Keogh to find out what was happening and Keogh told him to meet him in the Gresham Hotel in O'Connell Street, Dublin to "discuss the matter". S noticed that when the cop arrived, he seemed very wary, arriving into the hotel through the back laneway entrance. He spotted S but he had a good look around before he approached him. The two men had a meal in the restaurant and discussed the matter. S offered to give £200 to a charity of Keogh's choice but the garda said, "that's not enough". Increasing the offer to £500, Keogh brushed it aside and came out with his own demands, saying he had a £40,000 mortgage to pay off. He demanded £10,000 to "drop" the case. S was speechless – he couldn't believe what he was hearing. Seeing his shock, Keogh said he'd take £7,000 and told S to meet him at the hotel the following Sunday with the cash. Keogh later changed the meeting, saying he'd call to S's business premises, the following Wednesday evening at eight.

I got the call the day the meeting was to take place. After a quick consultation at my offices, I arranged to meet S at his business, when we checked out the premises. We had just a few hours to set up video and audio surveillance and to show S how it worked, before we took up our surveillance positions in an adjoining warehouse, waiting for Garda Keogh's arrival. With a clear view through a window connecting the darkened warehouse to the well-lit office in the main building, we could see if any transaction took place. Our cars were concealed under tarpaulins in the warehouse, so as not to alert the blackmailer to strange cars in the area. The only car outside was the client's Merc. We checked and rechecked our equipment, monitoring the client's telephone on headphones to ensure everything was working properly. Covert surveillance was also maintained in and around the premises, waiting for Keogh to show up. Everything was working perfectly; it was just a matter of settling down and waiting for something to happen.

After our meeting, the client had withdrawn the cash in old notes, as demanded by Keogh. We made sure it was all in small denominations and I noted the serial numbers, photocopied the notes and covertly marked them with my initials with a special invisible marker, which can only been seen under ultra-violet light. As eight o'clock came and went,

I began to wonder if the cop had got cold feet. At half past eight, I heard a car pull up and then a door open. In the brightly lit corridor, I saw a thin, dark-haired man in his thirties walk into the client's office. Normally we would have visually identified the target before the surveillance operation, but in this instance, time wasn't on our side.

After some initial banter, the cop got down to brass tacks and said, "Well, you know, I don't know what I can do for you, I mean it's difficult, you know, even without the doctor. I could get around that but it's not easy. I could maybe not call the doctor, you know, but don't worry about that. I could maybe reduce the charges, dangerous driving maybe – that'd be better than drunk driving now, wouldn't it? I mean, after the last time, it's three years this time, you know. Three years is a long time without a licence and you in business and all." S was so nervous, he'd forgotten he hadn't given a "sample".

S said, "What about the other guards?"

Keogh replied, "It's entirely in my hands, I'm dealing with it, do you know. I might have a bit of a problem with two sergeants – well, one anyway – but I'll take care of that. It's entirely up to me, I'm dealing with it you know. You do understand I'm doing you a big favour – I mean, after all, three years, £10,000 is not much to get you out of that bit of trouble, you know."

S asked him to reconsider, saying, "It's an awful lot of money."

The cop said, "Sure it's nothing to you; you can make that in a couple of months, in two months even. It will get me over a bit of a hole and, remember, it's the other thing as well," referring to the lesser charges he had intimated.

S said, "You mean I have to pay you and I'm still in trouble."

The cop replied, "I'll look after it for you. Sure we probably won't have to go to court at all, you know."

S said, "I'll have to take it out of the company, I'm not the sole owner, you know."

The cop said, "Oh, aren't you, I didn't know that." He then reminded S what had happened when he'd lost his licence once before. S had been forced to hire a driver for the year-long disqualification and, at the end of it, the driver, who spent the time taking his business contacts, had gone into business in opposition to him. He couldn't afford to let that happen again.

The blind girl, as Keogh reminded him, was another problem – how could he explain that to his wife, a formidable lady firmly in charge of the purse strings?

S asked, "What about the £7,000 you mentioned the night in the Gresham?"

The cop said, "Ah sure, it wouldn't be worth my while putting my job on the line for £7,000. I mean, I never did anything like this before – it would have to be the £10,000 you know."

S said, "Well, I'd have to write a cheque for cash and give it to you each week." Asked what he meant, S told him he couldn't explain £10,000 missing from the account.

There was a pause in the conversation as the cop seemed to be thinking about it. Finally, he said, "Well, okay, a thousand a week."

S said, "I'll give you £900 here and now."

We listened and watched as the cop counted the money out in tens and twenties up to £900 and S said, "I'll give you two £50s as well."

The cop re-counted the money, saying: "£1,000, right, that's grand." He told S to meet him in the Gresham the following Sunday morning at eleven o'clock. Keogh then used the office phone to call his wife. As he left he said, "You needn't worry now, you know. I'll look after everything. Don't mention this to anyone – *anyone* – that's very important. I'm doing you a really big favour now, you understand that?" Repeating his warning, he said, "I'd better be going now, I'll see you on Sunday."

The cop left and I heard his car drive away. The time was 9.09 p.m. We left our positions and went to S's offices. He was a nervous wreck. In a shaken voice he asked if we'd heard everything. We reassured him we had – loud and clear – and had recorded everything. He asked what happened next. I said I would be contacting a senior Garda officer, as it was a serious criminal matter.

S was very upset and said he felt obliged to contact a garda friend who'd been advising him on the matter. I was very surprised. It was the first mention of anyone else's involvement other than his financial advisor. He'd said nothing about a "garda friend" before. If I'd known about it, I would never have taken on the case.

He made a call and, much to my surprise, Sergeant B arrived within minutes, despite the fact that the premises was remote from easy access. I was uneasy and very suspicious. The "friend", Sergeant B, didn't know about my involvement and was visibly surprised to see me. He asked S to give Keogh a chance "on humanitarian grounds", saying: "You should phone Keogh and tell him you recorded the conversation and that on the return of the £1,000 and an undertaking that the garda would take no further action against him, they could both forget the matter."

I smelt a very big rat. His sudden appearance had been suspicious enough, and now this. I was certain Keogh and

Sergeant B had set S up for the sting. I told S he had no option but to report the matter. Sergeant B asked to be left alone with S to "have a chat". His intention was to persuade S not to make a complaint against Keogh. I made my position unequivocally clear. I wasn't being a party to a cover-up. Blackmailers always come back for another bite of the cherry. I gave S an ultimatum – either you report it or I will.

I arranged to meet them an hour later in the Skylon Hotel, in Drumcondra, but they turned up within minutes of my arrival. Sergeant B said he now agreed the matter should be reported – I'd given him no choice. He found himself between a rock and a hard place and decided to stop digging in the hope that he wouldn't be dragged into it. My associate, ex-Chief Superintendent Maurice O'Connor (formerly of C3, the nerve-centre of Garda intelligence operations, who took early retirement to join my organisation), contacted a senior garda at home and told him what had happened. He offered to meet us immediately, but it was close to midnight – it had been a long day – so we agreed to meet at his office the next day at 9.15 a.m.

Next morning, accompanied by Maurice O'Connor and the client, we met with senior gardaí. We discussed the matter and gave statements as to what had happened. The senior investigating gardaí asked us not to discuss the matter with anyone and, in particular, the press, and we agreed. I had no intention of exposing my client to media scrutiny.

Meanwhile, unknown to me at the time, in a follow-up action, the Gardaí decided to set up their own "sting" operation. At the request of senior investigating officers, S agreed to go along with it, to help their internal investigations. He was told to tell *no-one* about it. He did as they'd said, too scared to even tell me. They got him to keep his appointment with Garda Keogh at the Gresham that Sunday and on their instructions, he phoned Keogh to confirm the arrangement. The garda gave him £1,000 in marked notes, noting the serial numbers, exactly as I had done. They put the money in a marked envelope and told S to give it to Keogh at their meeting. Covering all angles, they bugged the public phone in the hotel lobby and "wired S up", attaching two listening devices to his clothing. Keogh never showed up. S's police "handlers" got him to phone Keogh at home from the bugged hotel phone. He was surprised when Keogh asked him if had left a message for him the night before. He got the distinct impression that Keogh had been "tipped off" not to show up – that it was a trap.

If there was a tip-off, it could only have come from inside the Gardaí, as the operation was, supposedly, "highly confidential" and on a "need to know" basis. The Garda "sting" failed. Despite their resources, it appeared that they had a security leak. They immediately dispatched two senior officers to Keogh's home, where a detailed search turned up the money, some of which was found still in the boot of his car. All the seized notes matched the serial numbers I'd recorded and my initials showed up on every note under ultraviolet light testing, exactly where I said they'd be. It was effectively an open and shut case.

The Gardaí had other ideas and launched their own full-scale investigation. They sent "experts" to examine S's offices, to establish if we could have observed and videoed all that our statements said we had from our positions in the warehouse – already self-evident on the video. As part of the initial plan in setting up our "sting" operation, I made sure the surveillance positions gave a clear view of the deliberately well-lit glass office area, while I and my investigators were hidden in the darkened warehouse. They queried every last detail, taking away all the equipment I'd used for "technical examination". They checked out everything, sending the Technical Bureau to photograph and map out the area. Initially, I thought they were just doing a thorough job but, after a while, it felt as if *I* was under investigation and that they were actually trying to disprove I had such a watertight case against one of their members, rather than concentrating on the attempted blackmail.

It was essential to ensure that the equipment was working properly and that it could and did record the attempt to extort monies, as stated in our case – without such evidence, a prosecution case would collapse. However, here the evidence was irrefutable. Perhaps it was the fact that they themselves had been unable to obtain any evidence, despite their resources and equipment, and they felt it would reflect badly on them. Was there any genuine reason for the actions? I'm still not sure. As a professional investigator, if I hadn't had enough hard evidence to support the burden of proof required in a criminal case, I wouldn't have called them in. My equipment passed all the rigorous Garda Technical Bureau's tests.

The garda's blackmail demands had been proved beyond doubt, as evidenced on the recordings. There was also our additional "eye-witness" evidence and the garda's phone call to his wife at home had also been recorded. Telecom records later confirmed the call was made from my client's office, at precisely the time stated in my report. The marked money was found in Keogh's possession, just one more nail in the coffin.

The next time I heard anything about the case was months later, from a journalist asking me to confirm the story. He'd had a tip-off about a garda who'd been charged – not with attempted blackmail, but with "accepting" a bribe. The journalist heard that the case had something to do with me and that the garda was due to appear that day at the local district court in Swords village, as opposed to the more usual Circuit Criminal Court in Dublin, given the seriousness of the matter and the amount of money involved. As the prime witness, I wasn't even told Keogh had been charged, much less given a subpoena calling me as a main witness. I never got a phone call.

By that evening, it was front-page news. Keogh was charged with conspiring with my client to pervert the course of justice by agreeing to accept a bribe. This was quite different to what had actually happened, in that it was Keogh and the sergeant (who had "befriended" S for the purposes of setting him up) who had laid a trap and demanded the bribe. The client found himself caught in the middle with nowhere to go. He couldn't contact the Gardaí, afraid of what might happen to him – he didn't trust them, with good reason. He had come to me on the advice of his legal and financial advisors.

The Garda plan to dispose of the case quietly might have worked, but for two strokes of bad luck – the journalist who informed me, and the "own goal" scored by Garda Keogh, who decided to plead "not guilty". Had he pleaded "guilty", the matter could have been disposed of without the need for a full hearing. Indeed, that appeared to have been the intention, as counsel for the prosecution told the court he'd been instructed to proceed with the matter as "expeditiously as possible". Obviously, a quick guilty plea in a local District Court, attracting no publicity, would suit the Gardaí. There would be no need for witnesses, especially me, and the garda would probably just get a slap on the wrist. Job done, nice and clean – an easy way out of the dilemma.

For some inexplicable reason, Keogh decided to plead "not guilty", stymieing any hope the Gardaí had of a quick and quiet end to the matter. The case was adjourned until the following October.

In the case of a "not guilty" plea, it is of paramount importance to ensure that all witnesses are in court to give evidence for both sides, but particularly in the case of the prosecution. If the prosecution witness doesn't turn up, unless the accused pleads guilty, the case will be dismissed and the accused will be free to go, with no blemish on his character. The usual procedure is to issue a subpoena to the witness to attend court on a particular day and time. Once again, the Gardaí failed to issue a witness summons or notify me of the impending case, even though Keogh was pleading "not guilty". But for the media, I would never have known that the garda's case was before the court. In the end, despite his not guilty plea, I was not called as a witness, and only read about his conviction when it appeared as front-page headlines in the evening paper.

I'd obtained the evidence and presented it "gift-wrapped" to the Gardaí, who then asked S to repeat the exercise for them, which he agreed to do. The fact that they failed in *their* efforts to get the evidence shouldn't have effected S. Despite his bringing the blackmail attempt to the attention of the highest-ranking gardaí; despite his total co-operation in their failed sting operation; despite my handing them a watertight case on a plate; and despite their promises that no action would be taken against him – S was sent for trial in the Circuit Criminal Court.

Not for him a quick disposal of the case in the local district court, away from the spotlight of the media, which was to have been the fate of the corrupt cop. The man took the courageous move of standing up to police corruption and was rewarded with a criminal prosecution. S's legal team made an application to the High Court to prevent his trial going ahead, on the basis that S had brought the matter to Garda attention and had been given their assurances and co-operated with them fully.

Mr Justice Blaney rejected S's application and said that there had been "no question of unfairness" towards S. Incredibly, he was convicted of attempting to corrupt a member of the force. He got the Probation Act. S felt very bitter – understandably so. He had done no more than they had asked him. If their "sting" had been successful, would they have prosecuted him for that too, despite having established the guilt of Garda Keogh and his associate beyond any doubt? S was also angry with me, as he believed I had leaked the story to the papers.

Meanwhile, Garda Keogh was convicted and got an eighteen-month prison sentence. In his summary, Judge Kevin O'Higgins described Keogh, a garda with twelve years' service, as "an extremely tragic" case. Keogh, who eventually admitted to attempting to obtain the money (and had obtained it) said that he was "very ill at the time and didn't realise what I was getting into". He later told the *Sunday World* that his prison life was "pure hell". "I had to be isolated in a cell on my own because I was a garda . . . only for my faith and prayer I don't think I would have got through."

A second garda – Sergeant B, S's "friend and advisor" – was also charged with the crime. As I'd suspected, he was directly involved with Keogh and, together, they had "set up" the businessman. He contacted the Association of Garda Sergeants and Inspectors asking them to represent him in the case, but they refused due to the weight of evidence against him. The Sergeant had been moved previously from other duties because of similar allegations. Sergeant B never got to Court. Tragically, he committed suicide before the case was heard.

Commissioner Laurence Wren stated in a letter to Garda Keogh that he was "not in any doubt as to the material facts" and dismissed Keogh from the force. At the end of the day, there were no winners in this sad case. Sad for all the families concerned, who were the victims, some more than others, of the crimes not of their making. But at least the Gardaí took *some* action and were seen to do the right thing (at least in the public perception) in the face of the clear and irrefutable dishonesty of a serving member.

I still feel a sense of outrage at S's treatment. He was in a no-win situation. Had he paid the blackmail money, it would never have ended; he'd have been at their mercy at any time. By trying to bring it to the attention of the people charged with keeping the law, he found himself not treated as a victim of corrupt cops but before the courts himself as the villain of the piece – hardly actions likely to encourage the public to come forward with information on Garda involvement in illegal activities. There will always be bad apples in any organisation but when they are in the law enforcement agency of the State, it is harder to accept. When they are identified, immediate action must be taken, and seen to be taken, to eradicate this element and restore confidence in the public they supposedly serve. Otherwise there is little difference between them and their prey.

Disciplinary action is not always apparent today in the face of the issues such as the Donegal gardaí scandal, which I spent several months in Donegal investigating and writing about, where certain gardaí perverted the course of justice over a long period of time. Donegal was not a stand-alone situation, as over the years I have investigated many allegations against gardaí. It was, however, the biggest Garda scandal to be publicly uncovered in the history of the State. After Donegal, there is a public awareness of the vulnerability of any organisation. Donegal is possibly just the tip of the iceberg.

17

Watching the Detectives: The School for Scandal . . . Or How to Investigate It

In the middle of all these investigations, I was conscious that there was no real organisation in Ireland for private investigators, as was the norm all over the world. I was already a member of numerous international organisations from Switzerland, Germany, the UK, the US and elsewhere, and despite the fact that we had managed to attract several international detective conventions to Ireland over the years, we still hadn't got our act together to organise ourselves into a cohesive professional body.

The British Association of Detectives had held their convention in Dublin in 1966 at the invitation of my father and it was an outstanding success. Some years later, in 1974, he persuaded the World Association of Detectives (WAD) to hold their convention in Dublin, in the Burlington Hotel. PIs from Alaska, South America, the UK, India, the US, Africa, the Nordic countries, Japan, Thailand and Australia all descended on our tiny island and loved every minute of it – so much so that just a few years later, in an unprecedented move, they held another WAD convention in Ireland. It was a great opportunity not only to showcase Ireland but to develop our business links and show that Ireland was to the forefront in business and investigative expertise.

Following on from this, my dad, Bill Kavanagh, together with myself and other well-respected members of the profession in Ireland such as Gerry Kenny, Liam Brady, Mick Foley and Charlie Miller, got together to form the Institute of Irish Investigators. It was a professional body that had stringent membership requirements, as detailed in a lengthy membership application and police clearance requirement.

It was not unusual for less-than-scrupulous people to hang up a shingle and advertise their services as private investigators. There was no legislation governing PIs in Ireland and nothing to prevent convicted thieves, fraudsters and conmen from setting up shop, offering their services to an unwitting public, despite the fact that my father had called for licensing of Private Investigators and security companies, having it raised in the Dáil as far back as 1963.

I continued this campaign with every Justice Minister on my watch but no action was taken by the subsequent governments until 2004, when the Private Security Services Act – operated by the Private Security Authority (the PSA) came into being, which included a one-line reference to private investigators. Four years on, there is still no licensing system in force for private investigators in Ireland and we remain one of the few countries in the world not to have licensing for PIs. A spokeswoman for the PSA told me there are no plans to implement such licensing for the foreseeable future – as they are still trying to cope with the burgeoning security industry. At present, it is still a free-for-all for conmen, fraudsters and charlatans to prey on people.

Many who hold themselves out as PIs have no experience in private investigations but nonetheless they dish out "advice" which is often legally incorrect. Time and again I came across problems of this nature and I could usually identify the culprits before the name was mentioned. Some of these chancers were well known to the police, having done time for various crimes. One in particular had convictions for impersonating a policeman, robbery and assault. While working in a factory, he was moonlighting as a PI. Others are just Walter Mitty types who, though not intentionally malicious, can create great problems, misleading clients and compromising a case. Obviously, by the very nature of the business, a client's problem is not something they want publicised in court and they're unlikely to make a claim against the incompetent or dishonest would-be PI.

One example was the case of a man purporting to be a PI who regularly dealt with family law matters, without having any experience in the field or knowledge of family law. When a woman – and it usually was a woman – came to him about her philandering husband, almost inevitably a wealthy businessman, he made contact with the husband and offered him a deal for a fat fee. The hard-done wife then paid him his fee for a "report" that gave her husband the "all-clear", showing him to be a hard-working businessman. It confirmed his late-night business meetings and she was relieved that her suspicions were wrong. The so-called investigator then got paid handsomely by a husband who had now been alerted to his wife's suspicions and most probably was moving his assets out of reach, in the event of future problems.

Yet another advertised their services without having a manned office in Ireland. They used a secretarial service who passed on their mail or dealt with telephone enquiries from clients. Nothing illegal about that but in an area that demands a high level of confidentiality, it afforded little or no control over who was dealing with potential clients and their problems or whether, in this village called Ireland, it could have been a friend, relative or associate of the person under investigation. Most reputable agencies will ensure that all staff sign a client confidentiality and non-disclosure agreement. On one occasion, someone from that particular agency actually phoned me to ask if I could send someone to the serviced offices to check if any cases had come in! The same person had a colourful background, to say the least, not to mention a conviction for attempted kidnapping.

A common practice was that some companies advertised investigation services without actually providing them, merely acting as "agents". Sometimes security or alarm companies accepted instructions from clients relating to what was an investigative matter. Having neither staff nor experience to deal with the cases, they would inevitably pass them on to me and would then add a "top-up" fee to "their" client for the report. This didn't make them dishonest or disreputable, but the trouble was, if the matter came to court, our agents had to appear, swear affidavits or sign the reports under my name. The companies never disclosed to "their" client that the case had been subcontracted out. What if the client didn't want to use me or my agency for some reason? Perhaps they knew me personally and were embarrassed or it was a conflict of interest. Perhaps I was already acting for the "other party" and yet the file, disclosing all *their* information, was passed on to me without checking first.

Like every profession, the investigation business has its share of rogues. So how do you really know if a private detective is reputable or proficient at their job? I consider it important that you choose your investigator as you would your doctor or solicitor – and even then, as we know from recent accounts, there is no guarantee. Recommendation is one good way. Solicitors and barristers, as well as insurance companies, banks and accountancy practices, are high-end users of PI services and may be in a position to recommend a good agency. After all, who wants to go to a complete stranger and tell them your most private and confidential problems, be they business or personal. This is particularly true in a small country like Ireland, where everyone knows someone who knows you – the six degrees of separation theory reduces to three in Ireland. You need to be absolutely certain that your private problems are as safe with a professional investigator as they supposedly are in the confessional.

My motto has always been "Trust but Verify"; after all, better safe than sorry. Often the matter is a one-off and perhaps just too private or sensitive to ask anyone for a recommendation; or maybe you don't even know anyone who has used the services of a PI. The biggest advertisements are no guarantee that they know their job and will provide a professional, honest and reliable service. They must be aware of the law and ensure that the information is legally obtained, otherwise it may be of great interest but no value in a court case, as information illegally obtained is inadmissible, regardless of how crucial or accurate it is.

What is the PI's background? Were they in a police force or another agency? What training, if any, did they have? How did they get into the business? What kind of cases do they handle? If they are merely debt collectors – something most reputable PIs don't handle – they won't be much use investigating a major commercial fraud or even a straightforward family law matter. They must be aware of the requirements of proof in any given case and be able to give clear, concise and accurate evidence they can support in a court of law. If they have no experience of court, regardless of the strength or accuracy of their evidence, under cross-examination they may well appear incompetent. A good barrister will readily pick holes in their case, throwing doubt on their overall accuracy and reliability.

Price should not be an issue, although I appreciate that in some cases, particularly some family situations, it *is* a very big issue. A busy professional practice will always do a certain number of *pro bono* cases. If one company charges a cheaper fee than another agency, it doesn't mean you will get a better service; after all, there is no substitute for experience in any field. Although I was aware that my fees were far higher than charged by other agencies, I had no problem justifying them based on my experience, contacts and, ultimately, my results. Being a former police officer is not in itself always enough to become a successful private investigator. Many police officers have little practical investigative experience or background, having worked only in traffic, administration or other areas unrelated to investigations, especially where international contacts are needed.

Over the years I have given talks and lectures to various organisations, from the Law Society to the Military Police, from insurance bodies to security professionals and other "end users" either directly involved in providing investigation services or to direct corporate clients such as banks or government agencies. As a result, I saw the need to set up a course in professional investigation, which was run through the auspices of the Institute of Irish Investigators. It was a ground-breaking course, the first of its kind in the world outside of government agencies.

The course was held in UCD at Belfield between 1986 and 1990 and consisted of introductory, intermediate and advanced lectures on such diverse subjects as the Irish legal system; civil, criminal and family law; legal terminology and documentation; court procedure; Rules of Evidence; surveillance and observation; photography; fingerprinting; DNA; Land Registry information; drugs investigation; questioned documents and handwriting analysis; fraud investigation; forensic analysis; fire investigation; and counter-technical surveillance measures, to name but a few. Lectures were given by the leading experts in the relevant fields and included barristers who also taught at King's Inns (the training ground for barristers) in their specific areas of law, while drugs investigation and the identification and location of concealed drugs was done by the Garda drug squad. I lectured on various subjects including surveillance and observation, fraud and court procedures and other issues.

Practical "on the job" tasks were set for teams of students, who were given specific "targets" to pick up and follow. Teams were given a description and photograph of their subject and the general location and time they might expect to find them. They were to maintain a discreet surveillance and report back with details of the subject's movements, where they went, what they did, who they met or spoke to, a detailed description of what they were wearing, car registration numbers and photographs. It was a fun exercise, as many made basic mistakes. When they spotted a "target" go into a pub, some students waited outside for the subject to come out, in case they were "spotted", while others gave them a few minutes before going in, not wanting to appear to be following them. What they didn't consider was that there was more than one exit. The "target" simply went in one door and out another, losing their "tail" in the process. Basic surveillance rules but there's nothing like practical experience to make you remember your mistakes.

Another test in basic observation set them thinking. Sitting in the lecture hall, without warning they were asked to describe the person sitting immediately behind them, giving specific details of what they were wearing, their hair and eye colour and anything else of note that would identify them in a crowd, all without looking around. Despite the fact that they'd been sharing a classroom with their fellow students for weeks and socialising with them at the coffee break, only one student managed to give a complete and accurate description. A good exercise for observation, identification and description of subjects and an essential requirement for all investigators.

Experts from the UK, members of the Forensic Science Association, gave lectures on forensics, fire investigation and hand-writing analysis. The final class was a court-room re-enactment, presided over by Judge Gillian Hussey. Students played out the roles of witnesses and investigators giving evidence, while they were questioned and cross-examined by barristers. It was a resounding success, proving that there is no substitute for experience, as despite all the lectures, basic mistakes were made when it came to a court-room appearance, with "nerves" being a big factor.

The final test – written exams in all the subjects they'd studied in each category of the basic, intermediate and advanced courses – was then marked "blind" by the relevant lecturers who only had a student number to ensure impartiality. The course was a great success and attracted attention from the UK and the Indian government, who later set up a similar course. The BBC did a radio documentary on this, the first-ever course on private investigation, with their reporters "sitting in" on one or two lectures for research purposes. Many of those who passed the course are still involved in the business today, while others are working in areas such as insurance fraud investigations, banking and related areas.

Due to the relatively small population in Ireland, the course was always intended to be a short-term one. However, I have no doubt that there would be an opportunity for Ireland to establish the first degree programme for private investigators, which could attract international students to Ireland, given the lack of available professional courses world-wide. The skills of private investigators can be very useful in other professions, particularly in the area of journalism and in investigative journalism in particular. There are, of course, correspondence courses in private investigation regularly advertised, but they need to be approached with caution. While they may impart a certain amount of basic information, they can in no way substitute for proper instruction and on-the-job experience which is only gained by working alongside an experienced investigator.

18

Family Law: You Think You Have Problems?

The area of family law – or matrimonial investigations, as it was called in my father's day – has always been part of a private investigator's job in every jurisdiction in the world. It can be a harrowing task for the investigator and client alike, as some marriages are so appalling as to be almost beyond belief. The general perception that marriage break-up – or rather break-down – has increased since the introduction of divorce legislation is far from the truth. Some marriages never worked, but for religious or other reasons – what the neighbours thought or the family's reaction to a split – many people endured a life of misery.

Perhaps my view has been coloured by what I saw – not alone the cases I dealt with but the many others from my father's files or in other jurisdictions. Whatever the reason, I believe in marriage – but I also believe in divorce. For some, it is the only "life-saving" solution to an awful situation and an opportunity to start again. There is no reward for enduring a miserable marriage. No-one will thank you or think you are a wonderful wife or husband. The bottom line is, life is too short to be a martyr. You owe it to yourself and your children, if you have any, to have a full and happy life and to pass on the "good news" story to them, rather than allowing them to believe that all marriages are made in hell. Few marriages are perfect all of the time and into every life a little rain must fall, but while not all marriages are made in hell, some very definitely are, if some of the cases I dealt were anything to go by.

The cases written about here were not subject to the "in camera" rule of the current family law courts, which precludes reporting details of a case. Some were pre-Irish divorce legislation, when the only recourse was to obtain a judicial separation *a mensa et thoro* – literally, from table and bed. It gave no right to re-marry and was little comfort to a distraught spouse, be they the husband or wife. During my father's time, the law considered a wife "a chattel" of her husband – a possession, much like *his* house or *his* car. A wife had little recourse to justice in a bad marriage, even if she was being physically abused or neglected or her husband was having an affair. On the other hand, a husband could sue the "other man" if his wife had an affair. The "injured" husband had several options open to him, such as "alienation of affections" and "criminal conversation" against the "interloper", who would most probably be found guilty and ordered to pay the "injured party" substantial damages.

These arcane legal reliefs were still in force in Ireland as recently as the late 1970s and, far from being neglected laws, they were put to use where a charge of "criminal conversation" was brought in a case of adultery. Werner Braun, a German national, sued his wife's lover, Stanley Roche of Roches Stores, and sought "damages" for the alienation of her affections, despite the fact that he was a notorious ladies' man himself. Until law reforms were enacted, the "servile position of the wife" was the issue at law and the areas to be considered were (a) "the actual value of the wife to the husband" and (b) "the need to compensate him for injury to his feelings and the blow to his marital honour". It is hard to believe that we are not talking about a law that prevailed hundreds of years ago – these were matters dealt with in a report by the Law Reform Commission as recently as December 1978. When the case was heard in the High Court, Mr Justice Butler addressed the jury telling them that the husband was entitled to damages as his wife had been "seduced and kept from him". Obviously, as a chattel, she had neither a mind nor a will of her own under the law in Ireland at the time – a law that was a throwback to British rule and one which had been abolished in England 115 years earlier.

In his judgment, Justice Butler said that "a wife is regarded as a chattel just as a thoroughbred mare or cow". It remained only for the jury to decide the extent of the damages they felt he was entitled to as to the "value" of his loss of a wife and the hurt to his feelings. The jury didn't waste much time and came back with an award of £12,000 – a substantial sum in 1972, approximating to €1 million today – to compensate the poor man for the embarrassment, hurt and loss of his wife to another man. It mattered little that he himself had attempted to seduce and alienate the affections of more than one married woman and had succeeded in hurting his young wife – she was eighteen when she married her then thirty-six-year-old husband – both physically and emotionally, bringing women back to their marital home with no regard for her or their children, as evidence obtained in our investigation on behalf of Stanley Roche proved. Unfortunately, the law at the time did not take such behaviour by the husband into consideration. But Werner's feelings had been hurt and he would get his pound of flesh. Heide Braun later married her lover, Stanley Roche and they remained inseperable until his death in July 2008.

Generally speaking, when a partner has suspicions they are frequently right but, on occasion, investigations have exonerated a spouse who, for various reasons, was acting in what their other half viewed as "suspiciously". One example of this was a case of a husband who went out for several hours two or three nights a week. The wife had visions of an affair, as he was neither a drinker nor a gambler. She could think of nothing else that would explain his absences, despite his many and varied excuses. It turned out to be a simple case of a down-trodden man being married to a nagging wife. He "escaped" on a regular basis, just to get some peace. His affair – well, he regularly went to down to the local church and sat alone, no doubt contemplating his situation and hoping for a miracle!

Not every case is so straightforward, however, and while each situation is a source of unhappiness and stress for the people involved, some are seriously traumatic and on occasion even life-threatening. Of the thousands of cases I undertook, I'll give you a brief insight into just a few. Most were on behalf of women but many were at the instigation of men – some of whom suffered untold misery and could share it with no-one, such was the anti-male bias that prevailed. It still does to a great degree, especially in cases where men seek custody of their children due to the mother's behaviour.

Such cases transcend the barriers of wealth, position and power. Many of the worst offenders came from educated and wealthy backgrounds, which, to their minds, gave them a

God-given right to act as they pleased. In some instances, money talked, as they hired the best lawyers or threw money at the problem in the belief that they were untouchable. In a few cases, thankfully, the law showed them otherwise.

A Question of Sex

Some cases are quite straightforward for the lawyer or private investigator but are nonetheless shocking for the partner, when they find their suspicions are justified. Sometimes what unfolds is even more hurtful than anticipated, as was the case with one "family law" matter. I was contacted by a lady who had concerns about her husband. Married for more than ten years to a prominent businessman, well-connected and known in Ireland, they had a "normal" happy marriage and family. In recent months she'd felt that something was not quite right and suspected that her husband was having an affair. His business meant he was working erratic hours and always travelling around the country but she was used to that and he was a wonderful family man, she explained.

It didn't take long to get to the bottom of the matter. After a relatively short investigation and surveillance operation, we had the answer. The client, as is often the case, had been right in her suspicions – but she was in for a shock. Her husband wasn't having an affair with her friend, as she had believed – he was gay. He was frequenting gay bars and clubs and having one-night-stands on a regular basis. Not exactly an affair or a long-term attachment, but nonetheless, he was being unfaithful and apparently putting her at risk of contracting Aids.

For the shocked client, it was worse than she had ever expected. She could have coped with an affair with another woman, but this was different. She had had absolutely no idea that he was bisexual – if in fact he was. When she began to think about it, she realised that he had probably only married for appearance's sake to please his family. They got along well together but theirs had never been a great love affair. Maybe now she knew why. She said she felt as if she'd never really known her husband and wondered if he'd always known he was gay and tried to suppress it by marrying her. She was devastated. I don't know what eventually happened to their marriage, whether they worked through it or moved on, but it just shows, you can never tell what will turn up when you start an investigation.

It wasn't the first nor the last time we investigated an affair for a "happily married" spouse and found to their complete surprise that their other half was gay. Whether it was the old bias in what used to be a very Catholic country or the pressure of family to meet their expectations, who knows? Hopefully in a more open society this charade is less likely to happen and people won't be "forced" to marry to keep up appearances.

Mad, Bad and Dangerous to Know

Unless there were exceptional circumstances, most of my "new client" appointments took place at my offices. Certain days were set aside for appointments, which started at nine in the morning and ran all day until at least six in the evening. As we were booked months in advance, it was easier to structure things that way. From time to time, even long-booked appointments had to be rearranged as cases came to a head or a court case came up, such was the unpredictable nature of the business. One such case came about as a result of a call from a very distressed lady who wanted me to call out to see her. My PA, Annette Beecher, explained it wouldn't be possible due to our workload, but when the lady explained that she was in a wheelchair and housebound, naturally I made an exception.

It turned out that the lady had been married a few years when she became pregnant and had a wonderful healthy baby boy. Unfortunately, she was diagnosed with a condition that had rapidly left her in a wheelchair, trying to care for her active baby as best she could. Having four children myself, I could only imagine how difficult that was. Her husband organised an au pair to help out but that arrangement soon ended when he went into the young girl's room uninvited during the night and tried to rape her. Naturally, she left but she made no formal complaint against him for the sake of his wife. A replacement au pair was found, an older lady and, with her help, the wife contacted me.

I met her in her beautiful house in an expensive part of Dublin and, but for her unfortunate health situation, she appeared to have everything. Life can be deceptive, as she explained how she was a virtual prisoner in her own home. Her husband had reluctantly taken her out in the car from time to time, until he had an accident. Someone had damaged the passenger door of his car and he'd never had it repaired, using it as an excuse not to bring his wife out shopping or for a drive – anything to get out of the house. There were high circular steps leading up to the front door, making it impossible to manoeuvre a wheelchair, and he refused to put in a ramp. She couldn't understand why he was doing this. Was there somebody else? She needed to know. Trapped as she was, with no access to the outside world, she contacted me.

The husband was so confident that the little woman was tucked safely away and wouldn't be able to find out what he was up to, that he was quite open in his womanising. He had a girlfriend who knew nothing of his situation or background and he was enjoying the "single" life. Having established what he was up to, we prepared our report for the client's solicitor but, before she could take any legal action for a divorce, her husband was killed in a car crash coming home drunk after a night out with his girlfriend. Poetic justice, maybe? I don't think anyone shed a tear for him, least of all his wife to whom he had been so cruel.

An American Nightmare

Another case which I investigated that falls into this category was located in the same area. The lady was married to a tall, very well-built American, who looked like he worked out. They'd had several children but it was far from being a happy marriage. Her husband was an aggressive man and she was terrified of what he might do. She had been trying to leave him for some time, having made previous unsuccessful attempts. You may well think she would call the police or get a barring order. It sounds simple, but there are many reasons why women can't always do that – sometimes they are too terrified, embarrassed, afraid for the children or they just don't know what to do or who to turn to.

In this case, the man had threatened the safety of the children – in fact, he'd done more than that, he'd actually scalded his two-year-old with the contents of a hot-water bottle. The woman was pregnant again and couldn't bring herself to stay with him any longer. She couldn't prove her case, as he threatened to tell police she'd done it as she was depressed. She came to me in desperation. After a relatively short surveillance and investigation, we established that he was seeing various other women and was known to be extremely aggressive. He was a regular at a body-building club and was believed to be on steroids, increasing his already aggressive character. We had evidence that he had threatened and beaten others, who were too afraid to press charges.

On my advice the woman contacted a solicitor and the husband knew that she was really leaving him and this time she meant business. He "visited" her in hospital while she was heavily pregnant and attempted to rape her – impossible, you might think, barbaric and incredible, but unfortunately true. She got a barring order against him but all the while she was terrified as to what he would do when she returned home from hospital. Despite the barring order, when she got out of hospital, she found he was still living in the family home and he had even moved a "girlfriend" in. Neighbours said she had been there while she was in hospital.

The police were called on foot of the barring order and he left the house. She moved back in with the children, still frightened at what he might do. Within days, he turned up under cover of darkness and poured petrol around the house. He sealed up all the windows, doors, even the letterbox, and set fire to the place – with his wife and children, including the new baby, inside. But for the fire brigade, they'd never have survived.

The husband was arrested and got ten years in Mountjoy for his trouble. But what happens next time – when he gets out? Ten years is not ten years in Ireland, where even the most hardened criminals get time off for "good behaviour". It is time our laws were properly implemented and let the punishment fit the crime. At present here is no real deterrent to such people. Whether he was mad, bad or both, who knows? It doesn't really matter. That is one ex-wife that won't be hanging around to find out! He is still a threat to his family.

Madness!

They say truth is stranger than fiction and I well believe it. One "family law" case from my father's time that fits that category was when a man arrived with a bizarre story. He claimed his sister-in-law was trying to have his brother "sectioned" under the Mental Health Act then in force, which meant that he would be committed to a mental institution without his consent. The man said his brother was perfectly sane and that the "plot" had been contrived by his wife and her lover, a medical practitioner. It required two signatures from medics who were not related to certify that the "patient" needed treatment in a mental hospital. The "lover" had persuaded another medic that "Tom" was psychotic and imagining all sorts of things.

The cuckolded husband had found out about their liaison and was intending to throw the wife out of the family home and leave her with nothing. This was at a time when the "chattel laws" still prevailed. Determined that she was having the substantial property and all that went with it, the lovers had been "laying the ground" for some time and people were starting to believe the brother was sick. My father's client didn't know what to do or where to go, so it was in desperation that he turned to a PI for help.

Having kept surveillance on the pair to establish that they were in fact having an affair – their "motive" – and confirmed that they were telling their friends and associates that poor "Tom" wasn't well and was imagining things, there appeared to be grounds for the man's concerns. My Dad arranged for "Tom" to be independently examined by two leading psychiatrists – one in the UK and one in Northern Ireland. Neither could find anything wrong with "Tom" and their reports gave him a clean bill of health. In a belt-and-braces move, he also arranged for a friend of his, a psychiatrist attached to St Brendan's, to examine "Tom". He too, found nothing wrong with "Tom". Between the investigative evidence and the independent medical reports, they had enough to ensure that "Tom" was going nowhere, much to the disgust of the conniving lovers.

The Runaway Bride

A very distraught man came to see me. His wife was missing. They had been together two years and had recently married. Back from honeymoon, they moved into a new house in Cork. Come Monday morning, they both went back to work. That evening, he couldn't wait to get home to his new bride. She greeted him at the door with a nice meal cooking away in the oven. He couldn't have been happier. It was the start of summer and the new wife asked her husband to dig out the weeds in the back garden to plant flowers she had bought – saying she wanted "somewhere nice" for them to enjoy when they came home from work. After a long day's work, he could have done without it, but he didn't want to disappoint her, so he got stuck in, digging out the weeds and planting the flowers and shrubs.

Finally finished, he went back into the house, but his wife was nowhere to be found. He called out, checking the bathroom and the rest of the house, to no avail. There was no note and he couldn't imagine where she'd gone. As the hours went by with no sign of her, he began to get really worried. He phoned everyone he knew but no-one had seen her. He sat up all night long in the hope she'd come back. As morning came, he was frantic and began searching the house for any clues. He opened the wardrobe and was stunned to find it completely empty. All of her clothes were gone.

He didn't know what to think. They'd had no argument and she'd given no indication that anything was wrong. He tried contacting the hairdressing salon where she worked and was shocked to learn she'd left over a month before the wedding. Over the following weeks, he was too embarrassed to tell people what he now knew. She'd left him. He had no idea why. There had been no hint of it – ever.

He came to me to find her, if only to find an answer to the age-old question – why? Armed with as much information as he could give and her photograph, the hunt began. None of their friends had seen her or knew anything about her departure, either from work or from her marriage. Checking on her credit card, I found that at least she hadn't left the country – it was being used hundreds of miles from Cork for groceries and "bills" that suggested she wasn't just on a holiday. With no known friends or relatives in the area, it seemed worth a visit.

Checking around the locale, the small supermarket she'd used and the local pub confirmed that the woman had recently moved into a nearby apartment with her "husband". Keeping this apartment under surveillance, her identity was confirmed. Now at least we knew *why* she'd left – though it was still difficult to understand why she'd gone through with the marriage in the first place. I gave the news to my client, the real husband, letting him know she was alive and well.

An investigation into her "new" or at least "newer" husband revealed that they had been seeing each other for over a year, while all the time she was planning her wedding to my client. The new man in her life didn't know she was married – she'd apparently told him she was going on holiday "with the girls" to think about their relationship. When she got back she agreed to move in with him and just disappeared overnight. Whether she didn't know or just didn't care about the devastation she'd left behind, who knows? It seems she wasn't brave enough to call off the wedding or honest enough to explain to her heartbroken husband why she'd just "done a runner". I can only imagine how she explained herself to her new man – makes you wonder if either man could ever trust a woman again?

"Family law" cases for a private investigator extend beyond marriage and cover everything including cohabitation, same-sex relationships and of course children, be they adult or otherwise, as you will see from some of these cases.

Strange But True . . .

One case that falls into the "strange" category struck me as being like something out of the backlands of hillbilly country. I was asked by a Health Board to investigate a family they had concerns about. They lived in a very remote part of the west of Ireland – their nearest "neighbours" being the occupants of an old disused graveyard halfway up a mountain. The family wanted no dealings with any figures of authority and kept to themselves, being rarely seen by people from the town, some distance away. As I made my way in the depths of winter to this godforsaken spot, travelling up mountain roads that appeared to have been abandoned to nature, I began to think I'd taken a wrong turn somewhere. There was nothing to be seen for miles and miles, except a very occasional small cottage.

Eventually, I came upon the rustic and overgrown graveyard. On very high ground and surrounded in mist, it had an eerie feeling and I remember thinking that, if anything happened me here, I probably would never be found. I still couldn't see any sign of life in the area but as I walked around the graveyard, I came across a path leading up to a wooded area. Walking along the path, I noticed what looked like a garden shed on concrete blocks. As I approached, I saw a boy aged about eight or nine staring at me from the dirty shed window. This couldn't possibly be the "house"; I couldn't believe anyone could actually live in the dilapidated shed.

I banged on the door, there being no knocker, and it was answered by a young woman in her late twenties. I spoke to her under a pretext of being an American tourist looking for relatives buried in the old graveyard. The woman never answered me and when I asked her if she was "Miss Z", she just nodded. I walked in, not waiting to be invited, in case I was refused.

Once inside, I saw five people – the young woman; a man, probably in his fifties but looking older; a woman of the same vintage whom I presumed to be his wife; the young boy I had seen at the window; and a girl of about eleven. They all looked dirty and dishevelled – and somewhat strange. The sight that awaited me was unbelievable. The shed, which was about twenty feet by twelve, was laid out as one single room. It had a double bed, a broken arm-chair and an old television set, which was sitting on a wooden crate. On another box was a two-ring cooker attached to a gas bottle. The only other furniture appeared to be a small kitchen table and two rickety-looking chairs. I could hardly believe my eyes.

There didn't appear to be any heating or toilet facilities and I'd seen nothing in the way of an outdoor toilet when I did a quick recce before approaching the shed. It was obvious they were reclusive and appeared to be mentally slow. Coaxing them into conversation, the girl told me that the elderly couple were her "mammy and daddy" and the children were hers. The old couple didn't speak during the time I was there; they just sat staring at me. The father sat in the armchair, looking straight ahead at the television, which wasn't even on – there were no electricity in the shed. It was somewhat unnerving, to say the least.

Given that the Health Board had asked me to check out the situation independently and it wasn't an insurance claim or other routine case, I had expected something different – but not quite this. When the boy called his grandfather "daddy", it became clear – but just in case it was a colloquial term, sharing my bag of sweets around, I made conversation with the children, who didn't appear even to know what school was, much less attend one. Both children called the younger woman "mammy" and referred to the grandfather as "daddy". There was no sign of any other male in the house and no indication that anyone in the room thought anything amiss with their setup. The older woman, who was both the mother of the younger woman and grandmother of her husband's two children, said nothing throughout the time I was there.

I had seen enough to file a report to the Health Board and they in turn got an Order under the Mental Health Act to ensure that the family were taken into care and received the treatment they so obviously needed.

To the Ends of the Earth: The Falklands Father

Some parents will go almost to the ends of the earth in trying to protect their kids from anything that can hurt them. In one case in particular, one man did just that. A father living on Ascension Island in the south Atlantic Ocean, thousands of miles from Ireland and worlds apart, contacted me because he was concerned about his daughter who was living and working in Ireland. He wanted the best for her and, although she was an adult, he believed her to be in an unsuitable relationship that would ultimately make her very unhappy. Interfering parents? Maybe – but he was genuinely worried about her vulnerability, as a previous boyfriend had been killed in an accident and, naturally, she was devastated. When she met someone else, she fell head over heels and by the time her family found out about it, she had agreed to marry him.

I got a call from the British Embassy asking me to contact the man, as a result of which he arranged to fly from the Ascension Islands to the Falklands on a British military flight to Brize Norton RAF base in the UK and then on to Ireland for our meeting. It was just a few months before the planned wedding; he knew little about his future son-in-law and was worried that his daughter didn't know much more. Following an urgent investigation, his worst fears proved well founded. Unknown to his fiancée, the local Romeo had an "interesting" background, having been sacked from several jobs. In one, he had operated a "dead men" fraud – claiming salaries for employees who didn't exist and pocketing the money himself. He had been charged with sixteen counts of forgery and had served six months' imprisonment.

He was no sooner out of prison when he was in trouble again in his next job, borrowing money from customers that he never repaid and "borrowing" cars, one of which he crashed, refusing to pay for the damage. Again, he had been sacked – an embarrassment to his boss, who was losing customers as a result of his behaviour. He moved on to another job and suddenly appeared to have money, buying into a local business. Within six months, the long-established business went bust and he disappeared. He came to the attention of the police yet again when he was charged with obtaining goods by false pretences. In court, he asked that the case be adjourned as he was getting married, but he was refused. The case went ahead and he was again convicted of fraud.

Investigation showed he had been sacked from virtually every job he'd ever had and was well known around the country, having left a trail of "bounced" cheques along the way. Bouncing cheques wasn't his only claim to fame, however, as I turned up numerous girlfriends. All of them admitted to giving him money and on more than one occasion, he was found to have had two or even three girlfriends "on the go" at one time – each one knowing nothing of the others.

The client was kept informed of developments and every second Thursday, he made the round trip of almost 16,000 miles from Ascension Island to Dublin to meet me and get a personal update on the developments in the case. It was also an opportunity to keep in touch with his daughter to see how she was doing.

The final straw came when my investigation took a new turn. Far from being single, the fraudulent fiancé had a wife whom he'd forgotten to mention. Apparently, he didn't feel the need to tell his fiancée he was already married or that he had several "current" girlfriends, who were all supporting him financially.

He was undoubtedly an unsuitable husband in anyone's book and certainly not what this father had in mind for his intelligent, well-educated daughter, for whom love was blind. The Trojan efforts of a loving father undoubtedly saved this girl from years of unhappiness.

This was but one of hundreds of cases of concerned parents over the years – some justified, others not – but at least they loved their children enough to go to such lengths.

A Young Man's Fancy

Protective parents can be overpowering, but then again, it's their job to look out for their children – it just depends on when they eventually let go of the reins. One young man from a wealthy business family was less than impressed with his "interfering" parents, when he brought home his girlfriend to meet the folks. She was a very attractive English girl and his parents made her feel very welcome, but as the months went on and the relationship began to get serious, so did the family's reservations.

When their son "popped the question" and announced their engagement, they were horrified and decided to have the love of his life investigated. They had never done anything like this before but something was really bothering them, and try as they might, they couldn't quite put their finger on the problem. The girl was well-mannered and polite and held down a well-paid job in marketing. She certainly had expensive tastes in clothes – but still, they had doubts and wondered if the family fortune was part of her attraction to their only son. You may think that hiring a private investigator to check her out was a bit drastic but it is not uncommon and is quite the norm in other countries, particularly in South America and Europe, where wealthy families "vet" their sons' or daughters' suitors.

The girl, who was in her late twenties, was kept under surveillance for a while and it soon became clear just what the problem was. Following her to work, it turned out that she worked in a massage parlour, which was, ironically, situated directly opposite a police station. That was her "day job". At night, she plied her trade in the Leeson Street and Baggot Street Bridge areas, being one of the more active and successful prostitutes on the game at the time. A check revealed that she was working under an alias but was "well known" to the police and had numerous convictions in England, although, at the time, none in Ireland, despite her plentiful supply of customers.

The future parents-in-law were horrified – it was not what they'd expected. They had no idea how to tell their son, afraid of his reaction. How they broke the news to him, I don't know. I do know that the young man had absolutely no idea about his fiancee's "career". He was shocked beyond belief and immediately called off the engagement, much to the disappointment of his fiancee in "marketing". She hadn't exactly told them a lie – I suppose she *was* in marketing . . . of a kind.

A Gentleman and Scholar

Not all domestic violence is at the hands of drunken, unemployed and uneducated men, as is often the stereotypical image. Many cases I have investigated have shown that women are as likely to suffer domestic abuse and violence from well-educated professional men, some of whom may even be in the medical or legal profession and themselves dealing with domestic abuse on behalf of a patient or client. I was shocked at the number of cases that fell into these categories.

One such case involved an elegant lady who came to me for help. The fact that she was a professional, well-educated woman herself didn't prevent her from becoming a victim of abuse by her womanising, equally professional husband, who regularly beat her when something – anything – irritated him. In the past, she had suffered broken bones, extensive bruising and had even been slashed with a knife. She was both embarrassed and ashamed but she was in a difficult situation. This was at a time when the police were reluctant to get involved in "domestic" issues, especially when professional people – particularly within the medical and legal professions, well connected and with no shortage of funds – were involved.

It was a serious case of street angel, house devil, but she had no proof. She was never prepared to go to court to expose her sorry relationship to friends and colleagues. Despite the "in camera" nature of the family law courts, the legal system in Ireland is still small enough to be a hotbed of gossip and word inevitably gets out. It was a matter of getting the evidence and using it as a means of curbing her husband's violent outbursts, for fear of his exposure. Having kept him under surveillance and "monitored" the situation at the family home – not to mention his "extra-marital" activities – there was enough evidence to ensure that he kept his temper under control where his family were concerned. The wife's solicitors "discreetly advised" him that court proceedings would be initiated, which was definitely not in his interest, if he didn't change his ways. At least he now knew that it was no longer just a "family" secret and that independent investigators with a track record for "clean hands" had the goods on him. He wasn't very happy about it but, given his profession, he could see he had little option but to take their advice and an anger management course to boot.

A Sporting Divorce – of Sorts

Another "gentleman and scholar" was playing away from home, while making life hell for his wife – herself equally qualified in the same profession as her spouse. Despite years of suspicions, constantly denied by her husband, the mental torture became too much and she called in the professionals.

The man thought he was clever, always covering his tracks with legitimate business or sporting trips, away rugby games or horse racing, all part of the game that is called business. Keeping tabs on him, we waited until the next big "away" game was on and kept him under surveillance. He made a point of having his wife drop him at the airport, where he met all the "lads" and gave her details of where he was staying and his hotel room number.

A check on his bookings confirmed that he was booked into a single room at the hotel in question. Surveillance was maintained and we joined him on the flight to the UK with his buddies. When he left the baggage area, we weren't surprised to see him being met by a glamorous blonde in her early thirties. They were obviously old friends from the "warm" welcome she gave him and he appeared quite happy to be seen by his pals kissing her passionately, as they all grinned and waved him on. The "couple" left together, parting company with his friends and jumping into a taxi outside the airport building.

For only the second time ever, I told a cabbie to "follow that car", much to his delight and excitement. Despite the traffic, he kept us in clear sight of our target, even radioing his "mate" in the first cab to ask him where he was headed. The other taxi pulled up outside a small hotel outside the city. I gave the taxi man a large tip. He was delighted, saying, "I'd have done it for nothing, luv – wait 'til I tell my mates!" He probably thought I was the man's wife, following him!

The pair checked into the hotel as Mr and Mrs, and spent the entire weekend wining, dining and partying. Little did they know that the "Irish paparazzi" were tracking their every move and their photos would be back in Dublin before they were! Covering his tracks, as he thought, his mates had checked him in to the "rugby" hotel and whenever his wife phoned his room, the desk clerk said he was "out" but they'd put a message under his door, which they did. Following one arranged call, we watched as one of his pals checked his room one night and picked up his messages. He obviously provided an excellent secretarial service for his friend, as he immediately passed on the message from the wife and the dutiful husband phoned home, claiming he'd "just missed" her call. The lady decided to leave him in the dark until his return – why spoil his fun now when he was facing a very expensive divorce when he got back?

On his return, her husband was shell-shocked – he had totally under-estimated his wife, after years of taking her for granted. His business partner was not impressed when he learned what had been going on. A very family-oriented man, he split up the partnership, with each man going their own way – a business divorce, you might say. Strange thing was, despite all the evidence, the wife gave him another chance – but only after he had transferred substantial assets into her sole name. Not so dumb after all.

Mayhem on the Motorway

Forrest Gump's Momma said, "Life is like a box of chocolates, you never know what you're gonna get."

Another family law case, the story was the same routine. It was the middle of winter but the husband was out until all hours at night and had no decent explanation. More recently, he was displaying all the habits of a man out to impress a woman. The wife was suspicious – a woman can usually tell when something is up – the expensive new clothes, new after-shave, underwear, attention to personal hygiene were all tell-tale signs, if they are not the normal habits of the man. She wanted him watched to see where he was late into the night.

Surveillance was going well – we were turning up some very interesting information – but as yet there was no sign of a lady friend. The guy didn't appear to be gay either, so it was a matter of waiting it out and seeing what he was up to. He was hanging out in rough pubs and snooker halls, not exactly the place to pick up a girlfriend, but anything was possible. Some of his "friends" were very dubious and well known to the police, who would undoubtedly be interested in the people he was meeting.

One night we followed him to a spit-and-sawdust pub on the northside of Dublin, popular with his mates from the flats. Propped up at the bar with three or four buddies, they were overheard discussing "business" – something to do with "moving the gear" before the weekend. Unfortunately, their discussion was interrupted when the girlfriend of one of the men turned up. She shouted, "Howya, Mick," as she walked into the pub, drawing everyone's attention. She was a big busty brunette – though I doubt anyone other than her boyfriend could have described her later. As she opened her coat, it was obvious that she was wearing nothing more than a smile. A shocked but delighted crowd – well, the men anyway – cheered her on. A brave girl, given that it was the middle of winter! Apparently "Mick" had broken off their relationship and this was her way of enticing him back. Nothing to do with our family law case, but the nearest we got to seeing "our man" in female company!

Surveillance continued for a few more days but, with no sign of any females, it looked like whatever our boy was up to, he had more on his mind than an affair. From his movements, snatches of conversation and his known associates, it seemed they were planning something big. Before we could tie it all down, however, things came to a head.

He phoned home, telling his wife he wouldn't be home, that he was meeting some people in a pub in Clondalkin. Certain he was meeting an ex-girlfriend, she wanted us to keep an eye on him that night. Now familiar with him and the car he drove, it was a routine surveillance.

Arriving in Clondalkin, I did a recce around the area for his car without finding it; nor was he in the pub, as he'd said. Either he was late or there'd been a change of plan. With no sign of him, I did one last "circuit" and was about to call off the job when, out of nowhere, a car revved up and tore after me. The noise alone was enough to draw my attention and as I glanced in my rear-view mirror, I saw our man in the driver's seat. It was obvious he was gunning for me.

He was gaining ground fast. I saw a man in the passenger seat. I couldn't make out who it was, nor did I care – I just knew it meant trouble. I tried to shake them off but, with the narrow roads and traffic, there was nowhere to go. Getting away from the congested village, they began to gain ground and the passenger stuck what looked like a sawn-off shotgun out the window. I drove like hell, mounting the path and weaving left and right to make it difficult for him to get a good shot, taking sharp right turns, which would force him to fire across his bonnet at me, making a more difficult target. With no room to pull up on my inside, he'd have no clear line of fire. He did his best to stick close-up and personal as I wove from side to side, avoiding his line of sight as best I could, knowing he needed to be close up to do any serious damage. A sawn-off would have a wide scatter effect, so it was critical that I put as great a distance between us as possible.

Eventually I made a break for it up Monastery Road. The adrenaline rushed in as I put the boot down and tore up the road. I was never so grateful to be driving a gutsy car, a Honda Prelude, which didn't let me down. I made my escape out onto the Naas Road and shook them off. Constantly checking my mirror, I turned off the main road as soon as possible – all the time wondering if they'd "pop up" and thinking out loud, "Where the hell is a cop car when you need it?" If I'd been a drunk driver, I'd have been arrested by then!

I was just thankful that they never got a shot off. But perhaps it was more of a warning rather than an intention to do serious damage, which would draw fire down on them from the Gardaí. Finally heading home, I had a well-earned G&T and chilled out – thinking, not for the first time, *they call this glamorous!*

I phoned the client and told her what had happened. She "confessed" that in the heat of an argument the night before, she had told him she'd been having him followed. Our standard instruction to a client is to keep quiet. No matter how suspicious they are or how heated an argument they have, they should never, ever give any indication that they

157

know what their "loved one" has been up to or even hint that they are being followed. At best, it could blow up in the client's face; having spent money on fees, they may well have wasted the chance to get any decent evidence. At worst – depending on the person involved – they could get a good hammering. Either way, it was never in their interest to "win" a battle by saying, "I know where you were last night", only to lose the initiative and the war.

He'd no idea he'd been under surveillance until his wife broke the golden rule and talked. He was furious she'd exposed him and his "gangster" associates to close scrutiny and was afraid he'd be "taught a lesson" if they found out. He'd set a trap for her – and ultimately for me.

Luckily it all came to nothing, but as far as I was concerned that was the end of the case. We couldn't work on a case in which our cover was blown by the client. The confidentiality rule goes both ways and, when she breached it, putting my life in danger, whether it was just a warning or not, the information on file was passed on to the police. The man was a small cog in a paramilitary smuggling gang involved in various criminal activities including money laundering and, apparently, gold. Guess he just didn't have that Midas touch after all!

Washing Your Dirty Laundry in Public

One family law case gave a wronged wife a great deal of satisfaction, after years of frustration at the hands of her philandering husband. Despite having reared several children, the wife was continually short of money while her husband had the best of everything. No holidays or weekends away for her, as she stayed home to mind their brood. After years of neglect and putting up with her lot, she despaired of ever having a life, until one day she'd had enough. She'd had her suspicions for a very long time but had been too weary to do anything about it. She couldn't afford to anyway, until she read about an open meeting on family law I was holding at my offices.

In the early days of family law, marriage difficulties in Ireland were still considered a taboo subject, not to be discussed in public. The attitude was, you'd made your bed and you had to lie in it, especially if you were Catholic. A panel of experts drawn from the legal profession, family support groups such as AIM (Action, Intervention and Mediation) medical support and myself, as an investigator, dealt with numerous questions throughout the day. The media were there in large numbers as it was a unique event, the first of its kind in Ireland. Finally, somebody, somewhere, was standing up and saying that Holy Ireland had bad marriages too.

After the initial embarrassment, one after another, the crowd found the courage to ask specific questions. How could they sort out their problems? What did it cost? Where would they start? What rights did they have? It was as if the floodgates opened and many new friendships were made that day, as women – and it was women in the main – shared their troubles with another kindred soul, no longer feeling like the odd one out. Many of these women came to me after the meeting for personal advice on their situation and we helped as many as we could.

One of those was the long suffering lady I've already mentioned – but she could be one of hundreds in similar situations. Having discussed her situation, I agreed to take on her case. It seemed that her husband was often away on "business" and I agreed to check out just what kind of "business" this entailed. It turned out that his next "business" trip was to Spain – but he'd neglected to mention that he was bringing along some female company for the two-week trip. We joined him on the "holiday" and our client saw his holiday snaps before he did. It was obvious that the only business he was involved in was "funny business".

Unknown to me, the wronged wife was determined to give her husband a warm welcome when he arrived back at Dublin Airport. As we waited in arrivals, I was surprised to see her, with her eldest and now adult daughter, standing behind a pillar. To my surprise, she said she was there to meet her husband. She wasn't kidding. She surprised her husband with a welcome he – and indeed his fellow passengers – will never forget. As he came through the arrival doors, she stepped forward and emptied a suitcase full of his dirty clothes on the ground. In a voice loud enough for everyone to hear, she said, "Since your lady friend has been taking care of your needs for the past two weeks, she can look after your dirty laundry from now on as well." The shocked couple didn't know where to look as the bemused passengers tried to stifle their laughter.

The lady said it was the best thing she had ever done. For over twenty years she had been bullied and dominated by her mean husband. Now she'd found her own voice and intended to make a new life for herself. I never saw a happier reaction to finding out a husband was having an affair – and I have to admit, it was funny . . .

The Serial Deceiver

This could be one of many cases; a lot of the characteristics fit more than one person. A wealthy businessman who courted the press and enjoyed a high profile was not the Prince Charming he claimed to be.

His wife contacted me because some years previously I had dealt with a case for her sister and she wanted someone she "knew and trusted". She had had her suspicions regarding her husband's infidelity for years and had even gone as far as contacting a private investigator she'd picked at random from the Yellow Pages – but the husband was the wealthy one and client confidentiality or loyalty wasn't one of this particular PI's qualities. Seeing an opportunity to make even more cash, he tipped off the husband – for a fee. The man tackled his wife, telling her she was mad. From then on he kept a close eye on her movements, including secretly installing closed-circuit television and bugging devices around the house. She was convinced he was still having affairs.

Married for more than thirty years, his wife saw him for what he was and was no longer impressed by the image he portrayed to the world. He needed to get his adulation elsewhere and a fat wallet went a long way to attracting women less than half his age. I'd heard the story a million times – middle-age crisis and the need to prove they still had pulling power – nothing to do with their bank balance, of course!

From what I'd been told, the husband seemed to know his wife's every move and she was nervous about meeting me in case he found out. Cautiously, she and her sister met me for a "casual" coffee – just another pastime for the "ladies who lunch". Having spoken to her at length, it was obvious that her home had been bugged and the first thing to do was to establish that for certain. When her husband went abroad, I arranged to sweep the house from top to bottom and came up with an array of sophisticated "no expense spared" bugging devices located in a "bunker" beneath the entrance steps to the large house, set in private grounds. It was like a veritable "war room" with endless recordings of each day's telephone calls, visitors and related matters. We left it in situ – but now my client knew not to made any calls or talk to visitors about her suspicions.

Keeping the spouse under surveillance, we had little difficulty in recording his activities with various young women, from hairdressers to barmaids and professional executives. He left the company of one woman only to escort another for dinner, drinks and whatever came next. Even the bad weather didn't deter him. Ireland was then in the grip of what the media described as "Arctic conditions". The country's sporting fixtures were cancelled – and yet our suave would-be seducer managed to keep a date for his own sporting fixtures and we, very reluctantly, tagged along with him.

Finally, we had enough evidence to go to court and the wife was delighted. But like many cases before, things changed before the court date came up. The lying Lothario persuaded her it was all in the past – she was the only woman for him. She cancelled the proceedings and hoped to live happily ever after. I don't know if she did, but judging by his appearances around town in subsequent years, I very much doubt that the leopard changed his spots – although he has certainly slowed down. Perhaps she was happy to settle for the fact that he now knew she could go to court at any time in the future and relieve him of some of his ever-increasing wealth. As I see his smiling face staring at me from the newspaper pictured at some business function or fund-raiser, I think it's probably only a matter of time before some PI gets a call about her errant husband. The old evidence would no longer be of use as, under the law, she condoned the situation, having accepted him back. It would be a whole new ballgame – and he is still a player.

As a young girl, I appear unimpressed to be in the company of Bing Crosby (with binoculars) at the Curragh in Kildare

My father, Ireland's first private investigator, Bill Kavanagh (left) with Scottish PI John Grant

Dad (left) with famed San Francisco PI Hal Lipset, who was Chief Investigator for the Senate investigation into the Watergate affair

Me standing beside my father and other guests at Association of British Investigators meeting

PIs attending the World Association of Detectives convention in Dublin in 1974; (back row, left to right): unknown, Henry Bawa (India), Bill Philips (Canada), Sumio Hiroshima (Tokyo), Matti Westerholm (Helsinki), Kevin (Chicago), my father Bill Kavanagh (Dublin); (front row, left to right): Tony Kinghorn (UK), David Almog (Tel Aviv), me, my mother Helen Kavanagh (Dublin) and Zena Scott-Archer (Liverpool)

Youngest detective . . . Miss Sandra Kavanagh.

Detectives

IN the Gresham last night more than 200 "private eyes" from all parts of the word met for the annual con-ention of the Association of British Detectives.

Among them was a 16-year-old girl, still at school, but determined to make a place for herself in this essentially masculine world.

She is SANDRA KAVANAGH, daughter of Ireland's best known private detective, BILL KAVANAGH, of Dublin.

Said Sandry: "My aim is to become Ireland's top woman detective. I am already helping daddy in his work and I want to go into the business full-time when I leave school.

"Actually, I cannot think of a more fascinating life. Most of my friends want to be nurses or air hostesses, but I want to follow in daddy's footsteps and play my part in the battle against crime."

During their stay in Ireland the detectives will visit beauty spots in Dublin and Wicklow in addition to attending a series of conferences in the Gresham and Hotel Moctrose.

Newspaper clippings highlight my early interest in becoming a private investigator

WHEN PRIVATE EYES ARE SMILIN'

Private eye Bill Kavanagh.

All tied up in organising a conference—girl investigators Jane Thompson, 22, Marie Tingleton, 21, Shirley Slater, 18, and Sandra Kavanagh, 16, work hand in hand.

THRILLER fans can relax . . .

Glamorous girl detectives with stunning figures and nimble brains really DO exist.

A group of them are helping to organise the Association of British Detectives' annual con-vention in Dublin next month.

The girls work for Dublin private eye Bill Kavanagh who persuaded the association to switch their convention from London.

The 100-strong staff of Bill's K Security agency are as excited as he is about the "capture." His attractive girl sleuths will help with hotel book-ings and sightseeing trips for the visitors.

"Of course, all our staff can't be released from duty," explained a cautious Bill. "We will still keep our patrols

guarding the big stores, factories, and race-courses.

He added: "I would like to warn pickpockets not to venture into the Gresham Hotel, where we are meeting.

"They are likely to end up in handcuffs."

Bill's firm is a family affair, with his wife Mary and sixteen-year-old daughter Sandra on the staff.

Sandra is hoping for a repeat of the drama at the conference two years ago.

While eighty of Britain's top detectives were in the convention hotel in

Tools of the trade: An early polygraph machine (lie detector)

Dad "tests" me on the lie detector in New York!

The famed "martini cocktail", which both Hal Lipset and Manny Mittleman claimed they had invented along with minox sub-miniature "spy" camera which I used to photograph documents in undercover operations

Me with Irving Shumbord and my mother on Rockaway Park Beach, New York state

Me with Sumio Hiroshima of Japan at a World Association of Detectives convention

The Association of
BRITISH INVESTIGATORS LTD.
2, Clements Inn, London, WC2A 2DX

Name Miss S.M.Kavanagh

Membership No 492 MARA

Signature

This identification is invalid
without a current Certificate
of Membership ──────→

My Association of British Investigators
membership card

DNA Fingerprints now used here by Private Eyes

By Colm Keena

DNA "fingerprinting," which was used for the first time in the conviction of a rapist in the UK two weeks ago, is already being used by private investigators in Ireland.

The President of the Institute of Irish Investigators, Sandra Mara, said that private investigators are using the new process, sending their samples of body fluid or tissue to a private laboratory in the UK.

Irish investigators use the process if the client is prepared to pay for it," she said. In her own work, with her firm, K Security Private Investigations, she had recently used DNA analysis in a case of alleged homosexual rape.

The case involved a family who did not wish to report it, and a young man. Semen samples were sent to a laboratory in the UK, and this led to a positive identification.

Body fluids, tissue, or even spittle can be used to positively identify their owner, in much the same way as fingerprints. Everybody's genetic material is unique.

Mr John Hayward, a British consultant forensic scientist, who is to give a lecture here on Tuesday next, to private investigators, said that the new process will be used mainly in rape and sex murder cases, and can now be used to "absolutely prove paternity."

There is, as yet, no definite plan to set up a private laboratory in Ireland, though the matter has been discussed. A considerable level of expertise is needed to carry out a expected that DNA "fingerprinting" will soon become an accepted tool of forensic investigators here.

DNA analysis, according to Mr Hayward.

As yet the Gardai's forensic scientists are not making use of the process, nor have they the facilities needed. However, they have taken a strong interest in it, and it is expected that DNA "fingerprinting" will soon become an accepted tool of forensic investigators here.

UCD teaching private eyes to get their man

by MICHAEL ROSS

THE stories she could tell you . . . but every case is confidential of course.

Sandra Mara is tall and slender. She wears a white blouse and the hair falling over her spectacles is flame red. White teeth glisten in the crescent of her smile.

Gerry, one of her first students, in UCD's new course for would-be private eyes, does not look like a private investigator. He has no soft hat, no macintosh, just a suit that could have been mistaken for a deckchair. Though the smoke from his cigarette does curl up towards the ceiling of the lecture hall as Sandra spoke.

"I am in insurance. I want to get involved in investigation work," he said. Gerry is one of 14 who have signed on for the course. There are nine men and five women. Six of them are smokers.

Sandra Mara, private investigator, our lecturer for the evening, was preceded by a tubby, balding man with a brown anorak and an American accent.

The fat American was standing in front of the blackboard. He had chalk in his hand. This was circumstantial evidence. Behind him on the board was a triangle of words.

Who - What - Where - When - How - Why. Above were two lines in the same hand, 0001 hrs = 1 minute after midnight; 2400 hrs = midnight. This made no sense to me at all. A private eye, however, must make sense of things.

The students have paid the Institute of Irish Investigators £225 to angle in on the basic tricks of the trade in 19 lectures over ten weeks.

Most of these people come, one of the course organisers says, from banking, security and insurance, also the gas company, for some reason.

Sandra the premier gal in the business, according to the investigation £225 to angle the institute people were fine, but that there were shady operators in the field. "A person can come out of prison for fraud or blackmail and hang up a PI sign."

The students jot down all the buzz words; pretext, research, report, source, surveillance, fraud, forensics, photographs. They want to know about insurance fraudsters, pole-vaulting whiplash victims, that sort of thing. Sandra has handled a great number of these cases.

"Some people claim much money, some too little."

She knew of a man in an accident. He sued had to get a foot amputated later as a result of accident, but didn't s it in his claim. He have got more money like to see people fix you can. The privat with the heart of gold

Another student, M trying to start a new himself. A bad spinal in a car crash six yea took away his livelih taxi driver and has le careful and shy. determined to strike an investigator.

He reckons that he work again otherwise he's too old. There's amount of crime out he says . . . especial manufacturing busi We're living in a word. Democracy has cards stacked against investigator can even up a bit for democra

Move over Magnum, say Irish PIs

MOVE over, Magnum PI and Remington Steele, Ireland is currently producing a new strain of private detectives fit to take on the underworld.

But the romantic TV image is out — instead aspiring "dicks" need patience and keenness to work long erratic hours.

This year sees the second course in private investigation taking place at UCD under the direction of the Institute of Irish Investigators, an organised body of private investigators.

According to the Institute president, Sandra Mara, last year's course, which was the first of its kind, was enormously successful with hundreds of applicants for just 30 places.

This year will see an intermediate course which allows last year's students to continue their studies. It will be in conjunction with the original course which was on offer last year.

The course covers topics as formation services, internal theft, drugs, types of fraud, industrial espionage, surveillance and observation and bugging.

Sandra described the type of people that made up last year's class. "Many of the students were practicing investigators at the time of their enrolment. Others included bank officials, semi-state employees and company directors.

"I attended a World Association Conference in Singapore recently and they were quite impressed with the success of our course, so much so that then others have been set up, a London course among them."

This year's course has attracted applicants from all over the country. Enquiries have been received from banks, wholesalers, personnel departments in various industries and other private individuals. The course begins on October 8 next and details can be obtained by contacting the secretary of the institute at 101 Richmond Road, Drumcondra.

One of the biggest problems facing genuine private investigators and the public is that there are no licensing laws to control 'cowboy' investigators whom Sandra claims are can "rip off clients giving all private investigators a bad name. "We are currently lobbying for suitable licences to be applied," she added.

She lists the qualities needed to be a good investigator as follows: patient, hard working, observant, honest and adaptable to erratic hours.

She added "Those who see the job in terms of a romantic TV situation are in for a very sharp shock."

More newspaper clippings, highlighting the early use of DNA fingerprinting and the course for detectives which I initiated at UCD

Me today

Leading a Double Life

One case that comes to mind was that of a well-known businessman. He ran a large successful business and was happily married with a young family. As the business continued to grow, he was away "on business" more often but his family saw the fruits of his success, moving to a bigger house and enjoying exotic holidays. His wife was very proud of her husband – he worked hard and life was easy for them, but gradually she began to resent the amount of time he spent away from home, meeting clients, playing golf and networking. What good was all that money when he seemed to have less and less time with his family? In desperation, she came to see me. Given her "charmed life", as she described it, I wondered why, although I had my own suspicions. She was obviously concerned about something else.

The businessman was kept under surveillance for a couple of weeks and it wasn't too long before I realised that his wife had good reason to be concerned. Despite not wanting to believe ill of him, she had been worried that he was seeing another woman. She was right, but there was a bit more to it than that. Not only was he seeing another woman, but he had in fact "married" her and they had two young children together, the younger being just four weeks old at the time of my investigation. His "new" family lived in a new house thirty miles from his home and neither woman knew of the existence of the "other" family.

My client couldn't believe what she was hearing, but the photographs and video proved it. It showed him kissing his "other" wife and family as he left for work in the early morning. The client had absolutely no idea her husband could be so deceitful. Bad enough to be having an affair, she

163

couldn't understand how he had gone as far as "marrying" this other woman, never mind having had two children with her, and she'd never suspected a thing!

She'd never thought him a devious man and not once had he ever let slip the name of his "other" wife or their children. Funny that, as it is often a giveaway when an affair is going on. One of the early signs can be the frequent mention of a name in conversation. The client was sick with shock. She felt she didn't know this "other" man, the father of her children. I can only imagine the conversation in her house when her husband came home that night – if he did come home, that is!

Loving Father, Drunken Mother

One particularly sad case was the uphill battle a loving father had to protect his children – both just babies aged one and two – from their drunken mother. Both parents held down respectable jobs in semi-state bodies, but the mother, a very attractive girl in her early thirties, had a drink problem that led to her "socialising" at all hours of the day and night whenever the mood took her. She "hung out" with inappropriate people and had liaisons with fellow travellers along the way, and was believed to be having an affair with her middle-aged boss.

The family had bought a house in Dublin and the children were cared for in a local crèche while the parents worked. Due to the nature of his job, the father's hours could be erratic and frequently he arrived home to find the mother had collected the children, only to dump them in their cots, while she went drinking, nowhere to be found. Gradually her behaviour got even worse. She would come home in the early hours of the morning with "new friends" in tow or he'd find her in a drunken sleep on the floor.

As the months went on, things went from bad to worse. Often she wouldn't turn up for days and, but for a few good neighbours, the father wouldn't have been able to cope on his own. His family lived in the country and he didn't want them to know his desperate situation. He began to hear rumours and worried that the situation was even worse than he'd thought. By the time he came to me, he was desperate. He'd tried everything else and was unable to get any direct help from the social services.

At his request, we kept the mother under surveillance for some time. Even we were shocked at her behaviour and incredulous that she could continue to hold down a job, given her binge drinking. On one occasion, she left home with an overnight bag and met a man in his fifties. They went to the overnight ferry in Dun Laoghaire, where he bought her ticket and carried her bag to the gate, kissing her as she boarded. On board, she headed straight for the bar, picking up a young man in his early twenties, who bought her a drink. They obviously didn't know each other, but they spent the night drinking together, despite the very rough seas. When the ferry docked at Holyhead, they were last off, the worse for wear, and they caught a London-bound train together. Throughout the journey they continued to drink and were seen kissing and cuddling.

What happened next shocked both me and the male detective with me, not to mention passengers in close proximity, as the two sprawled on top of each other, oblivious to their fellow passengers. A couple of people shouted at them and they stopped, at which point the woman fell into a drunken stupor, lying across the man, her mouth wide open.

When the train arrived in London, he couldn't wake her and a number of people offered to help. She eventually came around and they left the train, again being the last people off. She took a tube, heading alone to a clinic. En route, she was overheard asking some men what time the pubs opened – it wasn't even ten in the morning.

In a sad reflection of her chaotic life, she'd become pregnant and had arranged an abortion, apparently not for the first time. It was the ultimate shock to her partner, who knew nothing of her pregnancy. The one thing he was sure of was that it wasn't his. He adored his two children and wanted nothing more than to protect them. He'd tried everything to help her, despite her drinking and her affairs. Now his only concern was for his children. The trouble was, he wasn't married to the mother and had no solid legal rights; he was virtually powerless. The best we could do was to refer him to a lawyer, an expert in the area, and hope that sanity prevailed, but experience has proved that the law rarely has all the answers and all too often the law really is an ass.

Just an Illusion

Not all cases that fall into the "family law" category involved married people. Many are just living together – what used to be termed "common-law spouses" – which they wrongly believed gave them legal rights to property and inheritance. Certain cases related to people who were separated or divorced and involved in another relationship. Some were nervous about getting "burned" again or, on occasion, it was the single partner who had cause for concern about their new found "love", suspicious that perhaps they were still married and living with their spouse but were playing away, claiming to be separated or divorced, which was quite common. Others claimed to be single – forgetting they had a spouse and children waiting for them back home.

This case involved a glamorous, vivacious and intelligent lady who had her pick of admirers but was swept off her feet by one persistent professional man, who was charming, courteous and very attentive. Things were going well and, when he proposed, she was thrilled and agreed to marry him. Ever the romantic, he gave her a magnificent diamond ring and organised a romantic wedding, to coincide with a trip down the Nile, a fitting setting for his Cleopatra lookalike. It seemed like a fairytale come true, yet something was obviously bothering the princess – a personal friend of mine – as she asked me to "check up" on her fiancé before the imminent wedding.

Following a detailed investigation, I met her with the report. It made for interesting reading, and not what she wanted to hear. Nonetheless, she was going to hear it anyway, especially as she was a life-long friend. Her Prince Charming was the original Jekyll and Hyde. He had an "interesting" background, having left a trail of destruction in his wake. He'd been a well-qualified medical professional, struck off the medical register for personal drug abuse – writing his own prescriptions for class A drugs. He had a history of alcoholism and bouts of violence and he'd been barred from various private clubs, pubs and other venues over the years. Worse still, although separated from his wife and large family, he had never divorced and was legally not free to marry.

She was devastated and it was very hard to have to pass on this terrible news – the man she loved was just an illusion. At this stage, it was so close to the wedding that he'd gone ahead to make all the arrangements. She was due to follow within days. What transpired afterwards was even more bizarre and I only heard about it later. There are times in our lives when we all do things that, with hindsight, make absolutely no sense, but who knows how people will react under severe pressure. The lady, shocked to her core, devastated, but still in love, flew to Egypt and met up with her fiancé. Together they went on a Nile excursion and, as they cruised along, she confronted him with my report, which she'd brought with her. He was livid. She later said she thought he'd probably have thrown her overboard but for the other people around. Even more bizarrely, he talked her around and even persuaded her to go ahead with the "marriage" and honeymoon in the land of the Pharaohs. They returned to Ireland and moved into her apartment.

It wasn't long before the honeymoon was well and truly over, as he reverted to his old ways. Try as she might, she couldn't extricate herself from him and he refused to move out – virtually "squatting" in her home while she went to work. She bided her time; he'd have to go out sometime, and when he did, she had locksmiths ready to change the locks. After a couple of months, her opportunity came but as the workmen were in the middle of the job, to her horror, her "husband" came back.

It eventually took the long arm of the law to persuade him to get out of her life for good. At least she didn't have to go through the messy and expensive business of divorce but it was an emotionally expensive lesson, not to be recommended, but proof positive that love is after all, truly blind. As I always say, everything passes – good or bad, and she later met a real "Prince Charming" and they are living happily ever after.

19

Nursing a Grudge:
The Boston Burglar

The case involved a ninety-year-old widow from Boston, Massachusetts. It seemed the old lady, Dorothy Wirth, was missing a few items from her home. Could it be a case of a bad memory, Alzheimer's disease even, or was there something more to the story? I was about to find out.

Strange thing was, it came about at the same time as her personal nurse/housekeeper decided to go on vacation or, as she put it, a mission of mercy, to look after a sick relative in Australia. The nurse, Barbara Joyce, was in her early forties and had been working for the old lady for several years. Mrs Wirth totally relied on her. Reluctantly, Mrs Wirth agreed to a temporary replacement nurse. Nurse Suzanne Sakr took over Barbara's duties and, within days, while checking the household bills, she noticed dozens of cheques that were unaccounted for, while others were made out for large amounts to stores all over Boston. She found credit card bills in her employer's name showing purchases for furniture, electrical items and clothes. She knew the ninety-year-old Mrs Wirth wasn't interested in shopping – she had everything she wanted and none of the items appeared to be in the old lady's house. Rather than worry Mrs Wirth, she called the old lady's attorney, Michael Riley. He took one look at the accounts and called the cops. Then he called me.

It seemed that the caring nurse, now supposedly looking after her sick relative in Australia, had been looking after herself just a little too well. Barbara Joyce, the missing nurse, was Irish and they wanted me to track her down. Mrs Wirth's bank account was missing over $400,000 and that wasn't all. Old she may have been, but senile she was not.

When Dorothy Wirth complained that she was missing a "few items", she was right on the money. The trouble was, she was missing a hell of a lot more than that. It all started when Mrs Wirth, the widow of a wealthy Boston restaurant owner, hired Barbara Joyce to work as her live-in housekeeper/nurse. Within months, Mrs Wirth authorised Barbara to draw cheques on an account she held at the Bank of Boston, to pay the household expenses. It didn't take long before Barbara and her "husband" Patrick Joyce (also known as Patrick Joseph Fahy) embarked on a plan to criminally and fraudulently convert Dorothy Wirth's money and personal property for their own use.

Over the following three years, Barbara Joyce withdrew substantial sums of money from the Wirth accounts for her own use. She made out cheques for large sums in her husband's name and in the name of others. Other cheques for very large amounts were made payable to friends and family. She even went as far as using Mrs Wirth's chequebook to buy expensive pieces of jewellery and furniture for her own use. Then Barbara's avarice took over and she began to draw cheques on other accounts held by Mrs Wirth in the State Street Bank and the First National Bank of Boston. Again, she bought numerous pieces of jewellery, including diamond rings, silver and other valuable pieces, together with furniture and antiques, and a grandfather clock.

It didn't stop there, as her greed knew no bounds. Surreptitiously, she began removing pieces of Mrs Wirth's personal property from the Lime Street mansion. The "haul" included diamond jewellery, pictures and silverware, as well as furniture and antiques, including another grandfather clock. Having accumulated a hoard of goods to rival Aladdin's cave – including American electrical goods, fridges, freezers, televisions and laundry equipment, all specially ordered to conform to the Irish voltage – Barbara told Mrs Wirth she had to go away for a while to look after a very sick relative in Australia. Far from such humanitarian motives, Barbara had no intention of going to Australia, it was just a ploy to buy her time to get away with her haul. As the investigation progressed, I had discovered she'd already set plans in train to return home to Ireland in June. The Boston Police Department were now on the hunt for the missing nurse and her husband and an arrest warrant was issued for the missing pair, now wanted on suspicion of conspiracy and embezzlement.

Meanwhile, back in the "oul' sod" I was working on the case and making good progress. Investigations showed that Barbara Joyce was born Barbara Grealish and was from the village of Muckinagh, near Carraroe in County Galway. She'd married locally but the marriage didn't work out. Barbara left for America where she lived with Patrick Joyce, originally from the west of Ireland. They were believed to have married in 1984.

Patrick Joyce was from a family of five sisters and three brothers. Many Irish working in America were coming under scrutiny as illegal immigrants. With no "green card", they were restricted in the work they could get and had to opt for cash-in-hand poorly paid work and it was not unusual to use the identity of a family member who legitimately had a green card.

Patrick Joyce was one of the lucky ones. He had a green card, as did his brother John. Our investigations confirmed that John (Sean) Francis Joyce was safe and well, drawing unemployment benefit in the west of Ireland, awaiting delivery of a new boat, a thirty-six-foot long vessel still under construction. The contract price for the vessel was £75,000. Half the purchase price was being grant-aided by the European Union and Bord Iascaigh Mhara, the Irish Fisheries Board.

Our investigations were also progressing in other areas. It seemed that a series of cheques issued in Boston had made their way into a bank account in the name of Patrick Joyce at the Bank of Ireland in Galway. Eight cheques, ranging from $5,000 to $8,000, totalling almost $54,000, were drawn on the Mount Washington Bank, the Massachusetts Bank and the Shawmut Bank of Boston, all in a matter of weeks. In another twist, we discovered that Barbara and Patrick Joyce had paid £30,000 cash for a house they bought from a local garda at Derrykyle, in Rossaveal. The policeman believed they'd made their fortune in America. He'd no idea about the scam the Joyces had perpetrated on the elderly widow back in Boston.

Not satisfied with taking the ninety-year-old's money, over a period of months they had been stripping her house of valuables and personal effects, including paintings and a valuable diamond ring. They stockpiled the loot until they had full container loads and then shipped it to Ireland to furnish their new house in the west. Several container-loads of furniture and valuables had already arrived from Boston. At the time of our investigation, the house was undergoing major reconstruction and a large extension had already been completed. The work was halted when it was discovered that the Joyces had no planning permission and our information was that they were expected "home" within a week to resolve the problem.

On the other side of the Atlantic, the Boston Police Department were still working on the case. We discovered that the Joyces were still in the Boston area but would be leaving for Ireland within days. We passed this information on to the investigating detective unit in Boston, and they checked out all flights heading to Ireland within the next week or two. Based on our information, they hit the jackpot and arrested the Joyces on 2 July at Logan International Airport, as they tried to board a flight to Ireland. Police searched them and found jewellery belonging to Mrs Wirth and $25,000 in cash. Another $50,000 in cheques was found concealed in their suitcases.

The cheques were eventually traced back to a "John" Joyce who had "acquired" them earlier in the year. He was already under investigation for a money-laundering scam, transferring funds through several accounts before finally sending them on to Ireland. The theft and embezzlement had been going on for over four years, on an industrial scale. Documents relating to the purchase of the thirty-six-foot customised boat were found in his possession, while a search of their home revealed carbon copies of money orders payable to Mr Joyce. Handwriting analysis linked the couple to the forged cheques.

The Joyces were held in jail awaiting a court hearing for a "probable cause" on 14 July and it was deemed certain they'd be bound over for a full criminal prosecution. When the case came before the Boston Superior Court on 9 December 1987, the two reversed their previous "not guilty" pleas when they learned that my investigation had uncovered substantial proof of their scam in Ireland, as well as in the US. The evidence was stacked against them. They pleaded guilty to charges that carried possible jail sentences of over 140 years in a US prison.

Boston detectives discovered that they'd sold real estate valued at $155,000 in the City of Boston, the day before they boarded the plane They say timing is everything and I have to agree. While we were in Rossaveal, in the middle of our ongoing investigation on 10 July, three vans and two cars pulled up at the Joyces' new house. News of their arrest in Boston had obviously got through, as large amounts of furniture and personal effects were removed through a rear door of the house. Most of the furniture was covered in protective wrappings and heavy brown packing paper common to long-distance furniture transportation.

We maintained surveillance and watched as the wrappings were torn off and the incriminating packaging was burnt at the back of the house. The goods were hurriedly loaded into the waiting vans and moved to "safe houses" elsewhere.

As in most "crime scenes", every contact leaves a trace and this time was no different, as they left incriminating evidence behind which helped us track down the legitimate warehouse and freight company that shipped the goods to Galway. The stuff had been transported to Ireland by a Boston freight company on the instructions of Barbara and Patrick Joyce.

Back in Boston, detectives acting on our information visited the company and confirmed that the Joyces had been shipping large quantities of furniture and household goods in containers to Ireland. The first load left Boston some months earlier and the Joyces had delivered more pieces for shipping to Ireland just days before Barbara left Mrs Wirth's employment. This shipment hadn't yet left Boston and was still at the warehouse.

Boston police got a search warrant and seized the load, pending the court proceedings. When the cops opened up the containers they were amazed at what they found. There were over 6,000 items. A treasure trove of household goods, including fishing gear, exercise bikes, artificial plants, ashtrays, door handles, antiques, silverware, shower doors and, to their disbelief, a brand new top-of-the-range Mercedes!

Boston detectives were overjoyed at their haul. Their investigations found that Barbara Joyce had sold another property at 41 Dracut Street, Dorchester, Massachusetts and was waiting to pick up a cheque of over $130,000 from the sale. A week after Patrick and Barbara Joyce were arrested, while they were still in police custody, a man using the name "John Joyce" picked up the proceeds of the sale of Dracut Street.

Attorneys for Mrs Wirth applied for an injunction and an order restraining the Joyces or their agents from disposing of any property or monies, pending the outcome of the case. Lawyers acting for Mrs Wirth in Ireland took similar action through the Irish Courts. Peter Kelly SC (now a High Court Judge) acting for Mrs Wirth told the High Court there were believed to be large sums of money held in the Bank of Ireland, Galway and that the financing of the boat, the *Bláth na h'Óige*, was also part of the major fraud before both the Irish and US courts. Sean Francis Joyce of Rossaveal, described as the skipper of the boat, agreed in court that the vessel would not travel beyond twelve miles from the shoreline and would not berth nor dock outside the jurisdiction. An order freezing all the assets of Barbara and Patrick Joyce in Ireland was granted.

Back in Boston, Detective Lieutenant Eddie McNally told the court that the Joyces had been scamming money from the elderly widow for over ten years. What had come to light as a result of the recent investigations was probably a drop in the ocean, he said. The Joyces were jailed when they failed to come up with bail money, amounting to $100,000 in cash, as demanded by District Attorney Gerry Malone, who told the court he'd requested the steep bail conditions because the Joyces had sold their assets and were arrested trying to board a flight to Ireland.

Defence Attorney Philip Tracey said his clients' passports had been impounded, making it unlikely they would abscond. Their bail was reduced to $20,000 each plus a surety of $100,000. The couple pleaded guilty on all counts and faced 147 years in jail and thousands of dollars in fines. Sentencing was put back to allow them time to make restitution. They agreed to sell their home in Galway and other assets to repay Mrs Wirth. If this was done, Mrs Wirth's lawyers agreed that Mrs Joyce should get a six-month jail sentence, while her husband would get away with a suspended sentence, as due to her age, Mrs Wirth was reluctant to have to give evidence in a criminal case in two jurisdictions to recover her money, which up to that time had been conservatively calculated at over $550,000.

Patrick Martin Joyce and Barbara Joyce née Flaherty, of Crimnagh, Lettermore, are no relations of, nor are they in any way connected with the above-mentioned Barbara Joyce or her family, either through marriage or otherwise, nor have they any involvement with or connections to any parties referred to in this story.

20

Without a Trace

On a regular basis, we hear news reports of people who have gone missing . . . disappeared without a trace. One of the most common cases a private investigator deals with is that of missing persons. In some instances, it is a simple case of someone just "dropping out" from their daily lives. The most serious cases can involve kidnapping or even the murder of adults and children.

People go missing for all sorts of reasons – some because they are ill and don't realise what they are doing; others "disappear" to avoid debts; while many more just leave home to live with another partner, giving no hint of their intentions. Some might say that, for those who deliberately abandon their families without explanation, it is a coward's way out. Their reasons differ, from not being able to "face" their spouse to hoping they won't have to pay maintenance – it takes all sorts!

Then there are the "runaways", usually teenagers who are going through those "difficult" years when parents "don't understand them". Their answer is to run away from home. The distraught family turn to the Gardaí for help but, unless they are under-age or they consider the person to be "at risk", there is little they can do about it.

Time factors are critical in such matters, as the earlier it is investigated the greater the chance of locating them before the trail goes cold. For those who can afford a private investigator, it is often their best hope, although nothing is guaranteed.

Over the years, I have investigated many such cases, not all with happy endings. Only the families themselves can understand the hurt, loss and anguish they go through waiting to hear any news of their loved one. They clutch at every snippet of information, possible sighting or reason why. In previous years, not many people had mobile phones, making it difficult to trace their movements. Today, tracking someone's movements from their mobile phone is standard practice, with e-mail and CCTV a further aid to investigation.

Perhaps anyone contemplating such a distressing move will read this and think again – there is *always* another way! Unfortunately, not everyone has control over such decisions. They could be suffering from an illness such as Alzheimer's or severe depression, unaware of the devastation they leave behind. The cases dealt with here are just a very small cross-section of the hundreds I've dealt with. Some minor details have been changed to protect the identities of the families involved.

Infatuated by the Wrong Side of the Tracks

I was asked to find a missing teenager. The parents, my clients, were distraught and feared the worst. They had notified the police but there had been no news. The teenager had been gone for over a month but there had been no sightings and nothing heard from them in that time. As far as the family knew, they'd no money or access to money and had taken nothing with them – no clothing or personal belongings of any kind. It didn't look good. Armed with photographs of the teenager and as much information as could be gleaned from the devastated parents, I set about looking for them in all the usual places teenagers hang out – from pubs, clubs and shopping centres to cinemas and gaming halls.

Friends and associates were questioned for any clues of their whereabouts or any plans they may have made but they knew nothing – or if they did, they weren't telling. A close examination of their personal belongings turned up a letter from a friend in London and while it said nothing of much interest, I went to London to find out if the friend knew anything more of the teenager's plans. Realising the seriousness of the situation, the friend told me the missing teenager had been hanging around with a new crowd unknown to their usual friends and although they didn't know much about them – they weren't "their type". He gave me a name and general idea of where they hung out.

Back in Dublin, we checked out the name of the "new friend" and found that he was well known to Gardaí as a small-time drug pusher and user. He had numerous convictions for burglary, larceny and similar crimes – not the kind of guy you'd want your teenager hanging out with. I assumed he wasn't holding down a job and found he was collecting the dole every Tuesday morning. Keeping the dole office under surveillance – at one point I actually joined the queue myself to ensure I had the right guy – I followed him as he headed to a block of flats in Rialto.

Surveillance was kept on the flat in the hope that he'd lead us to the missing teenager, with nothing to report for two days. Late on night three, the missing teenager arrived in the company of three others. I had found out that the group, all in their twenties, had been squatting there for about three weeks. I contacted the family with the good news that we'd found their sixteen-year-old and the dangerous company they were in. The parents were worried that if they just showed up, the teenager would run away again. Before they made contact, they wanted to have their child made a ward of court. I told them that, realistically, as they would be seventeen by the time it got to court, it would be difficult if not impossible to enforce. The family went to their solicitor and were making plans what to do when events overtook them.

The drug squad arrived at their door with the news that their teenager had been arrested and was being held in Mountjoy following a preliminary hearing. It seemed they'd been involved in a break-in at a chemist's shop in which a large quantity of drugs were stolen. At the time of their arrest, the missing teenager was under the influence of drugs and was in the company of a known convicted drug-pusher, who was in the process of dealing. They were remanded in custody and were due to appear in Court the following Friday to face further charges.

My clients were in total shock. They were a respectable family and couldn't believe what they were hearing. The four appeared before the court and pleaded "not guilty" but were found guilty on all charges. A three-month suspended sentence was imposed and a hefty fine. Three of the group, including the client's teenager, had no previous convictions.

Luckily, it was the wake-up call the teenager needed and the family made sure they had no further opportunity to "relapse", keeping a close eye on them from then on. Happily, the teenager realised what a close call they'd had and made a full recovery, in every sense of the word. In later years, they went on to become a TD.

On the Right Side of the Law

A lawyer went missing during the lunch break right in the middle of a high-profile court case. The case was of a "sensitive" nature, at a time when the IRA were particularly active, and it was feared that he had been kidnapped to prevent the case going ahead. Gardaí were alerted and a nationwide search was put into action but, for security reasons, the media were not alerted. I was contacted by the family to assist in the search but I advised them to leave it to the police as, by then, he'd only been missing forty-eight hours and the Garda resources were obviously far greater than mine.

The next day the family contacted me again and asked me to help so, despite my earlier advice, and given their distress, I agreed. It was all hands on deck as we pulled out all the stops, interviewing his immediate family, friends and colleagues, going through all the usual routine but extremely important minutiae. He had been in court on the morning of the case but, following a break for lunch, he never returned. He had not made contact with anyone, either by phone or otherwise, and as far as his secretary knew, he hadn't taken much money with him – just his credit card, as usual. His passport and other property were still at home and he only had a small amount of cash on him that morning.

Something about the case didn't stack up, despite all the hype about a possible kidnapping. As was often the case, it was more a case of instinct and intuition than hard facts, but something was nagging me about it and I persisted in following my hunch. I decided to check all flights, ferries and anything else that left Dublin the day he disappeared, but there was no trace of him. We spoke to taxi, bus and long-distance coach drivers, without result. Eventually we got a break when we showed his photograph to staff at Connolly Station and someone remembered selling him a train ticket.

While these investigations were going on, we had also been checking his credit card transactions and found that he'd used the card to buy train tickets, travelling from Dublin to Cork. From there, he criss-crossed the country on a single ticket to Killarney, where he stayed in a hotel for a few days. From Killarney he travelled between Limerick, Cork and Tralee. We double-checked to make sure we had the right man; his identity was confirmed when we discovered he'd bought both a train ticket and a ticket for the Rosslare ferry with a credit card, just a few hours before our enquiry. The station staff described him as being well-dressed if somewhat dishevelled, with a couple of days' growth of beard. They'd guessed him to be a businessman on a boozy weekend.

He had no connections in Wexford that we knew of and the train had already departed for Rosslare. Given the pressure he'd been working under, I feared the worst. There was nothing for it but to have the train stopped *en route*. It was extremely time-sensitive, and possibly even a matter of life and death. The rail staff radioed ahead, asking the ticket inspector to keep a discreet eye on him until such time as we could make it to Wexford, and head him off before the final stop at Rosslare Harbour, the departure point for ferries to the UK and France.

As we reached Rosslare Strand, the last stop before the port, by arrangement with Iarnród Éireann we had the train stopped without alerting the passengers or the missing man. Boarding the train with a doctor, the man was discreetly escorted from the train and given medical care. He had been under severe stress. He later admitted that his intentions had been to jump overboard *en route* to France – never to be found or heard of again. We were very pleased to have found him before he took such a drastic and very final step. It was a wonderful result for everyone.

After proper medical treatment and rest from exhaustion, he too was delighted to have been literally stopped in his tracks. He went on to live a full and happy life.

When I later learned that the police investigation was forty-eight hours behind us – too late for them to have had a successful outcome – I was all the more pleased I'd taken on the case, despite our limited resources when measured against those of the State.

The co-operation and kindness of the staff at Ianród Éireann played a major part in our success and I wrote both to the company and to the individuals involved, Eric Sexton and Michael Conway of Limerick, and Patsy Cannon of Cork stations, to thank them for their tremendous efforts and humanity in helping to bring the matter to a happy ending. They can never know just how much their efforts meant to that family. It was times like this that made the long hours and the hard work all worthwhile.

The Kid and the Cash

Paul was a bit of a loner. He came from a good family, his father was in business and doing very well, everything about the family was normal. They loved their kids and did their best for them and, as far as they knew, their kids were happy and well adjusted. But then, one day, thirteen-year-old Paul went missing. They looked everywhere but couldn't find him. Eventually, after almost eight hours, he turned up with little or no explanation – just that he'd forgotten the time and was hanging out with friends. Annoyed and relieved, they gave him a hard time but left it at that – until a few weeks later, when it happened again. This time he was grounded, with a severe warning that it was never to happen again.

But it did. This time it lasted a lot longer. The family looked everywhere, contacting the police as the night set in, but he was nowhere to be found. They couldn't understand what was going on. Nothing was missing from the house – no clothes, food or anything else they could think of – except his bike. He loved that bike, it went everywhere with him; but where could it be? He hadn't been spotted by any of the neighbours and no-one from his school admitted seeing him. It was a complete mystery.

Naturally, the family thought the worst. A parent's first thought is, *Has he been snatched by some paedophile? Or perhaps he's had an accident and is in hospital?* They rang around every hospital without finding him. With seventy-two hours gone by, they came to me. It was a needle in a haystack and, with the police already working on the case, given that they had still not found him despite their resources, we were up against it.

I checked out Paul's room for any clues. It was obvious that he wanted for nothing – he was their adored son. As I looked around the house, I noticed wads of cash lying on bedside lockers, kitchen worktops and on the hall table. When I asked about it, the father said he was paid in cash for a lot of his business. He usually just stuffed it into his pockets, emptying them out when he got home to count later. He said he wasn't much good at bookkeeping and sometimes he was so busy that days would go by before he got around to counting it.

It struck a chord with me. They had said that Paul had taken nothing with him but his bike. I asked if any money was missing. They said they hadn't even thought of it – he was such an honest boy, he'd never do anything like that. They had no idea if any money was missing, never mind how much, but I was certain there *was*. More to the point, Paul probably had enough money to buy food and anything else he needed to lie low for quite a while.

With this new information, we printed poster photos of the boy and showed them around the shops, cinemas and anywhere else that might attract a thirteen-year-old boy with money in his pocket. Eventually, someone thought they recognised him. He'd been spotted in a fish-and-chip shop some distance from his home two days in a row. The staff were sure it was the missing boy, but in these cases we often got sightings from all over the country, all equally "certain" that it was the missing person. But when they said that he'd left a blue and silver bike outside – the same as Paul's – we felt sure it was him. Surveillance was put in place, with no further sightings of the young lad.

We checked with his classmates and, although they didn't hang around with him, one or two threw some light on the matter. He was apparently being bullied by older boys who'd been demanding money from him. At first he had refused but then they began to threaten him and he was ostracised from the rest of the boys, who were warned not to talk to him. Frightened, he began to do as they demanded but, like all such schemes, their demands increased as the weeks went by.

He'd been stealing the money from the house to meet their demands until, eventually, he could take no more. When he couldn't come up with the money, he was too scared to go to school and ran away; but having no money, he was forced to return home. This time was different. He had been missing for days now and there was no news from the Gardaí. The parents were terrified something had happened to their only son and, given his young age, both as a parent and an investigator, I was worried too.

I alerted contacts throughout the country and issued posters offering a reward for information. Seeing one of our posters, the boy realised we were looking for him and that it was only a matter of time before we caught up with him. He wrote a note to his mother saying he was sorry for running away and for taking the money. He said he had a job as a lorry helper and when he'd earned enough to pay them back, he would come home. The letter's postmark was clear enough to point us to the general location. Though he could have just posted it as he was passing through, I felt sure he was still in that area.

Accompanied by his parents, we headed to the country to look for him. Between asking questions and showing his photograph around the area, we eventually found him at a small boxing club in the company of a middle-aged man. The man had told people the boy was his "nephew". The lad had been hitch-hiking and was picked up by the man, who had taken him back to his place. He had offered him bed, board and a job, which the innocent teenager had gratefully accepted. Not surprisingly, he turned out to be an unsavoury character and the young lad was very relieved to see his parents again.

The Gardaí were notified and the man was charged. He pleaded guilty, so the boy was saved the trauma of giving evidence against him. His parents had had absolutely no idea how much money was missing, but it was a substantial enough sum. They didn't care. They had their son back, alive and well. Paul was moved to another school but not before the bullies were reported to their school principal, who presumably passed the word on to their parents. As far as I know, Paul never got into trouble again and he learned that, if he had a problem, the best people to sort it out were his parents.

The Young Widower

The family of a young man in his early thirties contacted me. The man's wife had died and, after the funeral, he had just disappeared. He had contacted no-one and had left all his worldly goods behind. The family feared for his safety, but he wasn't missing long enough for the Gardaí to be concerned. The couple had no children and their lives had revolved around each other. Understandably, he was distraught at the loss of his young wife.

We checked his bank account; he'd made no effort to withdraw any money since the funeral a couple of weeks beforehand. He hadn't been back to work but they just assumed he was taking a little time off and that he would be back before long. He was a model worker and had been employed in the same job since he'd left college.

The weeks were slipping by with no sightings of the man and the family were getting increasingly concerned for his safety. Had he done something stupid, in his grief? After about six or seven weeks, we had a breakthrough. Having visited every hostel, doss house and drop-in centre, we found that he'd spent the odd night in the care of the Simon

Community – wonderful caring people who reach out to those in need, day or night. Although they remembered him from the photo we produced, he hadn't been seen for a while; but at least we knew that, up to that point, he was still alive. The next time he turned up, we managed to catch up with him and his family arrived and brought him home.

A happy ending, you might think. So did I. Yet months later, the family came back to me. He was gone again. Another search eventually found him in similar circumstances in the west of Ireland, where he had no connections. Again, the family brought him home to look after him – but, time and again, the same thing happened, until eventually they felt they could do no more. For him, his life ended when his wife died and, as far as I know, despite the best efforts of his family, he never got it back on track again. Hopefully, time was a healer and perhaps he eventually learned to live with his grief and move on. I truly hope he found peace and happiness – but somehow I doubt it.

Ain't No Sunshine When You're Gone

I got a call from a worried businessman whose co-director had "disappeared". He hadn't been seen for several weeks, his flat appeared to be empty and he wasn't answering his phone. He was worried about him and the business was suffering badly as they were joint signatories on the company cheques. Suppliers and staff weren't being paid and they were losing business. People were speculating they were in financial trouble, which was far from the case, but he didn't know what to do. He was worried that his friend and partner had done "something stupid".

He'd been separated from his wife for some time and was very depressed about it. No-one seemed to know where he was – even his immediate family hadn't heard from him and had reported him missing to the police. After several weeks without any contact, the businessman had exhausted all possibilities, which is where I came in. He had explained the situation to the staff, clients and suppliers and they had all agreed to give him some time to sort things out.

Our investigation began in Dublin, where we spoke to family and friends, trying to get some background on the man. Depression can be deceptive and, as far as friends and colleagues were concerned, while they knew he was upset, everything else had appeared normal and they hadn't noticed anything different about his behaviour. We contacted his landlord, who gave us access to his apartment. The rent had been paid in full and he'd had no concerns about a "missing tenant". There was nothing unusual in the apartment – the wardrobes still held clothes and many personal items were still there. There was stale food in the fridge – but being a lone guy, in itself that meant nothing; he could have just gone on holiday and not bothered to throw it out before he left. His letterbox was full of bills, junk mail and the usual stuff. It seemed he'd been gone for about a month, judging by the dates.

I decided to track his credit card for usage since his disappearance – not a guarantee, as it could have been stolen, but usually a good indicator. I discovered he'd bought a ticket to Florida, the sunshine state, a few weeks before he'd disappeared. Obviously it had been premeditated, as we found he had applied for a visa some time beforehand. Following investigations in Florida with immigration and other contacts, I established the date he'd arrived in the US.

With continuous monitoring of his credit card activities, I tracked him down to the South Beach area. I flew to Florida and found him working locally in a bar on South Beach.

I made an approach under the pretext of being a tourist. I got chatting with him and he told me he had got sick of life in Dublin and wanted out. He said he was fed up in his job and he hated the cold weather. He wanted the sun and something different – so he just took off without telling anyone. He never mentioned the business partner he'd walked out on.

After a while, I gained his confidence and came clean, explaining what a detrimental effect his actions were having on the business and the difficulties his partner was having. He hadn't thought about the business or about the need for his signature. He was so depressed he just wanted to get away from it all. There was no malice in his actions, just desperation and a lack of thinking things through. He agreed to return to Dublin to sort out the business issues, which he did, selling his interest to his former partner.

After the deal was done and his partner sorted out, he went back to a life in the sun.

Anything But the Bike!

Funny how something as innocuous and unimportant as a bicycle can turn people's lives upside down.

This was just another kid with a bike. For reasons the parents couldn't even remember, there had been a huge argument in the house over the same bike. Whatever had happened, the parents had warned the kid that the bike had to go – but the kid had other plans. The bike went, and he went with it.

The case had started in England and there had been a country-wide manhunt for the teenager, without result. The parents feared the worst, as would most parents, thinking he had been picked up by someone and possibly murdered. They did everything they could to publicise the case, postering as many places as possible, keeping it in the local news, contacting school-friends and anyone who knew their son, all to no avail.

A year went by, then two, and still they had no news of their son. They continued making every effort to find him but were getting nowhere. Their only glimmer of hope was in the fact that no body had been found and they hoped that perhaps there was a slim chance he was still alive, somewhere.

With renewed vigour, they contacted private detectives in England, Scotland and eventually us here in Ireland, sending the most recent photographs of their son, taken over three years previously. We copied the photographs and postered them throughout the country, while at the same time checking records and descriptions of anyone remotely fitting his description. After six months of trawling, investigations and eliminations, incredibly, we located the lad – David J, living in a small village in Wales. He had originally come to Ireland where he had some distant relations but, being a relatively innocent child, he didn't find them. Dejected, he got a ferry to Wales and, when his money ran out, he took a job as a live-in labourer on a farm. By the time we found him, he'd been working there for almost three years. He had wanted to make contact with his family in England, but he didn't know what to say to them or how to face them after what he'd done.

When we made the call to his family, telling them we'd found him, they didn't care that he'd caused them such anguish, not knowing if he was dead – nothing mattered but that their son was alive and well and coming home to them.

We got a wonderful "thank you" letter and our fee and we never heard from them again. I'm sure they realised that life is too short to fight over silly things and they never made the same mistake again.

A Cocktail of Depression and Prescription Drugs

A call from a garda sergeant led to another case. A family friend had gone missing and although the Gardaí had been notified and were making enquiries, after two weeks there had still been no progress and he had recommended that the family contact me.

It seemed the man had been in the house when his wife left to go shopping but when she returned, he wasn't at home. She didn't really think much about it, assuming he'd gone for a walk to get some fresh air, but when he hadn't returned later that evening, she began to worry. By the following morning, when he still hadn't shown up, she was really worried that something had happened to him and called the police.

On meeting them, I went through all the routine questions. What was his financial situation? Was business good? Did he have any health worries? Was he a drinker or a gambler? Could there be another woman involved? On and on the probing and intrusive questions went. Hard as this can be for a worried family, it is very important to the overall picture. In many such situations, the family may think they know the answers to these questions but it is not unusual for some people to have "other lives", other families even, totally unknown to their existing family.

Reluctantly, they admitted that he hadn't been feeling too well recently and had been treated for mild depression, although they could see no reason for it, as things were going fine. He was a businessman running a family business and, to all appearances, everything was going reasonably well – no better or worse than any small business and the family GP put him on an anti-depressant, Prozac, which had made the world of difference.

I did a thorough search of the house and confirmed that none of his clothes were missing; nor did he take his wallet, credit cards, money or any form of identification. Everything belonging to him was still in the house and his car was still parked in the driveway.

Something rang an alarm bell with me. I'd seen cases like this many times, when even the most immediate family don't realise the depths of depression that can ensnare a loved one. On the surface, everything appears normal, until they go missing. I liaised with the investigating gardaí, who were extremely helpful and gave me full access to their file at the garda station, but I was surprised that there was little or no information in it. It is a difficult situation for the gardaí. It is not a crime to go missing and unless foul play is suspected, there is little the police can do – and certainly not in the first few days.

I went back to basics and started from scratch, taking nothing for granted. I interviewed every family member, every friend, associate, worker or colleague I could find. I organised country-wide publicity, with radio appeals, placed posters throughout the country, interviewed security staff at shopping centres, airports, banks, truck drivers, courier companies, taxi drivers, bus and train personnel, as well as toll bridges and pubs – all were on the look-out for the missing man. All the hospitals country-wide, including psychiatric hospitals, hostels and social workers, were contacted without result.

Every client he did business with was interviewed in an effort to shed some light on his disappearance and alert them to keep vigilant, should they see him.

We had extra staff manning the phones and collating the information, as sightings were reported all over the country. Calls came from Donegal, Dublin, Limerick, Cork, Kildare, Mayo and Waterford. In virtually every county someone was sure they'd spotted him – we even got calls from gardaí throughout the country, who believed they might have sighted the man. Each and every "sighting" had to be investigated. Staff interviewed the callers as the nation got behind the search. The response was magnificent but, after extensive investigations, most of these sightings were ruled out.

There were only two sightings that seemed promising. One was from a lady who had spotted a man fitting his description a mile from his home a few days after he'd gone missing. The other sighting was even more promising, as it came from a woman who had known him for twelve years. She'd been a passenger in her husband's car when they drew alongside a jeep. She noticed the missing man in the driving seat and was surprised to see him driving a jeep; as she said: "It seemed out of place for him." She tried to catch his eye but he never looked around, staring straight ahead. When the lights changed, she lost sight of his car, which turned off. She had no reason to take the registration number at that time. This had happened a week after he'd gone missing and before my involvement. There'd been no publicity about the case and she hadn't known he was missing.

There was no mention of a white jeep in the Garda files, but I found out that he had a relation who drove a white jeep and who hadn't been interviewed by the Gardaí at that time. However, due to the long time-lapse since the day of his disappearance, this lead ran into sand.

The man's bank account and credit cards were checked on a daily basis to see if there was any movement on them – with no result. Although he'd left everything behind, it has been known that people planning to go "missing" get second credit cards, in the belief that when the original card has been left behind, it won't be checked.

It wasn't looking good and I was now convinced that the man wouldn't be found alive. It was the old mixture of experience and gut feeling, together with the fact that he had stopped taking his medication. I'd seen instances of it in previous cases, when a depressed person felt fine while taking their medication; then, resenting the "stigma" of being treated for depression, they stopped taking it. Coming off the drug without medical supervision can be extremely dangerous. In clinical studies, anti-depressants were found sometimes to increase the risk of suicidal thinking and behaviour in people with depression. At times like this, reason goes out the window for the patient, and the missing person is not responsible for their actions, such is their state of mind.

It was my immediate and most worrying concern, although I couldn't tell the family that. The family were understandably distraught. His wife and adult children were near breaking point. I already knew what the outcome was likely to be and tried to prepare the family for the worst as gently as possible.

I checked the tides around Howth and Dun Laoghaire, expecting that perhaps his body would be washed up. From time to time, I would get a call from the Gardaí when a body had been found. I would go and check if it was my client's husband – no point upsetting them unnecessarily if it wasn't.

Eventually, almost two months after he'd gone missing, a man's body was spotted on a cliff ledge by a tourist on New

Year's Eve. Rescue services were alerted and they recovered the body, which was identified as the missing man. It was a terrible situation for a family to face at any time.

Even today, writing this, I feel immensely sad for the family and can only imagine what they went through. Although I have investigated numerous cases of missing people, somehow that one has always stayed with me. It was a tragic end and there was nothing anyone could do to ease the pain of those left behind. It was one of those cases I could never forget. He had gone missing on my daughter's birthday and on that day every year since, I think of him and his family.

The Case of the Missing Twin

This is the strange story of a "missing" twin. The case came about when a client was searching for his identical twin sister. His story was bizarre but true. His parents were professional people, living in an expensive area. They had four children. As a teenager, their young boy was put into a mental institution and the family had never bothered to visit him. When he reached maturity, he was obviously well enough to be released – if in fact he'd ever really been mentally ill.

He returned to his family home, only to find that it had been sold years previously. The family had moved without notifying the hospital or leaving a forwarding address with anyone. He was devastated and not for the first time. Whatever their reasons before, they had abandoned him to the "system". Now, that abandonment was complete – they just didn't want him in their lives. He had no money, no job and nowhere to live – and now, he knew for sure, he had no family either.

We were contacted by a kindly solicitor connected to the Salvation Army Hostel where the young man was living. They had already exhausted the usual resources of the Sally Army's own investigation branch, which provides a wonderful service to people looking for lost relatives and friends. Investigations showed that his mother had transferred the family home into his oldest sister's name, months after they put him into hospital. His sister sold the house and moved away, giving her solicitors strict instructions not to divulge the family's whereabouts to anyone under any circumstances.

The man's father had since died but we established that his work pension had been sent on to his widow at an address in England, until her subsequent death. Investigations in England proved that one of the sisters had continued to live at the same address after the death of her mother. We paid her a visit but she made it clear that the family wanted no contact with their brother, despite the passing years and his reduced circumstances. Two of the sisters had married and had families of their own and they'd never even told their own families they had a brother.

Having tracked them all down, it became obvious that the sole purpose of the move to England was to ensure their brother never found them again. As they put it themselves, "We have gone to extreme lengths to avoid this". We had managed to find his family despite their best effort to hide. They were all extremely comfortable and living in the "stockbroker belt", but they wanted nothing to do with their brother. They refused to say why.

He wasn't looking for money – just his family. Though they were aware of his reduced circumstances, it changed nothing; they weren't prepared to share their good fortune or their lives with their only brother. Sometimes, despite our best efforts, there is little we can do in such circumstances. We found his family but he realised that he had lost them forever, many years before.

The Magician's Disappearing Act

Some years ago I was contacted by a number of people, all anxious to locate the whereabouts of Ronald Gold – better know as the entertainer and hypnotist Paul Goldin. Goldin made his name wowing audiences in the Olympia Theatre, when he hypnotised members of the audience and had them running out onto the streets of Dublin desperately looking for disappearing leprechauns. This time, he'd managed to disappear himself, leaving some very irate people, including his American wife, Patricia, and his son Richard behind.

He was supposedly spotted all around the world, from London to New York. Investigations revealed that he had been driven to Newry in his Bentley by an entertainer friend, accompanied by his receptionist, Mrs Maeve O'Brien, and her children. An arrest warrant had been issued for Mrs O'Brien, who had failed to get US visas for her children at the American Embassy in Dublin.

The group went to New York and eventually on to Honolulu, in Hawaii. At the time, Goldin left behind not only his wife and child but mounting debts, including a large sum to a private client of ours. He also owed money to a Cork car hire firm. Goldin hired the car and initially paid a cash deposit but then disappeared, taking the car with him. The car-hire company were looking for him, as by then he owed them a sizeable amount and they wanted their car back. The car had completely disappeared and was never seen again.

Investigations showed that Goldin had shipped his personal possessions to Hawaii prior to his disappearance, indicating that it had been planned well in advance. Goldin's wife Patricia got a warrant for his arrest in the Dublin District Court under the Children's Act, for abandonment and neglect. Her barrister, Mr Paul Carney BL, now Mr Justice Carney, sought to have Goldin brought back into the jurisdiction. Mrs O'Brien's estranged husband Patrick wanted the matter raised in the Dáil and asked the Department of Foreign Affairs to help him get his children back to Ireland.

Goldin was good at the disappearing act. He had been living with his wife of seven years, Patricia, in New York when, one October morning, he left their New York apartment to take a flying lesson. He never came back. Four months later, we tracked him to Raheny in Dublin. He "announced" his engagement to Mrs Maeve O'Brien, and his wife Patricia flew to Dublin to institute proceedings. Once again, Goldin disappeared.

Goldin wasn't just running away from family problems. With mounting debts, High Court actions against him and personal injury actions by people claiming to have been hurt when he hypnotised them and sent them in search of leprechauns during his show, it was more than he could take. He was also worried about a rival who offered hypnosis to stop smoking and for weight loss and there was a court case pending in this regard.

Years later, when the heat was off, Goldin returned to Ireland with his new wife, Maeve and family. He continued to live in Ireland until his death in 2008, when Paul Goldin disappeared forever.

The Disappearing Doctor

Not exactly a missing person case, this was more an investigation to find a doctor in a medical compensation case. It related to a claim by a young mother who was prescribed thalidomide during her pregnancy many years earlier. The drug was originally developed in the US as an anti-seizure drug but was found to be ineffective and the patent was sold to a German company. Following further testing, they marketed it as a sedative and later, as an anti-nausea medicine, prescribed for morning sickness in pregnancy, with disastrous effects.

My client had been prescribed the drug by her doctor while she was living in Anguila, in the West Indies. Eventually she delivered a baby girl who was severely handicapped by the thalidomide drug. A court case had been "pending" for several years but it couldn't go ahead, as the prescribing doctor couldn't be found. An international law firm had been trying to track him down for several years and had hired private investigators in the UK, the US and Canada without result.

Time was running out and they were anxious to get on with the case. There was some doubt about the nationality of the doctor but it was believed that he may have studied at the College of Surgeons in Dublin. Other than that, all we had was a name. Initially, we weren't having much luck, as lead after lead turned into dead ends. Reading and re-reading the file looking for an angle, I wondered if the name was correct – perhaps the patient had forgotten it or it was a typo, although checking with the clients, they assured us it was the right name. Doodling with possible variations of the name, I came up with another, similar surname – there were just two central letters that differed. Acting as I often did on a "hunch" rather than any hard evidence, I started all over again and this time, I managed to pinpoint the doctor as having been a graduate of the College of Surgeons. They *had* got his name wrong and by substituting just two letters, I'd identified him.

He wasn't registered in Ireland, nor had he ever taken out full registration here, having gone to England straight from college. The trouble was, he wasn't listed on the UK register either. Given the seriousness of the situation – the case could be struck out if we didn't find the doctor – and with the progress already made, the lawyers asked us to keep trying. After several more weeks, we got the breakthrough we'd been waiting for and found him in Canada, one of the countries already discounted by the Canadian investigators.

It was with great satisfaction that we told the client the man's address in Manitoba. It was the final piece of the jigsaw needed to resolve her case. It goes to prove – take nothing for granted, even when a client swears they gave you the right information.

21

Sleuths, Scams and Scumbags

A Slippery Job by the Customs Men!

No two days are the same in the life of a successful private investigator. You never know what sort of case will cross your door. Naturally, you'll get the usual fraud, theft, family law, missing persons, corporate disputes and investigations on a global basis but alongside these regular cases, you get the occasional case where people will do just about anything to make a quick buck.

One of these "strange" stories was the case of the slippery butter smugglers. It all started a long time ago, at a time when there were large amounts of cheap butter flooding the Irish market, marketed under all the well-known Irish brand names. We were contacted by the companies producing the genuine products, who couldn't understand how "their butter" was being sold so cheaply. We set up an initial investigation to find out if the butter was coming from the various legitimate factories. Perhaps it was "an inside job", with butter being "creamed" from the production line or from delivery trucks.

Having ruled out this source, we kept surveillance on various market stalls and shops throughout the country for evidence of the source of the butter. In each case, we made a "test purchase" and had the product tested by the relevant creamery that it was supposedly from. In each case, the results showed it to be an inferior product, not from the client's factory. Further investigation surrounding the packaging of the "counterfeit" butter identified that the labels were also counterfeit. While immediately recognisable as the well-known brands, closer forensic inspection showed up minute detail differences in paper quality and colour.

The scam appeared to be well organised and was raking in big profits for whoever was behind it. They were making big inroads into the butter market both north and south of the border. The legitimate companies were feeling the pinch as their sales plummeted. After all, the public were buying their "regular" brands at a fraction of the costs of the mainstream shops and, so far, they'd had no complaints about the quality.

Over a period of weeks, we "infiltrated" the "gang" in various ways. We approached them as they made deliveries and eventually became "wholesale" customers, buying large quantities of butter from them, and we also maintained surveillance on the delivery trucks, following them back to their source.

We established the whereabouts of their warehouses. Going undercover, we found boxes of butter labels which had been printed in both England and Northern Ireland. Some, though not all, of these printers were legitimate and thought they were supplying the genuine companies. Northern hauliers were bringing tonnes of butter on each trip into the south, with dozens of hauliers making numerous trips each week. The practice became so large that they even used pig transporters to move consignments and they still couldn't keep up with the demand, as customers were "limited" to two pounds of butter each.

As the butter scam spread countrywide, it was seriously hurting the genuine suppliers. The matter was also being investigated by customs officials and the Gardaí, who agreed to hold off raiding individual hauliers until solid evidence had been established. The black market in butter and butter wrappers was more valuable than the genuine commodity.

In a farce worthy of *Only Fools and Horses*, one evening, just as darkness fell, the butter smugglers were stopped by three customs men close to Skyhill in County Louth. The smugglers were on their way to the Republic with a lorry-load of dodgy butter, rewrapped in counterfeit butter wrappers, all bearing various "legitimate" brand names. The "customs officials" surrounded the lorry and seized over ten tonnes of butter bound for southern customers. When stopped, the smugglers abandoned the lorry and escaped across the fields. It was only later that the smugglers realised the butter wasn't the only bogus thing about the operation – the customs men were bogus too! A rival gang, dressed in genuine customs uniforms and driving what appeared to be "customs" cars, stopped and seized the load and simply drove away. The media later headlined it as "A smooth job by bogus customs men!" The outwitted smugglers were certain they would get their lorry back – the "word" had been put out, but they said goodbye to their butter mountain.

"Dealers" who ordered the butter paid up to £40 a tonne "extra" to have southern Irish wrappers on the butter, as it was considered the best quality butter and sold for more money. Kerrygold wrappers in particular were said to be worth "more than pound notes".

Like all good schemes, the scam was eventually broken when we identified the people behind it. It obviously took a lot of effort, between printing wrappers, acquiring the inferior butter and re-wrapping it in the various brand names, along with the risks in transporting it across the border and the time in "flogging" it to small outlets around the country – but the black market in butter made them a small fortune at the time. No doubt something even more lucrative such as diesel smuggling replaced it. Some things never change.

Off Their Head

Respectable companies that provide gas cylinders and replacement cylinders for everything from fizzy drinks cylinders to cylinders for cooking, heating and industrial use, both commercial and domestic, do so with the utmost care and attention to safety, both in the workplace and in the products they supply to their customers. They have a long history of good service and excellent security and safety records which they prize. But when you've worked in the investigation business for as long as I did, nothing surprises you and get-rich-quick schemes were never too hare-brained or foolhardy for *someone* to have a go.

The scam came to the attention of my clients quite by accident, when a load of empty cylinders from various outlets were returned for re-filling. As part of the safety check, staff are required to examine each cylinder for any damage that might have occurred. If there was any doubt about its safety, it was rejected. During a routine check, they noticed that a number of cylinders were not up to their standards and on closer examination, they realised that, despite carrying their colour scheme and markings, the cylinders were not theirs.

Worse still, far from being safe, they were crudely welded and positively dangerous. If refilled, they could explode and cause serious injury to life and limb. The company were shocked and contacted me to find out where they'd originated. Working through a list of their distributors and general hardware stores throughout the country, we kept a watching brief for any "new" gas containers dropped off for re-filling by unsuspecting customers. After a couple of weeks of checking out possible outlets, we discovered a number of dangerous soda cylinders in the south of the country. Our investigations led to a surveillance operation, which tracked down the people behind the "cloned" drinks cylinders.

They were operating out of a small, broken-down shed tucked away in the back of a small estate, close to the village of Blarney in County Cork. To our amazement, we saw a few lads working away with welding gear, welding the neck of a cylinder where it connected to the drinks machine. It was an accident waiting to happen and one of those cases where there was no time to wait. The illicit operation had to be shut down immediately for the safety of customers and for everyone else in the area, who were unknowingly working close to a time-bomb. I wondered how much money they could possibly have made for so much effort and high risk. Were they really that stupid, or was it just plain greed? Not only were they putting themselves at risk of serious injury or death, they were putting innocent customers and end users, often children, at serious risk too.

The clients took swift action in making design changes to ensure that such a dangerous enterprise couldn't happen again. They also took legal action against the counterfeiters, under various "intellectual property" laws, including breaches of the trademark, copyright and patents regulations.

Rip-Offs and Raiders

Long before CDs, DVDs, the internet and YouTube, there was a lucrative trade in pirated video and audio tapes, which cost the film industry multi-millions in lost sales and the tax man a fortune in VAT. Emanating mainly from the Far East, they were produced and on sale within hours of a film's release. Not always good copies, some videos were simply filmed in a cinema with a hand-held video camera and copied in their thousands, ensuing that a very poor copy reached the market stalls at a fraction of the original price. Nobody complained except the industry, who were losing millions to modern-day pirates.

Companies like Warner Home Video offered rewards for information on the video pirates. The racketeers operated country-wide in Ireland and all the major blockbusters were routinely copied by the highly organised gangs that released them in Ireland, months before they appeared in cinemas. For Joe Public, it was fair game. Why pay full price to see a film in a few months' time, when you can see it now for a fraction of the cost? The industry got little support from the public, who continued to pump money into the copied tapes.

I was asked to investigate the illegal trade on behalf of all the major international film companies such as Warner Brothers, RCA/Columbia, EMI, Disney, MGM, United Artists and 20th Century Fox. Our job was to track down the pirates and identify the outlets renting or selling them. We investigated shops, video clubs, movie rental libraries and pubs all over Ireland, from the smallest village to the biggest towns. Over the course of a few months, more than ten thousand tapes were seized. It was like a game of cat-and-mouse; as soon as we identified sources and outlets and eliminated them, new players entered the market. They were sold and rented out from shops, vans and market stalls and some publicans were even showing the bootleg films in an effort to boost takings. It became so lucrative that organised crime became involved, seeing it as yet another cash-cow to add to their many "ventures". They became so good at making the bootleg goods that they were almost undetectable from the real deal and the film companies were forced to introduce "secret markings" to identify their goods from the illegal ones.

At the time the only immediate legal redress was for the international distributors to go to court to get an "Anton Piller injunction" – a permanent injunction used to protect trademarks, copyright and patents. The injunctions granted by the High Court allowed us to search premises without prior permission and seize evidence. In order to meet the legal requirements needed before an Anton Piller injunction is granted, I had to establish a *prima facie* case on behalf of the clients.

Our evidence showed that there was real and potential damage to our clients' copyright and a real possibility that the perpetrators would dispose of, or destroy, any evidence, documentary or otherwise, before an *ex-parte* application (one-side-only hearing) – the usual remedy – could be made in court. The US responded to the unprecedented attack on the movie industry, bringing in legislation strengthening their copyright laws, with penalties of five years in jail and a $250,000 fine for those caught breaking the law.

The investigation continued for a couple of years. As we rooted out the dealers, the legal teams got the injunctions, seized the goods and destroyed them, often using a bulldozer for dramatic effect. The mass destruction of thousands of videos was frequently photographed by the press, the publicity acting as a warning to the "pirates" as to what they could expect to lose.

It was an ongoing battle but an easy enough investigation that became almost routine. It had an added attraction, in that we got to see all the new releases before they reached the cinema – just to be certain that they were really pirated versions. All in the course of the job, of course; we took no pleasure in it!

Like most scams, it didn't go away. Today it has been replaced by the twenty-first-century piracy of CDs and DVDs. Organised crime considers it an easy, low-risk money spinner. All it takes is a small investment in a few high-tech burners, printers and related machinery and, with a built-in distribution system, the money rolls in. This "black" industry currently nets criminals around €175 million in profits, funding the purchase of guns and fuelling their already lucrative drug trade. If they're raided from time to time and lose their equipment, its just an inconvenience and merely delays the operation for a few days at most.

Who's Been Sleeping in My Bed?

This is the story of a businessman who inadvertently got into trouble on two fronts, one with his wife and the other with his neighbours – all because he rented his Dublin 4 property to the wrong people.

The client was moving overseas for work purposes and decided that, for security reasons, it would be better to have his property occupied during his time abroad. He approached a letting agency who found him a suitable client, a European businessman who wanted to rent for a year or two and was happy to pay the stiff asking price. It suited everyone. The Irish businessman moved out and headed for the US, while his new tenant moved in a week later. All went well for a couple of months, the money was going into his bank account and he was happy with his arrangement.

However, his mail was being re-directed to his US address and he began to get letters from his former neighbours, complaining about the noise levels and the regular parties being held in his house. As an old client, he called me and asked me to check things out. We did. It seemed that his Dublin 4 house was now the busiest and most expensive brothel in town!

The client was shocked – how could he explain to the neighbours that it was nothing to do with him? He had, after all, introduced the European businessman to his neighbours as a "friend". His wife was furious. She blamed her husband for not "vetting" his tenant properly. My client immediately flew home and told them to get out, that their lease was worthless, as they were conducting an illegal business. He threatened to call the police if they didn't go.

In an effort to placate him, they offered him a "cut" of the proceeds, provided they could stay on. They were making a killing in this leafy upmarket suburb and they didn't want to have to find new premises. The client was outraged. How he kept his cool, given his rumbustious nature, was a miracle. He bluffed them, giving them the option of shutting up shop immediately or having their clients raided *and* the tabloids tipped off – something he would never have done, given that it was his family home. His bluff worked and the brothel-keeper left quietly, moving his "enterprise" elsewhere. My client went back to the US and had a relative "house-sit" for the duration of his foreign contract.

Charity Begins at Home

On more than one occasion I've being called in by registered charities who have fallen foul of scams perpetrated on them. Criminals recognise that there's a small fortune to be made in the charity game from money donated for a good cause. One of the most common scams is where a criminal gang "latches on" to a well-known respected charity as "organisers" or volunteers, offering to raise funds or get sponsorship for various events. Naturally, the charity are delighted with all offers of help, but they can't vet every volunteer. From time to time they get caught out and their fingers, not to mention their reputations, get burned. It's bad for everyone concerned and it undermines the charity, which loses the funds raised by the con-artist and public trust in supporting their efforts in the future.

One of the oldest scams is where a charity is approached by people offering to sell lines, get sponsorships or rattle a box to collect cash from the general public. Not for them the cold wet streets, standing around all day cajoling the public to part with their loose change. Theirs is a more sophisticated and easy approach to collecting the cash. Armed with their official Garda permit, ID and permission to act on behalf of the charity, they head off to a printer and order a batch of cards, sponsorship lines or charity boxes or whatever the genuine charity is using and readily identified with. From there, they "wholesale" batches of cards to middlemen, who distribute them around the country, recruiting people from all walks of life, from the housewife, the unemployed or students to anyone wanting to "earn" extra cash, offering them a chance to earn "easy money" by getting sponsorships or collecting cash for the charity. These people are usually just innocent pawns who believe they're earning a few bob, while

211

at the same time helping a worthy cause. The "feel good factor" is all part of the sales pitch in recruiting these people.

Now all the conmen have to do is sit back and wait for the cash to come in. As the "agents" or "recruiters", they alone have contact with this legion of collectors, and at the end of each day, they call and collect "their" takings, giving the collectors a small percentage of the funds. The incentive is always there; the more they collect the more they earn. To avoid alerting suspicions, they regularly hand over small amounts to the charity, who come to "know and trust" them, which sets them up for their next scam.

Some conmen have been known to be violent towards young collectors who were not pulling in enough money. With investigation, the key people behind the scams are inevitably tracked down. I was never surprised to find that they were living the high life, despite having no visible means of support. Invariably, they had no form of legitimate employment or explanation of their income.

Although my clients, the legitimate charity, had lost out on a lot of the funds donated by the public, an "arrangement" was arrived at where a generous "donation" was made by the conmen to help "compensate" the charity for their losses. This often happens in court cases where the criminal "makes restitution" for their crime. It seemed even more appropriate in this instance, given the nasty aspect of their theft. Charity frauds are usually dealt with discreetly, as bad publicity could have a long-term effect on the finances of an organisation totally reliant on the goodwill of the public and their continued donations. While my clients were on the alert for future scams with these con-artists, no doubt the latter moved on to another unsuspecting charity. It is one of those scams that inevitably re-emerges after the fuss has died down.

The Money-making Game

A professional client of mine had a serious problem. He operated a busy practice and when his receptionist went on holiday, he contacted a small recruitment agency run by two business partners requesting a "temp". Difficulties arose straight away when the temp proved unsuitable and the agency failed to resolve the problem. A few days later the agency "owner" called to collect payment for the "unrendered" services and when my client made his dissatisfaction known, an argument ensued. The client said the man was threatening and abusive and was told to leave or the Gardaí would be called. The man stormed out in a rage, witnessed by staff. There the matter ended until a few days later, when he had a visit from the Gardaí.

The man had alleged he'd been assaulted by my client and claimed the incident had been witnessed by his "partner", who had been sitting in a parked car across the road at the time. My client was shocked and completely refuted the allegation, but agreed to make a statement after he'd spoken to his solicitor. Within days, my client's professional body were also looking for a statement as they too had received a complaint from the man.

Coincidentally, a few days later, *The Irish Times* carried a court report on a case of an alleged assault by an employer on an employee. The chief witness was the same agency owner who had accused my client of assault. The judge strongly criticised his credibility and refused to accept his testimony.

Weeks went by without any developments. My client made several attempts to contact the garda handling the matter but never managed to get hold of him. He called to the station to check that the file on what he considered a "vexatious" complaint was closed. To his surprise, he was told that the

213

Gardaí intended issuing a warrant for his arrest, as he hadn't made a statement on time. He immediately contacted his solicitor but, despite their best efforts, the case went ahead.

My client and his staff denied the assault but, nonetheless, he was convicted in the District Court. A previously blameless professional middle-aged man now had a criminal record for something that had never happened. He couldn't believe the nightmare that was unfolding and immediately appealed his conviction. Worse was to come, when the agency boss brought a civil case for damages. He wanted compensation for his "pain and suffering" and his loss of earnings, claiming he had been unable to work for six weeks as a result of his "injury and trauma".

It was at this point that the client sought my help. He had availed of all legal avenues and was worried that, if his appeal failed, the criminal conviction would stand. The civil case would then automatically succeed, as the burden of proof in criminal cases is stronger and would be accepted as evidence in any action for damages. Given his profession, it would have a significant bearing on my client's practice.

Examining the documentation in the case, the witness statements and related information, it struck me as odd that the agency boss had claimed the alleged assault was witnessed by his unnamed "partner", presumably his business partner. Yet by the time the case came to court, the only "witness" statement produced was that of a female employee, Mrs P, a grandmother who had worked for the agency for about a year and was certainly not his "partner" in any sense of the word.

I checked out the background of this lady and, by all accounts, she appeared to be an honest, hard-working woman with no personal axe to grind. Even if she *had* been present in a car "across the road", it would have been virtually impossible for her to have witnessed anything, given the location, the heavy traffic, and the parking restrictions. I went to see her and, as my investigation had indicated, she was an honest woman who had wrestled with her conscience. She told me what had really happened.

The day after the alleged "assault", she got a call at home from her employer, one of the agency partners, who said that his partner had been assaulted the previous day. Two days later, the agency bosses told Mrs P that my client had refused to pay for the temp and wanted an amended account. The "injured" man re-counted his story, saying he "intended" making a complaint to the Gardaí and to his doctor. She said her bosses were very angry and were constantly talking about it, saying that they were "going to get him". She said: "I felt they were obsessed with the matter and no work was getting done as a result."

A week later, the "injured" man phoned her to say he'd made the complaint to the Gardaí. According to her, he said, "I've an awful big favour to ask you." She told him she'd do it if she could. He explained that when he'd reported it to the Gardaí, the guard said it was a pity he didn't have a witness, so, as he told her: "I named you as the witness." Mrs P said: "My reaction was one of shock and horror. I immediately said, 'I'm sorry, that's one favour I can't do for you.'" She came under constant pressure from him to change her mind. She said, "He initially tried to charm me in an effort to persuade me to go as a witness and, when that failed, he bullied and threatened me, saying things like 'You know me well enough to know nobody crosses me.' Initially I didn't take him seriously, but then he said, 'I could ruin you the way I know will hurt you most – professionally.' After several more incidents like this, I eventually felt I had no option but to give in and make the statement he had asked for to get him off my back, hoping it would come to nothing."

A few days later, the agency boss insisted she went with him. "He told me he was going to take me over the route he had gone and show me [my client's] office, as I had never seen it prior to that day. When we arrived, he parked his car in a side road, as there is no parking place on the main road, and he pointed out the area he wanted me to say the car had been parked, on the day of the alleged incident. He pointed out the front door of [my client's] offices. He dropped me back to the office and drove away."

Unknown to Mrs P, her boss arranged for the Gardaí to interview her at work. She said: "When the garda arrived, I was called into [the partner's] office and he took my statement in the presence of [both partners], so I had no opportunity to tell the guard that I was being coerced into making a false statement and that in fact I had been coached several times, by [the agency boss] as to exactly what I was to say, before making the statement. After the guard left, I went straight back to my office and refused to talk to [the agency bosses]."

Mrs P was disgusted. She gave in her notice and contacted the guard to withdraw her statement. Work had become intolerable. She claimed that her bosses falsified invoices and debts allegedly owed to them by Mrs P to coerce her to give evidence, knowing her financial situation was shaky.

On 25 September, Mrs P got a letter from the agency boss, telling her the case was being heard on 30 September. Her solicitor was away on holiday until the end of September and neither Mrs P nor anyone in his office were notified to attend court. On 30 September she was outside her solicitor's office waiting for him to arrive. He told her that in the absence of any official notification, she wasn't obliged to go to court as he believed that the case couldn't go ahead without her. Still worried, she said, "I then telephoned the clerk of the court and told her the situation and emphasised that my statement could not be used in the case. She assured me that the case wouldn't go ahead as it was being defended and unless the defendant pleaded guilty, it wouldn't proceed without me. I was happy to hear this and I left it at that. Two weeks later I heard what transpired and I was shocked and horrified at the outcome." The court wasn't told the witness wanted to withdraw her statement and the agency boss's partner, aware that Mrs P's statement had been "manufactured", did nothing to stop the proceedings. My client was convicted of assault.

I discovered that the agency was in financial trouble. The prospect of a claim was an easy way of raising funds. The man's business partner knew he'd been the first person to tell Mrs P about the alleged incident, yet she was to be the prosecution's main witness and he went along with it. When I tracked down Mrs P to check out her "evidence", she was relieved – not the usual response in such situations. She was happy to get it all off her chest. She never wanted to commit perjury and she had had no intention of going through with the lie, despite her boss's threats and intimidation. She was relieved to be able to make a sworn statement to me as to what had really happened and expose what she said was her boss's "efforts to pervert the course of justice". Given the level of threats she was under and her own personal circumstances, it took great courage for her to stand up and tell the truth. She went to great lengths to resolve the situation, at a financial cost to herself.

As a direct result of her evidence, the case against my client was thrown out on appeal and the civil action for damages died with it. Unfortunately, the law wasn't quite so enthusiastic in pursuing the offenders for attempting to pervert the course of justice or wasting police and court time in a vexatious action, designed not only to wreck one man's career but to relieve him of a substantial amount in damages. Her actions saved an innocent man from having a criminal conviction. After what had been a worrying and traumatic time, his wife and family were very relieved. Nice to know there are still a few honest people around.

22

Corporate Cops

Counter-intelligence or de-bugging was always on my case load, with many businesses exposed to industrial espionage and corporate spying. Everyone was looking over their shoulder, often with good cause. Over the years I provided these services for a diverse range of people – individuals and business, from government agencies to oil and energy corporations, mineral and mining companies, trade unions, manufacturers, industrialists, farming and related industries and even an organisation working on a project for the Ariane missile programme – the list is endless. Some, though not all, were victims of electronic surveillance or industrial espionage and in many cases their "intelligence losses" were down to a good old-fashioned lack of basic security.

Doing extensive surveys of these organisations over the years revealed that their weak points were almost always staring them in the face. Even those companies that prided themselves on high standards of "internal security" left themselves wide open, with swipe cards and coded access being readily available and basic things like filing cabinets left open or locked with the key still in, or sensitive documents or tenders left "lying around" for anyone to view and copy at their leisure. The attitude was that "Johnny" or "Mary" has worked here for years – they never considered that they could be a disgruntled employee or have been approached by someone offering "easy money" for a few bits of paper.

It all sounds too easy – but that's exactly what it is. One multinational organisation, which had lost highly sensitive information, had a huge internal telephone exchange and therefore assumed their phones were bugged. The investigation showed that the problem wasn't with their phones but with their "housekeeping", which was shoddy to say the least. Boxes of automated signed cheques were stored in the ladies toilet. Everyone, including visitors, had free and easy access to the area and no-one would have a missed few cheques from the boxes for quite a while. I also found several signed cheques, the smallest of which was for £100,000, behind filing cabinets. They hadn't even been missed, never mind cancelled! The very fact that I and an associate had the "run of the house" without anyone giving us a second glance was enough to ring serious alarm bells.

Companies always assume that their top executives are the ones to watch. They recognise the value of information and can trade it for better positions within a rival company. The fact is, while this can happen, it is more often the "unseen" cleaner, maintenance man or tea lady, who have "access all areas" and go unnoticed. Who better to infiltrate any organisation without suspicion once they get to know the routine and what they are looking for. It's easy, lucrative and carries little risk of being found out. Sometimes the simple schemes are the most successful.

Up, Up and Away

Private investigators are often called upon to bridge the gap between criminal and corporate business problems. The work is both international and diverse, with money rarely being a problem – except in the case of Aer Lingus Holidays.

Aer Lingus set up a subsidiary trading from Dawson Street, Dublin. They had access to the planes and were well placed to market their package holidays; yet despite its State-owned backer, it was losing money. Aer Lingus were shocked when ALH couldn't pay for the planes they'd chartered. Minister for Transport and Tourism, Seamus Brennan, told the Dáil that Aer Lingus Holidays was in trouble, under-estimating the losses by millions. Following a forensic examination by Craig Gardner, a massive deficit of over £15 million and evidence of false accounting was identified.

It became a matter for the fraud squad – and me. I was called in by Aer Lingus Holidays to investigate the missing funds, which appeared to have been used for the benefit of a certain party. Investigations led to the Canary Islands – to Gran Canaria and the Playa del Ingles region, and Lanzarote, both high-density tourist resorts. Apartments were being built like there was no tomorrow, all rented out by international holiday firms, winter and summer. It was a lucrative business, a sure-fire money spinner, much like the property market in the early days of the Celtic Tiger.

Subsequently, solicitor Des P. Flynn and accountant Peter Kealy were charged with conspiring together and with Peter Noone on dates from March 1987 to November 1988 to defraud Aer Lingus Holidays by using funds to buy property in Lanzarote in the Canary Islands for their own use and benefit.

When the case was heard four years later in 1998, Peter Noone wasn't before the court, and Judge Kieran O'Connor told the jury that "Mr Noone is missing".

The case lasted for thirty-five days, ending abruptly when Judge Kieran O'Connor ruled that evidence relating to money transferred to an account in the Midland Bank in the UK was inadmissible, as at the time of their original arrest in 1990, court rules didn't allow this evidence to be heard, as it had been discovered before the introduction of the Criminal Evidence Act in 1992.

The Judge told the jury that normally he would not comment on evidence in a case for fear it would contaminate the jury's consideration of it, but in view of what had transpired, he could now do so. He said that the evidence presented in the case showed that Aer Lingus Holidays "was run in a most appalling manner, with false accounting, to hide the fact that the company was, in effect, insolvent." He recalled evidence of false accounting that showed unquantified millions of pounds of losses had been suffered. Judge O'Connor said that, with no further evidence available, "the two accused are entitled to walk out of this court free against the background of all the evidence adduced in the trial." Addressing the two men, the Judge said, "You will never get a better Christmas present in your life than when I say to you that this is now the end of the matter for you and you are free to go."

As for my part – with no money left in the company to pay their bills, I was offered free flights in lieu of my fees, which I was happy to accept.

Gas Men!

One particular case was both intriguing and time-consuming. For weeks, a huge number of wage cheques, social welfare payment cheques and warrants drawn on accounts of the Paymaster General and the Dublin Gas Company (which was in receivership at the time) were being cashed in banks throughout the country. Initially the cheques were cashed without question but when they began to hit the various accounts, they noticed a dramatic increase in employees they knew nothing about.

Eventually the various bodies realised that something was wrong. Although identical to the genuine article, neither the gas company receiver nor the Paymaster General had issued the cheques. Perfect in every detail, they carried all the usual built-in security marks of genuine organisations. Obviously a major and very sophisticated scam was going on.

I was asked to investigate the problem. My first instruction to the client was to do nothing to alert the gang they'd been rumbled. The banks agreed to keep paying out the cheques for another while. If they refused to cash them, the fraudsters would know the scam had been spotted and disappear, leaving the "small players" who were cashing the cheques to take the rap, making it difficult to track down the "brains" behind the scheme and recover the substantial monies already paid out. I met with the head of the bank's internal security and made sure that all their surveillance cameras were working properly, as when we'd checked, some hadn't been switched on or the tapes were erased without checking; worse still, there were a few branches that had no cameras at all.

Cheques were being cashed around the country and the MO (modus operandi) was that a group of men dressed in boiler suits and with gas company ID badges would enter the bank to cash their wage cheques. Genuine gas company and other similar cheques were printed by security printers and neither the receiver nor gas company wages staff had any idea where the "additional" cheques were coming from.

An investigation into the security printing process and a comparison of the genuine and counterfeit cheques was undertaken. Even the genuine printing company were surprised at the quality of the counterfeit cheques. Forensic analysis revealed that there was a difference in paper quality, unnoticeable to the naked eye. The counterfeit cheques had been reproduced from scratch; the gang had prepared a new set of artwork and special magnetic ink was used in the lettering and security markings. They were virtually indistinguishable from the genuine article. In fact, experts claimed the copy was better than the original!

All bank tellers were instructed that if anyone, genuine or otherwise, presented a Paymaster General or gas company cheque, the video-recording was to be saved and I was to be contacted immediately. Within two weeks, there were dozens of such tapes and I set about the slow, tedious job of trawling through each and every one, looking for clues to identify the gang. Eventually a pattern emerged, as time and again the same characters presented the cheques in branches around the country. I took clips from the surveillance shots and made contact with various informers, cons and coppers – anyone who could put names to the various faces that kept appearing. It wasn't long before I had a number of positive IDs. The people cashing the cheques were generally small-time crooks who got a small percentage as payment for their efforts and the risk they were taking. Turning up in overalls with the "patter" of workmen and gas company IDs, they had no trouble cashing the cheques. The Paymaster General cheques varied and sometimes "men in suits" presented these for payment. Either way, they all got a "cut" from every cheque successfully cashed and everyone – except the banks – were happy.

Bank staff had no reason to suspect anything. The cheques were all made out to specific named people and the Paymaster's cheques even had the "home address" of the payee printed on them. The payee was obliged to write his name, address and bank account number and sign and date the back of the cheque as a security precaution.

The government pay warrants had a printed declaration which stated "I declare that for the period shown overleaf, I am entitled to the sum specified and I acknowledge its receipt", followed by a space for the Signature of Payee, their Address and Date. All the cashed cheques were handed over to me by the banks for handwriting and forensic analysis, which would be crucial at a later stage in the chain of evidence. When I identified the people cashing the cheques from the videos, which were timed and dated, I could later match them up with the signed and dated declarations. Naturally, they were signing a false name and address to match the printed one, but handwriting analysis could identify the fact that they were the same people identified on the videos as having cashed the cheques. The chances were, these "runners" had a police record already.

I identified one or two of these "small-time" players, some of whom had already come to "fame", being well-known criminals, having often had their photo in *Fógra Tóra*, the internal Garda "wanted" list. During our investigations, we discovered that the gang were also reproducing counterfeit social welfare, First National Building Society and ESB cheques, as well as Telecom Pay Orders, Ferry and Rugby Tickets, which were printed in Dublin, London and the UK Midlands.

The scam took advantage of an everyday business transaction. A highly respected company were responsible for printing security-encoded cheques and did virtually all the government and semi-state security printing. At every stage of the work, they maintained high standards of internal security. Ironically, in a move to increase their security, they'd recently brought in expensive state-of-the-art computerised printing machines, with extra in-built security features. The company were planning to sell the old machines but, unknown to them, a criminal gang had inside information and made a bid for the machines, with the intention of forging the Paymaster General and other cheques. It was a simple and effective plan and they got everything right, the security codings included. But for the fact that they used "old lags" who were identified from the surveillance camera, they might have got away with it. They were the "weak link" and we kept them under surveillance, which ultimately led to the downfall of the scam.

From our investigation, the "brains" behind the scam was a career criminal with numerous convictions for conspiracy and fraud. We identified him as having procured the paper used in reproducing the gas company cheques. He was also convicted in connection with a large well-organised forgery scam on a government department.

He was considered a dangerous and ruthless criminal – his gang of "twelve apostles", mainly foot-soldiers who did the donkey work, were "terrified" by him. When gardaí arrested one man in possession of Telecom Payable Orders, he refused to talk, saying, "If I do, I'll be a dead man."

I had a great sense of satisfaction in solving this case, after the mind-numbing hundreds of hours of watching videos from banks across the country. We found documentation showing that their next job was to cash batches of Eastern Health Board cheques they'd produced. It was justification for a job that, to this day, despite the technology, still involves a certain amount of "plodding", persistence and plain old tedious graft, but it paid off in the end.

Banking on a Deal

A business transaction turned into a long-term nightmare for one client when his former business partner, who had sold his interest in a financial business, turned up years later, looking for a second bite of the cherry. It seemed that, having agreed a substantial lump sum payout, he'd gone abroad and blown the cash. With nothing left, he turned up again, claiming he'd been short-changed. During the intervening period of several years, there'd been no contact from the former partner – let's call him "Tony" – until out of the blue my client found out that Tony was taking a High Court action against him and the company. I met with the client and his lawyers and advised them that our first step was to check on what Tony had been up to in recent years. Why had he turned up now, looking for more money that they believed he wasn't entitled to?

In such cases it is normal for a plaintiff – the person making a claim – to swear an affidavit, a sworn statement setting out certain facts. Tony had duly obliged, which gave me a starting point. He claimed he'd been living and working in Dublin for several years immediately prior to the action. I checked out his story. He appeared to have no RSI number nor was he paying any tax on his alleged earnings. A more detailed investigation led me to believe that he'd only recently returned to

Ireland for the purpose of taking the case, having lived abroad for several years. It seemed there was a lot more to this case than at first appeared. The hunt took me from Ireland to New York, Florida and South America before the full picture finally emerged.

Having cashed his initial windfall, Tony had gone to the US "on holiday", with the money burning a hole in his pocket, but he quickly managed to blow a large chunk of it on the high life. I tracked him to a rented property in Long Island, New York, where he'd been living for some time. He was supposedly "away on vacation" for a couple of months – obviously in Ireland staking his claim. A car registered in Tony's name was still parked in the driveway of "his" house. Investigations showed that he'd held a New York driving licence for several years – but anyone can have a New York licence; in itself, it didn't prove he wasn't living in Ireland.

A further bit of digging showed that he'd been working for a local company with a "dodgy" reputation. The Police Department, the District Attorney's Office and US Postal Fraud Investigators all told me the company was a "boiler-room operation", where victims are cold-called by fake stockbrokers and persuaded to buy shares in worthless, near-bankrupt or non-existent companies. Located downtown, the company had shut up shop overnight in suspicious circumstances, following complaints to cops about "white collar" crimes. Our guy Tony had listed the company as his employers for the four years prior to our investigation, at a time when he was supposedly living and working in Ireland.

A New York State-wide United Commercial Code search showed up Tony's SS (social security) number. I cross-referenced it to the SS number he'd given on various credit applications; it matched. I then checked it with the United States Social Security Administration. It turned out that the number had never been legally issued to Tony. Further cross-checking of "his" social security number against the three main US credit databases, CBI, Trans-Union and TRW, all showed Tony as listed at his New York address.

It was time to get to the bottom of this. It's not unusual for US social security ID numbers to be "stolen" and used by others. Initially, it was established that the SS number had been issued to a Hispanic woman named Mendoza. On checking with the office of the Inspector General, US Department of Health and Human Services, I established that Tony had committed a prosecutable offence and they were anxious to meet up with him. But Tony was on the "missing" list and he'd left behind a long trail of creditors who were all anxious to talk to him as well.

I dug up some more information about Tony and came up with another address in the Florida Keys. Also, a check with the Florida Department of Highway Safety and Motor Vehicles confirmed that Tony had applied for and received a Florida driving licence at that address two years previously. A copy of his hand-written application for a licence confirmed that it was the same man, with handwriting analysis proving it was his signature. He was regularly seen driving a car registered in his name (and had traffic tickets to prove it) at a time when he claimed to be living in Ireland. Given that it was the Florida area, I checked if Tony owned a boat or a plane, as the "word on the street" was that he made frequent trips to South America – specifically, to Caracas – on "unknown business". There were no records of him owning either. In the US, before 9/11, it was relatively easy and inexpensive to "rent" a light aircraft for private use.

An interesting piece of information was that Tony was about to open a business in Florida around the same time as his court case was due to be heard in Ireland. Maybe he was hoping for a little cash injection, courtesy of his old partner.

When we checked out Tony's "home" address, which he'd given on his Florida driving licence application, it turned out to be a false address. He'd combined the names of two adjoining streets to "make up" a fictitious home address.

He originally entered the US on a visitor's visa but later filed for the amnesty programme. From my investigations, he appeared to have given incorrect information to the US Immigration and Naturalisation Service on two separate occasions. Additional documentation sworn by Tony for the purposes of his Irish court case was in complete contradiction to information given on his US application documents – but then perhaps he was just confused; the court was the judge of that. Having left himself with very few options, perhaps he went back to South America; who knows?

The Wizard of Oz

You come across the same people, "the usual suspects", again and again. They turn up in fraud cases, theft, drugs, embezzlement, blackmail, industrial espionage and plain old adultery. They never give up; they just move on from one victim to another. When things get too hot at home they move on to richer pickings in England, America and Australia. They feel "safe" abroad and, despite their cunning, they appear to have no idea of the international network of private investigators that can track them down anywhere in the world.

Some years ago I got a case from a lawyer in Australia. He wanted to check the background of an Irishman who'd emigrated there with his extended family, a common occurrence, as people apply for high-powered jobs or are vetted for other reasons. The lawyer believed the man was wanted by the Fraud Squad in Dublin in relation to several matters. He had his name, age and description and a possible previous address. Investigations proved that the address was wrong but I tracked him down to an address he'd lived at before he left Ireland. He'd sold the property for a substantial sum and left in a hurry, leaving no forwarding address.

I felt there was a bigger story behind his quick exit but all checks showed he'd never been charged with any crime, nor had he "come to the attention of the Gardaí". Investigations showed the picture to be somewhat different from the lawyer's instructions, but nonetheless, his "gut feeling" was right.

The man had worked in the accounts department of a well-known building company for many years, during which time he kept a close watch on his bosses and how they operated their business. They subcontracted their work to other "companies", holding themselves at arm's length for tax and legal purposes. They operated through numerous "holding" companies, making it difficult to identify them as the beneficial owners of the business. He decided to follow their lead and do the same. He set up a number of obscure holding companies, making it extremely difficult to trace the beneficial ownership back to him. He then formed a building company with two smaller builders, using their names as the trading name. The "lads" were happy to take the glory as the "owners" of the new business – their "partner" claimed to be a retiring type who shunned the limelight.

His new partners knew him by a false name and had no idea who he really was, or the fact that he was actually working for a big building company. They were so impressed with his contacts and access to finance that they called him "the wizard". He dealt with all the financial matters from tendering to quotes, paying suppliers, wages and dealing with the bank. His partners were builders; they didn't understood the mechanisms of finance, nor did they care. The wizard had all that in hand and it was going really well. They had plenty of house-building work and they didn't have to worry about ordering or paying for supplies. They arrived on site, on time, and the wizard looked after everything else. Things were really looking up for them and business was booming.

What they didn't know was that their new "partner" had been paying their suppliers out of his employer's coffers. He had been made a director of his employer's company and they had the utmost trust in his honesty and ability. He knew his way around the various shell companies and routed payments and income through them. Everything seemed to be going well and his bosses were very happy with his performance. The man continued to work in his old job and was highly regarded by his employers, who promoted him.

By that time, things were going so well in his own building enterprise, he began to get greedy and started to go after the big contracts, which had been the preserve of his employers. Under various holding companies, he set up new companies in direct opposition to his bosses. He had drawn up the tenders for *their* work and he began to pitch for the same contacts, significantly undercutting "their" tenders.

They began losing out on major contracts and they couldn't understand how their competitive quotes were being rejected time and time again, while a new kid on the block, a seemingly smaller operation, was picking up business everywhere. Up to then, they'd had a free run at the business. They tried to check out who was behind the company that was scooping up all the work, but they fell at the first hurdle. The wizard had played them at their own game. He had set up so many convoluted shell companies in Ireland and abroad that the trail eventually ran into sand.

Despite his success, things were getting uncomfortable at work. The firm was losing out on contract after contract and there was friction at work. The wizard began to think that things were getting a little too hot in Ireland and decided it was time to move on. During his build-up to leaving the country, he amassed large sums of money, failed to pay suppliers and left his new business partners high and dry.

His partners, who had virtually no day-to-day dealings with him, began to get nervous when they couldn't contact him. Their supplies had been cut off, jobs were being left unfinished and creditors were banging down their door. By the time they found out the real story, it was too late. They had wrongly assumed they were directors of the new company, but when they realised that they too were being swindled by their "sleeping partner", they were too embarrassed to report him to the cops. Their business went to the wall but, in a way, as they'd never been registered as directors in the Companies Office, the wizard had inadvertently "saved" them from any personal liability for the debts. Despite the trading name being an amalgam of their surnames, they had no legal liability to the creditors. They meant nothing to the wizard, who saw them as just a couple of workers.

The wizard had disappeared, leaving a trail of debt and destruction behind him. His old employers, alerted by his sudden departure, began to trawl through their accounts and found a massive hole: payments to unknown suppliers; deliveries to sites they weren't working on; goods they never received; and numerous other discrepancies came to light. The matter was never reported to the police, however, as their employee had too much "inside information" as to just how his former bosses were running their empire and where the cash was stashed. There would be too many questions to be answered if they opened that particular can of worms, especially with the Tribunals in session. So they took the hit and learned an expensive lesson.

Afraid of being "rumbled", the wizard didn't wait around. He sold up and took his extended family to Australia, where he set up a similar operation, again with a number of new "partners". His sister met her husband shortly after arriving in Australia and he was persuaded to invest in a new realty scheme – an estate agents – which her brother had "run successfully for years" in Ireland. The new brother-in-law was impressed by the fact that when they'd arrived in Australia they had all the trappings of success. They bought an expensive property and appeared to have large cash assets. They were his "in-laws", it was a once-in-a-lifetime opportunity, and he grabbed it with both hands.

The wizard set up a successful business, operating as a Real Estate Agent and Building Consultant and he cut in his new brother-in-law. It was a great success and, once again, he kept himself at arm's length from any liability for debts. After less than a year of raking in the cash, he cleaned out the assets and disappeared without a trace, leaving his new "partners", including his brother-in law, to sort out the mess.

It turned out that the Australian lawyer was acting for a family member who had got involved and had been left to pay off the debts. He wasn't surprised to learn his new business partner had left Ireland leaving numerous debts, most of which he was not even legally liable for. What he found impossible to believe was the fact that no-one had reported the matter to the police. Hence his incredulity at our initial findings that the wizard had no criminal record, nor were there any charges pending against him in Ireland.

The wizard was responsible for several small contractors going to the wall. Numerous sub-contractors, small plumbing and electrical companies, many just starting out in business and anxious to get in on these "big contracts", were left high and dry. Banks, too, were left with substantial debts while the wizard laughed all the way to another bank in the sun.

A solicitor who had been dealing with the fall-out in Ireland made the following statement: "Mr X . . . left the country with a sum well in excess of £1 million which has been unaccounted for. If he ever came to reside in this country again, he would be assaulted with the issue of so many writs, that he would not know what happened. He is blamed for it all, he was a big spender."

During my investigations, I learned that the cheeky wizard *had* slipped back into Dublin to withdraw £6,000 he'd left in an account. Too mean to leave it behind, he took the risk of being caught, knowing that his accusers were unlikely to call the cops.

Because the wizard has never been charged or convicted of any crime, libel laws prevent me from naming him here. His former bosses declined to press any charges at the time, despite the large fraud perpetrated on them. They were adverse to any publicity about their business and are very successful builders in their own right.

Perhaps, by now, he has retired on his ill-gotten gains . . . or maybe he is just working on his next victims.

Barbados to Belem

The job of a PI demands that you be flexible, ready to go where the job takes you at a moment's notice, always carry your passport, cash and a credit card and be prepared to live out of a suitcase for as long as it takes. All this makes it always interesting and occasionally exciting, as you never really know what might happen. What might seem routine and mundane can prove to be exciting and challenging; equally, the cases that promise most often turn out to be run-of-the-mill.

A conflict of interest in a business matter – a straightforward breach of contract – turned into an international chase that led us from Ireland to South America, with many stops in between. Our client, a major international company, manufactured a branded product for sale in the export market under licence to a specific client, who was licensed to market it within a limited territory only. The client was concerned that the product was being re-distributed to other international markets in breach of their agreement and I was asked to track shipments to their customer to find out where it went from there.

When the product was dispatched, we kept it under surveillance as it was packed into containers and delivered to Dublin docks, which handles millions of tonnes of goods each year. Containers are piled like skyscrapers in the sky, bound for international markets. To the untrained eye, with the kaleidoscope of different colours and markings, it is difficult to tell one container from another. Cranes move them about on a regular basis, like a giant game of dominos, and it is hard to keep track of individual containers as they are loaded aboard the various merchant ships that dock at the port.

Round-the-clock surveillance was the only way to ensure that tabs were kept on "our" containers. Under cover of darkness, accompanied by another agent, we sneaked around the docklands, examining containers to confirm their identity from their ID numbers and seals, which we then photographed and recorded. The following morning, I watched as "our" containers were loaded on board a ship sailing under a Dutch flag. From the ship's manifest, I knew the first port of call was Santa Cruz in the Canary Islands, where it was due five days later.

Over the following weeks, I tracked its progress. I initially flew to the Canaries – somewhere I was already very familiar with. Assisted by local agents, a twenty-four-hour watch was kept on the ship in Santa Cruz for a couple of weeks as it off-loaded its cargo, before setting sail again. From there it headed to Bridgetown in Barbados, and I flew an agent out from Dublin to keep tabs on it. With English being the spoken language, it was easy enough to get around and check things out. The "tagged" containers were identified and followed to their end destination, while I went on to its next port of call, Trinidad, and eventually on to Belém on the Amazon River in Brazil – the final destination for the last of "our" containers.

Belém had its own problems; not alone was it a very "industrial" area, as are most docklands, but most of the workers spoke an indigenous dialect which I couldn't understand (not that I understood Portuguese!), but at that time, I had passable Spanish which is not dissimilar to Portuguese and I could get the general gist of things. Once again the World Association of Detectives network came to the rescue, sending an agent from their Rio de Janeiro office to assist me and help me report back to my Dublin office. The docklands weren't exactly the location or kind of job where a woman can "blend in" unless she was a "working girl" but, thankfully, on this case it was easy enough in places like Trinidad and Brazil to be a "curious tourist".

After three long months, the investigation was finally finished. You might think what an interesting case that was but on a personal level, it was one of the most tedious, boring and unexciting cases in a long time. The endless hours, just waiting for something to happen, in far-flung places not on the usual tourist trail but in dirty dreary docklands. I know that I was not alone, as my investigators, to a man – and they were all men, bar me – were delighted to get back home to the exotic shores of wet and windy Dublin. Yet again, another "glamorous" PI job.

Money for Nothing – For Even Better Value

In today's world, it seems impossible to understand how a national bank strike could last for months. But in the late 1960s and again in 1970, there were two bank strikes. The first, which lasted around three months, was surpassed by a fourteen-month strike four years later in 1970. It crippled numerous business outlets, which couldn't function without international bank facilities. Department stores and other "cash businesses" operated quite well, using the cash from customers to pay suppliers, wages and other bills. Awash with cash, security became a major concern for many outlets.

As security consultants and country-wide providers of store detectives and security to all the major department stores at the time, it was critical for my father's staff to be extra vigilant, on the look-out for everything from armed robberies to major fraud. Dunnes Stores, then run by Ben Dunne Sr, had their headquarters in Georges Street, Dublin. During the bank strike, their top-floor office was used as a counting-house. Cash was piled high on rows of tables, as the takings from each store arrived under security escort each night.

Like every other business, Ben used the cash to pay wages and his suppliers, including my father's company, which meant they in turn could pay *their* staff's wages. It suited everyone, but for some, it was a heaven-sent opportunity to take advantage of the "new" system and worry about it later. Many sharp operators traded away, knowing that the cheques they'd written for cash were worthless. With no money in the bank and no hope of trading out of the dilemma, they prayed that the bank strike would go on even longer. Many fled to the US, England and Australia before the proverbial hit the fan. My Dad's company had the task of tracking them down for banks and businesses throughout the country.

It wasn't long before word got out that Ben Dunne had become a "money changer", as more people asked him to cash cheques, and he frequently did. On one occasion, my father was in the "counting-house" when a well-dressed, well-spoken man called and asked Ben to cash a rather substantial cheque for him. My father, who witnessed the conversation, intervened and had a quiet word, warning Ben not to cash it, as the man was a con-artist, well known to him.

Ben would have none of it, saying he recognised the man and knew him from the race course – which he did. My father, who handled security for the Turf Club for all the racecourses, also "knew" him, having come up against the bogus "Major" on more than one occasion. Despite his warning, Ben cashed the cheque for the man, who claimed he was flying to the UK that morning to a race meeting. The "Major" thanked Ben profusely, telling him he had a good tip and would put a bet on for him as a "thank you" for cashing his cheque. Ben berated my father, saying the "Major" was a real gentleman. He was outraged that Dad could have thought otherwise.

It was too much for my old man, who insisted that Ben went with him to see just how much of a gentleman the "Major" really was. With great reluctance and a lot of grumbling, Ben accompanied my Dad, insisting it was a waste of his time. They crossed the road into the Long Hall Pub on George's Street, almost directly opposite Dunnes Stores, only to find the man himself regaling his cronies with the story of how he'd just conned Ben Dunne. My Dad knew it was a haunt of the "Major" and took a chance he'd find him there, once he had money in his pocket. He said later that he didn't know who was more shocked – Ben at having been conned and proved wrong; or the blustering "Major", who expected the Gardaí to arrest him at any moment.

To save face, Ben declined to press charges and got back what was left of his cash. As a parting shot, Ben told the "Major" that if he *ever* told anyone about it, there'd be dire consequences. Up until now, I don't think anyone did – at least not publicly!

Shanahan's Stamp Auctions

One of the most infamous cases to hit Ireland was that of the Shanahan Stamp Scandal in the 1950s and 1960s. For the most part, the story is well known in the annals of Irish criminal and corporate history, but the involvement of a PI – my father – may not be known.

The stamp auction was the brainchild of Dr Paul Singer, an Eastern European Jew who fled to Ireland after the collapse of his father's finance business. Singer was a director of the firm, which went bust, owing the equivalent of almost €14 million.

He moved to Dun Laoghaire and, while buying second-hand furniture from Shanahans for his tiny flat, he hit on the 'get-rich-quick' scheme of auctioning rare postage stamps.

The plan was that the company would be funded with start-up capital of £200 but that "investors", sourced by Singer, would provide the financing to make the purchases. When the stamps were auctioned off, the investors, the Shanahans and Singer would all take a share of the spoils, with Singer taking an additional 10 per cent on all transactions. He courted the press, ensuring he got coverage of his various "coups" buying sought-after collections. His plan was a simple, time-worn one, still used today – a pyramid selling operation, where gullible investors put money into a business, with a "cast-iron guarantee" of making a profit. If they worked, we'd all be millionaires!

Singer successfully operated the scheme for a few years as investors poured money into it, delighted with their "profits". What they didn't know was that, like all "pyramid" schemes, Singer was using investors' money to buy stamps and to pay out the "profits". Inevitably, it would all end in tears.

Living the life of the immensely rich, Singer hosted magnificent parties at his newly acquired thirteen-acre estate at Cairn Hall in Foxrock where champagne and caviar were the norm, showing off his treasures. His wife's diamonds, antiques and even the 1906 Ascot Gold Cup were paraded for the media and guests to admire. His staff included a butler, cook, liveried chauffeur, gardener and even a governess for his children, at a time when there were few jobs and little money in Ireland. It was just another stunt to attract investors and make them feel secure. His plan worked, as thousands of investors from all over the world poured millions into the scheme. At one stage, he paid £3 million to buy what was then the world's most valuable stamp collection. But like they say – if it sounds too good to be true, it probably is.

Things were about to turn sour for Singer. His lavish lifestyle, travelling the world allegedly on "business", his holidays abroad in Cannes, Israel and Canada, eventually caught up with him and the funds began to dry up. He'd been paying the "dividends" from investors' money – the rest was spent maintaining his lifestyle. By 1959, the bubble had burst and Singer needed an escape route.

He hatched a plan to explain away the deficit in the stamp stocks. In May 1959, there was a "break-in" at Shanahan premises and stamps valued at £500,000 were "stolen". Singer said he believed the robbery was "the work of teddy-boys who got a bit gay after the Spring Show". The haul included stamps from the Lombarda-Venetia collection, part of a famous rare collection, the bulk of which had been previously bought by an unidentified millionaire, who coincidently needed the "stolen" stamps to complete his collection.

Singer told police the stamps were "fully insured", but a week later when gardaí asked if the assessors had called, he said, "They haven't arrived yet" – despite the fact that it was the biggest-ever robbery in Ireland, equivalent to €15 million today. Thinking it strange, gardaí again asked if he was fully insured. He said, "Well, I have nothing to worry about." He then cheekily asked a garda if he knew how to smuggle stamps out of the country, saying, "It's quite easy . . . just post them out of the country in small quantities, in ordinary envelopes." This was a display of arrogance from Singer, who was, by then, the prime suspect.

Days later, in a swoop on Singer's home, he was arrested and taken to the station, where huge crowds gathered to see the famous Dr Singer, Ireland's next best thing to a movie star. Singer continued to plead his innocence, but he was remanded in custody to Mountjoy Jail, with no-one willing to put up the £100,000 bail money.

It was May 1959 and Singer's lawyers contacted my father, Bill Kavanagh, at his Dawson Street office and asked him to investigate the case on Singer's behalf. He interviewed Paul Singer in Mountjoy Jail several times between May and August and Singer gave him keys to Cairn Hall in Foxrock. The private investigation went on for three months and extended across Austria, Switzerland, the US, Canada, France, Israel and the UK. The more my father investigated, the more the evidence stacked up against Singer. Singer had claimed that the stamps for the Shanahans' first auction had been supplied by him from his "bank vault" in London, with his aunt, Martha Medak, supplying the rest.

My father found out that Singer actually owned no stamps but had taken a line of credit for £16,000 from a major London-based stamp auction house, Cyril Harmer. As soon as investors started putting money in, Singer began paying off some of his debts to Harmers. Despite the vast amounts of money Singer was pulling in from private investors, he was loath to pay back his personal debts, not alone to Harmer but to various suppliers in Dublin. Harmer wasn't happy with the irregular payments but when he found out that Singer had hired London-based private detectives to keep him under surveillance, he was furious. Immediately, he cut off Singer's credit line. In an early form of industrial espionage, Singer wanted to find out Harmer's contacts and source of stamps in an effort to put him out of business. With his credit cut off, Singer was livid and, from then on, hated

Harmer with a vengeance, seeing Harmer's actions as an obstacle to his plan to dominate the world of philately. He openly threatened to "smash Harmer and make him literally crawl" but at the time, it was put down to Singer's fiercely competitive nature. His personal vendetta against Harmer was unknown.

It emerged that Singer, despite his statement to gardaí, had no insurance. A strange situation, given the reported value of the stock. He had been offered insurance coverage of stg£500,000 by Lloyd's of London, for a premium of £400, but turned it down, saying Shanahans would carry the risk themselves. As a result of my father's international investigations, it emerged that, over twenty-two months, Singer embezzled almost £1.4 million from investors' funds, transferring it to his own name or in joint accounts with his wife, to banks in Switzerland, Canada, the US, Israel and Italy. Within a short time, he'd withdrawn most of it.

Armed with this discovery, my father reported his findings to Singer's legal team and visited Singer in Mountjoy on 17 July 1959. By then he had no doubt whatsoever that the ebullient "salesman" was a con-artist, who'd hit the jackpot in a naïve Ireland. Like every good conman, Singer was a charmer and tried to convince him otherwise, but my dad was not for turning. He handed Singer a letter and his fee account and was assured by Singer it would be paid immediately.

Five weeks later, with still no payment, on 28 August, he again visited Singer in Mountjoy. This time Singer said he'd arranged for the payment to be made through his solicitor, Des Moran. Seeing where things were going, my Dad wrote to Moran, advising him of his findings, his meetings with Singer and enclosing his final account. The letter said: "Having *fully* considered the position, I feel that the demand for our services is no longer required by Dr Singer."

Based on his findings, he believed his client was guilty and he therefore couldn't provide the legal team with any information that would benefit their client's case. In fact, if he was called as a witness regarding his investigations, his information could have been the final nail in Singer's coffin. Singer, having been appraised of his findings and the possible "difficulties" of the situation, ensured that he got his fees without further delay.

23

Compo Culture: Money for Old Rope

There has been an ideology in Ireland that making fraudulent claims is a victimless crime. After all, the business has to pay insurance anyway and the insurance companies are making millions – so, the argument goes, no one gets hurt!

This chapter deals with just a few "sample" claims cases but, for the uninitiated, the routine goes something like this. Generally insurance claims are fairly straightforward. An accident happens or not, as the case may be. A claim is lodged and the claimant's solicitor usually deals with the Personal Injuries Assessment Board or the insurance company's solicitors. Sometimes they go to court, are settled out of court or, on occasion, a claim is withdrawn, but this is rare. Most fraudulent claimants feel confident that they are in a win-win money-for-nothing situation, often having a "no foal, no fee" arrangement with their solicitor, which means if they don't win they don't pay, so there is no risk to them. A solicitor won't usually enter into this arrangement unless they believe their client has a good case.

In a claim-culture society, Ireland has always had more than its fair share of insurance claims. The genuine ones are no problem; that's what insurance is there for, after all. Fraudulent claims pose a serious problem, not alone for the insurance companies – heavy payouts on fraudulent claims mean increased insurance costs for everyone. This is where an experienced private investigator comes in. Insurance companies routinely check out a percentage of claims based on varying criteria. Perhaps it's the amount of the claim, the nature of the injuries, or it could be that the claimant had previous claims. It may simply be a random check on a genuine claim.

Some investigations are routine. The procedures are much the same in every case. The bottom line is that you have to investigate if the person's injuries are genuine; if their injuries restrict their lifestyle or ability to work or have a long-term effect on their quality of life; and finally, if the losses are genuine.

If the person who claims they can never walk again has a miraculous recovery, plays rugby or goes golfing every weekend with no obvious restrictions, whilst still in the process of making a claim, we have to provide sufficient evidence to satisfy a court that the claim is exaggerated or fraudulent. Many wait until a claim is settled to experience their "miracle" and it is not unusual in such cases to see a specialist's medical report which says something along the lines: "I do not expect the patient to make a full recovery until the claim is settled." Read between the lines. Sometimes the claimant is found to be genuine and the PI's report will be enough to recommend a settlement without the need for court.

There have been many professional claimants, especially in the days when rival insurance companies didn't share information on claims. The professional claimant would just move from one claim to another, claiming against department stores, government agencies, hospitals and local councils, over and over again, often for the same "injury". Entire families were often involved in this lucrative enterprise, giving "evidence" as witnesses for each other. It made sense – it was easier for them to remember their alleged injuries and many become experts on the symptoms of specific injuries. To add insult to injury (they having none), they were often found to be claiming unemployment benefit while working "on the lump" – cash in hand for other employers – *as well as* making their spurious claim, all in all earning them a tidy sum. Nobody cross-checked and the taxpayer paid out yet again when it came to claims against public bodies, county councils and government agencies.

On more than one occasion I've investigated such professional claimants, people I'd run across on several occasions, such was their bad luck to be so accident-prone. Insurance scammers come in all shapes and sizes – from the "prominent" businessman, sometimes in serious debt, looking for an easy way out, to the "chancers" who see it as easy money.

Not all subversives come from north of the border and we have many of our own home-grown boys, making spurious or fraudulent claims on a regular basis. They see it as their "employment" and it usually generated a good income for them until insurance companies began using professional investigators rather than internal claims people, some of whom were excellent at spotting a dodgy claim but generally were overworked clerical staff. Some of the insurance companies had been clients since my father's time, as every generation has their chancers, but in recent years it became a way of life, a cottage industry for what was "compo-culture" Ireland.

The following sample cases will give you an insight into the lengths some people go for "easy money". Over the years I've investigated thousands of insurance claims, some funny, bizarre, stupid or just downright brazen. I'll let you be the judge!

Dead, But Not Forgotten

They say that God loves a tryer – if that's the case, he must really have loved Marie. Marie's husband Tommy died in hospital while undergoing treatment for ulcers. There was no question that there had been medical negligence, in that he was over-prescribed medication which caused his sudden death, and the hospital accepted this. Three months later, Marie, his widow, put in a claim on behalf of herself and her eight children, saying that she was devastated by his death and could no longer provide for their children. Tommy, she said, had been the breadwinner and had never been out of work. The insurers passed it on for a legal opinion and the barrister recommended that I take a look at the case.

On the surface, it seemed straightforward enough – medical negligence. However, with further investigation, the case threw up some unexpected information. It seemed that Marie, although married to Tommy for several years, had an eye for the men and was known to "play away", to the extent that she had earned herself a reputation in the inner city flats where they'd lived. Tommy, a decent man, was very upset by her behaviour and, on one occasion, when he found out she was having yet another affair, he assaulted her. Arrested by gardaí, he got the Probation Act, as he had never been in trouble before. Marie refused to change her ways and Tommy stuck by her – she was all he had. As he'd been given up for adoption at birth, she was the only family he knew. Her behaviour became even more blatant over the years and he became depressed. In later years, suffering from ulcers, he ended up in hospital, where he met his untimely death.

What Marie didn't tell her solicitors was that she had left Tommy years before. I found out that she had been living in England with another man and had two more children – two of the "eight" children she was claiming for. In fact, on checking the birth certificates of "Tommy's children", it seemed that only two were actually his and they'd been born more than twelve years previously. Not all her children had a father's name on the birth certificate. Those who had were many and varied. Marie had been very busy; so busy, in fact, that she didn't find out that Tommy was dead until three months after he was buried. Hence the timing of her claim.

I discovered that Tommy had been treated for severe depression in another hospital but had neglected to mention it when admitted for his ulcers. Perhaps he didn't realise the importance as, if they had known, I understand the hospital would not have treated him with the particular medication that caused his death. In the course of my investigation to establish the true background to the case, I also managed to find a half-sister of Tommy's who'd been adopted by an American couple. Unfortunately, that discovery came too late for poor Tommy. Given the situation and the fact that I had established Tommy had been in and out of work all his life and had declared himself "unemployed" – claiming social welfare benefits for most of their time together – I doubt if Marie lived high on the hog as a result of her claim.

The Canary Sang a Different Tune in Court

Danger is not usually an ingredient of insurance scam investigations – unless you are getting into professional claimant territory. To them, it's a business that needs to be protected and anyone that interferes with their income will not be looked on kindly. For the most part, though, they are straightforward and, on occasion, even downright funny!

One such case that comes to mind involved a man who claimed a severe back injury as a result of a motorbike accident. He said he was no longer able to work and was surviving on sickness benefits until his claim was settled. The insurance company asked me to look at the case as a matter of routine. They had no real suspicions, it appeared genuine and was just a random check. Observation was kept on the man, who lived in a high-rise block of inner city flats. Although he was claiming to be unable to work or ride his motorbike, he was observed on several occasions running up and down the steps of the flats, jumping onto his motorbike and riding off – usually to do a "nixer", a cash-in-hand job here and there. Investigation into his social habits showed that he was a regular at a local inner city pub, especially at the weekend. I decided to join him, uninvited.

The pub was a "salt-of-the-earth" working class pub. I went in alone and sat in a corner, giving me a good all-round view of the place. A short time later, the place began to fill up as there was a live music session on that night. I was joined in my corner by a group of six or seven people, male and female. They knew I was a "blow-in" – my cover story was that I was supposed to be meeting someone from the flats and they included me in their conversation while I was waiting for "me mate".

It wasn't long before I spotted the claimant walking in. Well known by the crowd, he headed straight to my corner where he sat down with us, chatting away. I hadn't planned on such a "close encounter". The band played a few numbers and when they called on "singers" to come up, he was first up on stage. He sang several songs and gave a very energetic rendition of Elvis's gyrations, jumping two feet in the air and playing an "air guitar" without any difficulty, much to the enjoyment of the crowd.

His antics brought loud applause and the corner crowd filled me in on his efforts of the previous Easter Bank holiday, when he'd dressed up as a canary and went around "flying off stools and showing off". What's more, they showed me the photos to prove it! When he finally and reluctantly left the stage, he came and sat beside me and started chatting me up, asking me to meet him the next night for a drink. I couldn't believe it! After a few minutes, in the time-honoured manner of all PIs and journalists in a sticky situation, I made my excuses, saying I had to go home. He offered me a lift. I knew about his motorbike, but in my best Dublin accent I asked him, in an impressed tone, if he had a car. Before he could reply, one of his mates shouted out, "Yeah, love – a bleedin' go-car!" The place was in hysterics. As the women were heading for the ladies, I joined them, only to find that the "ladies" was outside and up another stairway. It was my opportunity to make good my escape, as I headed home for real.

Some time later, the case came to court and the claimant gave evidence of his life-changing back injury and how he was unable to have any quality of life, socialise or get out much due to the severe pain. I was then called to give evidence. It was the first time he had seen me since that night in the pub when he'd asked me out. He was speechless! His jaw dropped as I gave evidence of our findings and my observations on the night of his "star turn". Not only was he shocked – not having had a clue that he had been rumbled – he was doubly shocked when my accent was no longer the accent of a true Molly Malone. I wondered if he still fancied meeting me for that drink? I must admit, I couldn't help smiling. Needless to say, the case didn't exactly go his way.

A Run of Bad Luck

One unfortunate claimant, Mr F, suffered a leg injury when he walked in front of an oncoming car while carrying a large piece of furniture. According to witnesses, the driver had no chance to avoid him – despite which, he immediately made a claim against the driver. While he was undoubtedly injured, the question of his own contributory negligence was part of the defence. I was asked to look at the case eighteen months after the accident, as he was still claiming he couldn't work. It seemed a straightforward insurance claim, until the investigation began to throw up some interesting facts about the injured man.

In support of his claim for loss of earnings, he had supplied accounts to show he had been in the haulage business. At the time, under the Road Traffic Act, hauliers were required to have a Merchandised Road Transport Licence issued by the then Department of Transport. Investigation found that he'd never held such a licence, which in turn raised questions about the accounts he'd submitted. Further investigations turned up even more interesting information. The man, like many unfortunate claimants, seemed to have had a run of bad luck and accidents and had several other insurance claims over the years.

His misfortunes were not over yet, as two months after I took on the case, Mr F had another stroke of bad luck. This time it involved a shop he owned, which burnt to the ground over a bank holiday weekend while Mr F was abroad on holiday. Forensic investigation established that the fire was not caused accidentally and during the course of criminal investigations, it was found that plastic supermarket bags containing petrol had been tied at the top and thrown against the interior walls of the premises.

I found out that, prior to the fire, an elderly man had lived in a flat overhead for over fifty years. In an amazing coincidence, Mr F had visited his tenant a short time before the fire and told him he'd have to leave, as the flat was in a dangerous condition. No-one had been around to inspect the flat but obviously the owner was concerned as to the possible danger his tenant was in and needed vacant possession to repair it. Unfortunately, less than three weeks later, before any work began, the shop and flat were completely destroyed in the fire. Mr F made a claim for malicious damages. It was paid out, as the Gardaí had insufficient evidence to identify those responsible for the arson.

A few months later, Mr F decided he fancied a bit of hunting and applied for a firearms certificate for a shotgun, well aware that, given his well-known political background and associates, he would never be issued with a gun licence. Such applications are usually approved by the garda superintendent in the applicant's area. Undeterred by this minor detail, Mr F presented himself at the local police station, at a time when a certain "friendly" garda was on duty. The garda was going out with Mr F's daughter at the time. He handed over the application form and a letter of introduction from an arms dealer who'd already given him the shotgun before he'd even applied for the licence and the "friendly" garda put the application through.

On his return to work, the sharp-eyed superintendent picked up on the dodgy application and immediately issued a warrant to search Mr F's house and lands, where a firearm was seized. Mr F wasn't happy at such an intrusion and he went to the High Court to challenge the search and seizure. His case was thrown out and he was obliged to pay not only his own substantial legal fees but those of the State. The garda who'd put through the licence application was subjected to internal disciplinary action but no criminal charges and was transferred to other duties.

Meanwhile, Mr F was kept under surveillance in connection with his accident, where he claimed that he couldn't work anymore. He was seen operating in his various areas of trade on a regular basis and was often videoed single-handedly pulling a large trailer onto a high grass verge, dragging heavy tarpaulins, lifting them onto his shoulder and dumping them onto a trailer. His car, although registered in his name, hadn't been taxed for three years. Despite his "interesting" background and his non-mainstream political associations, the matter of the car accident would of course be judged on its own merits alone.

Love is . . . Taking the Rap

Not all insurance cases are investigated for evidence of fraud. Sometimes the investigations are to "prove" that the claimant was in the right and entitled to damages but for some reason they "slipped through the net" and were left without compensation for a genuine claim. This was the case in the following story.

That early "test case" set by Irving Shumbord in New York came in handy for me many years later when a law firm contacted me about an accident case. They were acting for a young man who had been involved in a motorbike accident several years previously. He had been in a coma for many months and, when he recovered consciousness, he couldn't remember the accident. He was so severely injured that he required residential medical care for life. His family had little means; they were simple people who didn't know how to cope with the situation.

The Gardaí had investigated the accident but had failed to establish the cause. They were of the opinion that the man himself was at fault, speeding on a bend, or else it was a "hit and run", probably by someone passing through the village. The trail had long gone cold. As far as they were concerned, the case was closed. Meanwhile, the insurers had not paid out, as the motorcyclist had only third-party insurance.

On reviewing the file and visiting the scene, things just didn't stack up. It was in a rural part of the country in an area where everyone knew everyone else's business, yet no one admitted remembering the serious accident. After driving and walking around the place several times, I went to the local County Council offices to inspect maps of the area. I discovered that the original road had been moved by several feet since the time of the accident to straighten what had been a dangerous bend. Either side of the new road were fields owned by a wealthy businessman who lived in the village.

Going back to the area, I went into the field on one side of the road, in the area where the accident had supposedly occurred. It was somewhat neglected and overgrown, close to the old road area. Armed with a shovel, I scraped away some of the weeds and grass closest to the edge and found the old road surface underneath. After some more digging and scraping, I found old skid marks, which appeared to have been "gouged" out of the surface, consistent with a motorbike sliding along the road. The metal bike-stand had cut a deep groove, which extended along the road for several feet. Taking photographs and measurements of the scene, the investigation took a new turn. From experience, I was convinced there had been someone else involved in the accident. Searching around the shrubbery, I found a long-abandoned car partly concealed by the overgrowth. It looked just like any other wreck seen in fields around the countryside, but the fact that it was there, so close to the scene of the accident, make me suspicious. The colour and make of the car were readily identifiable and with a bit more digging in the undergrowth, a broken number plate emerged. A check with vehicle registrations showed it had been registered to a local businessman, the owner of the field, at the time of the accident. The local council had been notified that the car had been sold about a month after the accident and a name and address of the "new owner" was listed as a man living in Belfast.

It seemed all too much of a coincidence. The timing, the location of the abandoned car and the false declaration of change of ownership – unless it was a "ringer" of course (usually a stolen car with false number plate already listed to another car). Investigation confirmed my instincts. The "new owner" never existed, nor did the Belfast address. The car had been owned, taxed and was insured by the businessman at the time of the accident. A full technical examination of the car was made and, despite the elements, after several years in the field, it was established beyond doubt that the vehicle had been in an accident. There were paint traces on the car matching the make and model of the bike. All indications were that the car had been in a head-on collision with the young man's motorbike.

It was enough to confront the businessman with the mounting evidence. He reluctantly admitted that his then seventeen-year-old son had been driving the car on the night of the accident. He said he was away on business and only found out about it a week later. By then, his son was so distraught, he just couldn't go to the police. The son had been sent to a relative in America a few weeks later and had only been back for a short visit earlier that year.

The businessman said it had been on his conscience but he didn't know what to do about it without involving his son. He agreed to accept full responsibility and made a substantial payment to provide long-term care for the young motorcyclist. My job was finished. I don't know if he was ever charged with the matter – I just moved on to the next case – but at least it was a relatively good outcome for one family, if you could call it that, under the circumstances.

The Ringer and the Clairvoyant who never saw it coming!

I got a call from a UK-based insurance company. For a reasonable premium, it offered self-employed people the opportunity to take out insurance in the event of their suffering an accident or illness that prevented them from working. They'd had a claim from a twenty-year-old self-employed Englishman who had a policy with them for just five weeks before making a claim. Nothing wrong with that – accidents can happen anyone at anytime.

The man had taken a full medical before taking out the policy and had received a clean bill of health. The unfortunate young man, who described himself as a painter and decorator, said that while loading a heavy tar-pot onto a truck, he'd injured his back and was unable to work. He claimed to be so incapacitated that he was only able to "lie on the floor". A local doctor certified that he was suffering from "back pain" and unable to work and the claim was paid out. Every month, regular as clockwork, a cheque for stg£1,500 came through the post. Every so often he returned to the doctor for another certificate. No one in the insurance company thought twice about it; it was an automated payment system that ensured his claim would be paid monthly until he was sixty-five, unless he notified them that he had recovered.

About a year later, a new claims manager was appointed and he decided to review the claims files, picking a few random files to check. One of these was the case of Greg, the twenty-year-old with the bad back, who was still happily sending in his medical certs. Strangely, they had no current address for him. His cheques were sent to a broker, who forwarded them on to another address. Having established that the broker was *bona fide* and not a suspect in a scam claim, I paid him a visit in London and he gave me some very scanty details from his file. He couldn't remember the man but at least I knew where he was sending the cheque every month.

This address was a large run-down house set in flats in a seaside town on the south coast of England. There was just one problem – the guy didn't live there and never had done. Was he using the address of a friend or relative or was it a case of a stolen identity? I arranged for the insurers to have a registered letter sent to Greg at the address and I monitored the post. When our letter arrived in a large coloured envelope, a girl, later identified as Greg's girlfriend, signed for it. With no further leads, we kept the girlfriend and the house under surveillance for the next two weeks, with still no sign of Greg. She neither met him anywhere, nor did he call to the flat. If he really was incapacitated, surely she would have at least visited him at home or in hospital?

I went back to the broker and insisted on inspecting his file as it's not unusual for us to pick up something that escaped a client's notice. It was worth the trip, as I realised that for months the broker had been sending Greg's cheques to an address in the West of Ireland and not to the UK address he'd given us earlier – a simple mistake on his part. Moving the investigation to Mayo, in Ireland, it seemed Greg hadn't been seen in the area for over a year. Whatever was going on, it was definitely dodgy. In an effort to root him out, I asked the insurance company to set up a "routine" medical check. The doctor's offices were kept under observation, but Greg never showed.

At this point I got the insurance company to withhold his cheque in an effort to flush him out. Greg obliged. He phoned to complain he hadn't received his cheque. When they asked why he didn't attend the medical appointment, he said he didn't get the letter in time. The insurance company pleaded a clerical error and asked him to confirm his address and phone number. He "confirmed" his UK address but refused to give a phone number, saying he was calling from a friend's. The insurers offered to arrange another medical appointment but he said he was staying with his mother in Ireland for a couple of weeks so she could look after him, as his back was no better. To facilitate him, the insurers arranged for him to visit a local doctor in Mayo and surveillance was set up again.

I still believed he was living in England and, for whatever reason, he might fly to Ireland, do the medical and go back home. A flight watch showed up nothing and, again, he didn't turn up for the medical. The insurance company stopped paying his claim and an angry Greg phoned them, claiming he'd had the flu but that he'd be happy to attend another medical at any time. They arranged one for the following day, at ten o'clock. At eight the next morning, our surveillance was in place. By ten, there was only one patient fitting the profile of our target, a young male, who matched the height and build details on the original insurance application. He arrived on time, wearing a back-brace and walking with a noticeable limp. After a short consultation, he left the doctor's surgery and went to a car "hidden" some distance away. He gave the impression he was having difficulty walking, limping from time to time and walking very slowly.

I followed him to a large isolated country house some distance from the town. A stroke of luck came my way when I saw a "For Sale" sign on the property. Investigation revealed that it was run as a B&B by Greg's mother and although she hadn't been in the area long, she was well known locally, offering her services as a clairvoyant. The "For Sale" sign was my "in" and I called at the house to ask about the property. A woman answered the door and offered to show me around. She introduced me to her son, "Greg", the young man I'd seen earlier at the doctor's surgery. He was in his twenties, almost six-foot tall and stockily built. He had no back-brace and was walking around normally, with no sign of any difficulties. His mother told him to show me around the property – a large five-bedroom house set in thirty-eight acres. It had additional run-down holiday chalets and a dilapidated leisure complex, which stank of mould and damp. Accompanied by her son, who seemed a bit strange, I trudged the grounds, climbing over stiles, gates and obstacles, as he showed no sign of any injury. His limp had remarkably disappeared. He spoke with an English accent and when I asked how long he'd been in Ireland, he said "years", saying he hadn't lived in England since he was a child, but was going over to his brother "Jimmy's" wedding soon.

Back at the house, the woman spoke to me at length about the property, saying she was a clairvoyant and could tell that "this is the right property for you". She said her powers ensured good health for herself and her family, who were never ill and never had to visit a doctor. It was hard not to laugh when she pointed to her son – the same guy I saw limping into the doctor's surgery just hours previously – as evidence of her claim! The guy sat cross-legged on the floor apparently trying to look up my skirt. I felt extremely uncomfortable in his presence, especially while he was giving me the "guided tour" of the remote property.

It seemed an open-and-shut case of insurance fraud but still I felt something wasn't quite right. Perhaps her clairvoyant powers had rubbed off on me, but instinct and experience told me there was more to this case. On my advice, the insurers restored payment when they got the medical certificate and allowed things to settle down, letting Greg think everything was back to normal. Meanwhile I checked out where he was cashing the cheques sent on to Mayo. It came as no surprise that they were regularly cashed in a Barclay's bank on the east coast of England.

The hunt moved back to the UK. Either Greg was flying between Ireland and the UK on a regular basis, which seemed unlikely, or else there was a "ringer" involved. (More common to horse racing or greyhound scams, the art of using "ringers" involves replacing a bad horse or dog with a good one at long odds, or a good car with a "cloned" banger carrying the same number plate. These are well-known frauds but are rarely used in personal injury insurance claims as the "stand-in" has to match all the age profile and physical characteristics of the claimant, as well as being a good actor.)

Surveillance and investigation was set up back in the UK, which led to yet another address for Greg – a three-storey house on the seafront let in flats. He shared the top flat with his girlfriend. It turned out that Greg owned the whole house, renting out the other flats. He also owned several other rental properties. Not bad for an infirm unemployed twenty-year-old. I found out that he was due to get married two months later, having romantically arranged their wedding for Valentine's Day, 14 February. It was to be a lavish black-tie affair at a local hotel. No doubt they were saving hard for the big day!

With the information that he owned the house he lived in, under a pretext, I spoke to a lady in one of the other flats. By chance, she was due to move and the flat was about to be advertised by her landlord, Greg. She gave me his mobile number and I phoned him about the flat. He said he was away but would be back the following Monday and I could look at it then. I phoned back and he offered the flat to me at £100 per week, with a minimum of a six-month lcasc, saying he'd several other properties to let if I wanted something different, but they wouldn't be available for a month or two.

Surveillance continued. It was mid-December, bitterly cold, with winter storms lashing four-foot-high waves over the roadside – yet again, the "glamorous" side of private investigation everyone talks about! Despite having spoken to

Greg by phone, there was still no sign of him. His girlfriend was seen coming and going, walking the dog and taking driving lessons. Eventually, though, patience paid off. One night close to midnight, a man closely resembling the man in Mayo, drove up in an open-backed truck, laden down with building equipment. He locked the truck and went into the house. Satisfied that he was settled in for the night, surveillance was resumed at six the following morning. The truck was still there and, to help me out, it even had his name and the words "Roofing and General Builders" emblazoned on the side.

At 10.45 he came out carrying ladders and threw them up on the truck, climbing up to secure them. He jumped down from the back of the truck with ease, loaded up and headed off. The chase was on! We followed him to Brighton where he was observed renovating a house and doing heavy building work without difficulty. With all his activities documented on camera, it was time to head home.

I reported to the clients, they stopped the payments and waited for him to call, as we knew he would. He duly obliged, demanding to know where his cheque was. Excuses were made and he appeared to accept it – but due to the "glitch", they told him he would have to submit another medical certificate. This was done for legal reasons, to ensure that he was still making fraudulent claims about his condition and inability to work *after* he had been photographed and videoed working. An appointment was made for 9 February with a GP in Mayo, just five days before his wedding. Surveillance was again set up and once again a young man in his twenties fitting our description turned up limping and wearing a body-brace. This time I recognised him as the real Greg, the man I'd kept under surveillance in the UK. Having pinned down the real Greg, I established that he had a brother, James, who was very similar in age and appearance, living locally with his mother. It was this man, Greg's brother James, who had turned up for the previous medical and had shown me around his mother's estate.

Giving him time to get home, and accompanied by another agent, I called on Greg at his mother's house in Mayo. His mother answered the door and was delighted to see me – presuming I'd come about the house. When I said that I represented the insurer, her attitude changed. Reluctantly, she agreed to let me in. She went upstairs and after a long time, returned with her son, introducing him as Greg.

Up close, this man was undoubtedly my "video star". Walking slowly and stiffly, saying he had a bad back, he dragged his leg as he moved. His speech was slow, in contrast to previous telephone conversations I'd had with him, when he was quick and witty. He said that because of his poor health he was living permanently in Mayo, saying he rarely went to the UK, where his brother "Jimmy" lived with his girlfriend. Greg was angry and demanded to know why his money had been cut off, claiming he couldn't work and had no money. When I asked him to confirm his identity, he said he had no passport or driving licence; instead he offered me a photograph of himself aged twelve and a birth certificate as identification! He became very aggressive and abusive, shouting obscenities and threatening to kill me. He made several attempts to strike out, only to be held back by his mother – a rather ample lady. His mother tried to calm the situation down and said that, due to her interest in faith healing, "Greg was planning to come off the insurance at the end of the year anyway – not because he isn't entitled to it – he is – but because faith healing doesn't work properly while he is lined up to the insurance." She said her earlier "boasting" about his big property business and how busy he was, was part of the process of talking positively about the person being treated with faith healing.

Greg attempted to talk his way out of his predicament but only succeeded in digging a deeper hole. Having failed to supply any means of positive identification, I took a photograph of him before I left. Despite his earlier aggression, the fight seemed to have gone out of him; he was too stunned to stop me!

The insurers were very happy. They had been paying out stg£1,500 sterling a month for over eighteen months – a total of stg£27,000. The indexed-linked policy potentially had another forty-four years to run if he'd continued to be unfit for work. It would have cost the company over stg£1 million, but for a random check. My fees were substantial but only a drop in the ocean it would have cost them if they hadn't investigated the case, and the insurers were happy to pay out on this occasion. For Greg, it was a wedding present he'd never forget!

The Miracle of Christmas

In one extreme insurance claim, the lady led me a merry chase. It came about when the Chief State Solicitor asked me to investigate a case against Ireland and the Attorney-General. Cases against the State are usually dealt with by the Chief State Solicitor's office and we frequently undertook investigations on behalf of various government departments. This one was a bit different.

The thirty-six-year-old "lady" in question, Ms X, had been a "guest" of the State in Limerick Prison when she fell down the stairs. Another prisoner bumped into her, causing her to stumble, hence the claim. She was claiming "severe personal injuries and substantial loss and damage".

There were two immediate problems. By the time I got the case, it had been seven years since the accident. The second problem was that the authorities had no address, photograph or even a description of the woman, who was claiming over £1 million (equivalent to €2.5 million today), plus additional special damages and costs against them.

A check with Limerick Prison and the Gardaí didn't help, as they had no records of any use to the State's case. It was a needle in a haystack – the kind of challenge I like. The trouble was, where to start? The medical reports were as good a place as any. As I read through it, it seemed that the field was somewhat narrowed. The lady said she was confined to a wheelchair, unable to walk without the aid of callipers and a walking frame. A later report was even more daunting and claimed her condition had seriously deteriorated. She was now reduced to paraplegic level. She had no feelings below her waist and had no response to standard pin-pricks or sensory examinations. She claimed to be doubly incontinent, with blurred vision and slurred speech.

As her health had declined, her claim had increased, along with her medical bills. She required special clothing; cushions; lifting poles; an ambu-lift hoist; an adjustable bed; portable telephone; medi-alarm; a special shower; structural alterations to her home; a specially adapted handicapped car; and a home-carer. These were just some of the claims in a very long list. Her solicitors were unable to provide a current address, as their client only contacted them occasionally by phone.

Meanwhile, given her long history of criminal activity, on a long shot I investigated in the UK, as it is not unusual to find that recidivists have "come to the attention" of police forces there. It was a lucky shot. She was "well known" to the UK police under various aliases and had been given a six month prison sentence for fraud, suspended for two years, just before she fled to Ireland. Caught for other crimes in Ireland, she ended up in Limerick Prison. It seemed she'd had an "interesting" background, with a history of bank fraud and deception. She'd also been involved in prostitution and heroin abuse since the age of sixteen.

I turned up a photograph and a last-known address in the UK, which, although years old, was the first real break I'd had in the case. A credit reference check produced a list of previous addresses, not to mention the debts she'd racked up, but no current address. It was going to be a foot-slog job. Cutting a very long story short, I tracked her down to an address in London.

The location was very difficult for observation – her flat looked out onto a busy roundabout at the front, the only entrance being via an enclosed courtyard, accessible only from another road. The courtyard was always busy, as tenants gathered to hang out their washing or to chat. The flats complex had a very active Neighbourhood Watch and strangers were immediately noticed, giving no cover for close-quarter surveillance.

A recce around the area located a wheelchair-adapted car similar to the one being claimed for, parked close by, but a check showed it was registered to someone else, which proved nothing – perhaps she just hadn't transferred the ownership details. There was nothing for it but to watch and wait. It looked like I was in for the long haul if she was as incapacitated as she claimed.

For ten days nothing happened, until one afternoon in December she finally left the flat. There was no question but that it was it the woman in the photograph I'd managed to get hold of, but she wasn't in a wheelchair! She walked quickly up the main road and across the busy roundabout, nipping in and out between the traffic without any apparent difficulty. She went into a local shop, where she was obviously on friendly terms with the owner – she went behind the counter and used his phone to order a pizza. She climbed onto a high stool without difficulty and sat chatting with him. An hour later her pizza arrived. Carrying the large pizza box, she ran to a car which had just pulled up outside and jumped into the passenger seat, as the male driver drove away.

From then on, it was straightforward. Over the following weeks I kept observation, photographing and videoing her miraculous recovery, as she walked on the local common or dragged a heavy shopping trolley with no difficulty for almost two miles, from the town centre to her home. She was extremely active and was caught on video hanging out large sheets and duvets, tending her small garden, cleaning her windows – it was almost enough to make you believe in the miracle of Christmas!

New medical examinations were arranged as a court date approached. Again, Ms X still had no response to the usual neurological tests. Doctors were puzzled. Was it perhaps a psychological condition? The answer was believed to lie in certain medications that could assist in a deception. For example, a dose of S-ketamine, a dissociative anaesthetic which depresses the central nervous system, would "mimic" symptoms associated with responses to neurological tests. Sometimes used in veterinary medicine, it is commonly known as horse tranquilliser. Often used on the battlefield, it allows surgery to take place while the patient is awake. Recreational use of the drug has grown over the past twenty years and it is a "class A" drug in many countries. The anaesthetic allows a person to talk and interact, but they feel no pain during procedures. Considered dangerous unless administered by a medic, it can be enough to suggest paralysis in an individual, who can suffer other "side effects" including the slurring of speech. It's a dangerous substance and not one to be taken lightly, but if the stakes are high, perhaps the risk involved would not be a deterrent.

I had been called in exactly seven years after the accident happened. Not alone had I found the claimant, but I managed to resolve the case within a relatively short time. Yet it was to be almost another three years before the matter finally came to court. During that time, I revisited Ms X on a regular basis to ensure there had been no "relapse". I got to know her "movements" quite well and had dozens of photographs and videos of her, summer and winter, up to all sorts of activities.

When the case finally came to court, numerous witnesses had been subpoenaed to give evidence on behalf of both the State and Ms X. Prison officers from Limerick prison were there in force, as were medical examiners, former prisoners, legal teams and a contingent from the Chief State Solicitor's office. My team arrived with equipment, ready to show the wheelchair-bound ex-con claimant to the court in another light. A private showing was arranged for both legal teams in the Chief State Solicitor's office in the Four Courts, prior to the hearing. The case never went ahead.

Ms X did receive a small settlement for her fall, but not the millions she'd been expecting, despite her Oscar-winning act and one hell of a lot of stamina to wait all those years! A good result all round. Well, for the State Solicitor's team anyway.

Ironically, the only "real" job Ms X ever had during her life was that of a clairvoyant. Yet another one who didn't see it coming. Makes you wonder if they're in the wrong profession?

24

In the Matter of a Solicitor

You might think this a strange title for a PI story, but that's the polite term the Law Society use when dealing with errant solicitors such as Michael Lynn and others. They call the proceedings "In the Matter of a Solicitor", which seems a somewhat arcane way of describing complaints against solicitors. It must be said that the Law Society, for their part, have to investigate every case to ensure it's not a mischievous or malicious complaint against a practising member. But for those found guilty of malpractice, fraud and related matters, why not just call a spade a spade?

With all the recent publicity surrounding errant solicitors, with their multiple mortgages on various properties not necessarily their own or the misuse of clients' funds, the spotlight has been on rogue solicitors and the vulnerability of the public who are exposed to them. Believe me, this is not something new born out of the Celtic Tiger as, for many years I acted for the Law Society on cases where a solicitor had acted dishonestly or improperly in their dealings with clients' money, property, wills and other matters. Very few came to public attention. After all, they may well say that any publicity is good publicity, but not if it dents public confidence in the legal profession.

In bygone days, the Irish public held their clergy, doctors and solicitors in the same high esteem. That is not the case today, as these professions no longer have an automatic right to respect. The Law Society requires solicitors to carry indemnity insurance but, as seen in the recent high-profile cases, the fund is unlikely to be able to cover all claims made against it, such is the extent of the fraud perpetrated by the recent high-profile cases alone.

Many of my cases investigating solicitors over the years came from members of the public and corporate business as well as the Law Society themselves. The cases involved, in the main, solicitors who had run up debts and "dipped" into clients' accounts to pay their day-to-day expenses or to support their expensive lifestyles. Always intending to "catch up" and put the funds back, they usually ran out of time or just lost count of how much they'd spent on the good things in life. When clients came looking for their money from a property sale, a personal injuries award or other funds, the well had run dry.

Although solicitors are strictly monitored and required to hold current "practising certificates" and professional indemnity insurance, all too often by the time the fraud emerges, it is too late. The legal machinations operate at such a slow pace that the door is often closed after the horse has bolted – as in the Michael Lynn case. Solicitors are no different from other members of society and, like other professions, be they religious, medical or any other walk of life, there will always be a mix of good and bad. Rogues come in all shapes and sizes. They come from major cities and small rural towns. I've come across them everywhere. Not everyone is out to fleece you, but a policy of "Trust but Verify", while not a guarantee, helps. Often life is just too busy to check up on everyone and everything, but it might just save a lot of heartache and loss.

Take the Money and Run

One of the more "colourful" characters I dealt with on behalf of the Law Society – and indeed the criminal courts – was Elio Malocco. I had already had extensive dealings with the firm of Malocco and Killeen before Malocco's fall from grace, when he was caught embezzling funds from the Irish Press Group's legal fund to the tune of IR£70,000. I acted for them on behalf of their many clients, from general investigations, family law and media matters on behalf of the Irish Press, which was a lucrative client for Malocco. Malocco was on the board of the Irish Press Group, having married Eamon de Valera's granddaughter, Jane de Valera.

I investigated allegedly libellous articles for the defence and dealt with general investigations required by the group. In the early days, I found the practice of Malocco and Killeen to be very much on top of their brief. They gave clear, concise instructions, backed up with detailed paperwork, and appeared to do a great deal for their clients, which was down to the Killeen end of the partnership. They were efficient payers when it came to my fees. In the latter days, however, there was a noticeable change and payments from Malocco's cases were being chased by Audrey who was in charge of matters financial, who alerted me to the situation.

It rang an alarm and I decided to call on him to find out what was going on. This was before the rumours started about his circumstances, personal and otherwise. He seemed a little shaken by my visit and to "reassure" me, he handed me a sizeable cheque to cover his liabilities. It didn't bounce but, from then on, it was money up-front. I stopped undertaking work for him in late 1990. It wasn't long before things came to a head and the rest is, as they say, history – and so was he.

In September 1991 the Irish Press Group discovered that monies they'd given Malocco to pay off case settlements were never passed on. Armed with this information, the Irish Press's Financial Controller and their accountant confronted Malocco, who denied the allegation. To "prove" he'd made the payments, Malocco forged a "Discontinuance Notice" for a circuit court case he had claimed to have settled. He also forged Bank of Ireland receipts for varying amounts involving huge sums of money. It was a stupid move and one that was easy to track.

Malocco was charged with forty-nine offences and was convicted of larceny and fraud. He was sentenced to five years' imprisonment. Being the first high-profile solicitor convicted of fraud, he made history for all the wrong reasons and the Law Society paid out over €2.5 million in compensation. He served his time in an open prison. On release, he published a men's magazine, which went belly-up. Despite all his experience with libel cases for the Irish Press, he fell foul of the libel laws himself when nightclub owners took an action against him.

There were a couple of ongoing libel investigation cases he hadn't paid me for when the bubble burst, but another major law firm took the files and as my evidence was crucial to the subsequent court proceedings, they paid my fees.

Playing Cat and Mouse with the Cash

One solicitor who had been in practice for less than a year got himself into hot water. His first stupid offence was that he didn't take out a practising certificate, which immediately drew the attention of the Law Society. They visited his offices and checked his books to ensure his accounts were in order, particularly his client accounts, which are generally monies held on behalf of clients, either for the purchase of a property or proceeds from a sale or other sources and are not allowed to be used for any other purpose – often, they are the first to be plundered. In this case, the books weren't balancing and it seemed that the "client accounts" were regularly being "dipped into", with cheques being written to pay his daily living expenses. When the shortfall came to light, he refused to co-operate with the Law Society. But they don't go away that easily. It's a long and protracted exercise, which eventually leads them to seek a court order against the solicitor.

In this case, the man made several excuses and promised to rectify the situation, claiming two clients had agreed to give him a long-term loan to resolve his problem. This was another stalling tactic. These clients had made complaints that they too had been defrauded of considerable amounts of money. One client lived abroad and hadn't been told that the proceeds from the sale of his property had supposedly been "invested" without his knowledge or consent. Time and again he asked for his money and was told that this "investment" had been "rolled over" to ensure greater interest – one of the oldest scams in the world (as "Patricia" could vouch for – see Chapter 10). The only money "invested" had been into the solicitor's back pocket.

By the time the matter finally came to a head and the Law Society were in a position to have him "struck off" – no longer allowed to act as a solicitor – several years had passed and all the time the clients were still without their hard-earned cash.

The solicitors' compensation fund will eventually deal with such claims but, on personal experience, clients are rarely compensated in full in the monetary sense or in the years of hardship and time it takes to sort out a mess not of their own making. It is not unusual that, by the time such matters are sorted out, some elderly clients cheated out of their money have died and it is left to their families to fight their corner.

Friend or Fraud?

Another case involved a well-established solicitor, then practising in Ireland. He was struck off, leaving substantial sums of money owing to former clients. The Law Society attempted to have him adjudged a bankrupt but technical and practical difficulties arose, preventing them from doing so. The Law Society contacted me and asked me to track down the errant solicitor.

I eventually found him living in the lap of luxury in a fabulous mansion abroad. A check on the ownership of this property revealed that it had been bought in someone else's name. Not content with his life of luxury abroad, I found that he flew back to Ireland from time to time to indulge his passion for gambling on the gee-gees.

Quite apart from the Law Society's action against the man, I found out that there were other proceedings for fraud being taken against him by a former friend, in relation to a property held in trust on his behalf. The "fraud" emerged when the solicitor's "friend" decided to sell his substantial property but was informed that it was actually no longer his but was held "in trust" for the solicitor himself. It came as a complete shock to the former friend, who was forced to sue for the recovery of his property. Due to this and other matters fraudulently dealt with by his former solicitor friend, the man got into serious financial difficulty which took him years to resolve.

These stories are a mere drop in the proverbial ocean of errant solicitors – the figures for which have risen dramatically with the corresponding rise in the numbers qualifying.

25

Forensics and the Private Investigator

While forensics are seen everywhere today, particularly in television dramas such as *CSI Miami* and other crime shows, the use of forensics has long been commonplace within the criminal investigation agencies of the State, be they police departments, crime labs, military forensics or forensic pathologists. As a professional investigator, I provided forensic services for many years. I was the first to offer DNA testing in Ireland back in 1985 when it first became available and, of course, handwriting analysis and fingerprinting was in everyday use.

Handwriting analysis is widely used to determine the validity of documents from wills, cheques, letters and various documents in a commercial capacity, for banks, building societies and in court cases involving fraud, contract disputes and even impersonation. Over the years, we have examined everything from Valentine cards to marriage registers, from threatening or poison pen letters to forged wills, bank documents, contracts and receipts. As seen in the Malocco case, people have even attempted to forge government forms and documents, right down to the "official" stamps. Some of the cases were sinister, others sad – but all proved that forensics don't lie.

Deoxyribonucleic acid or DNA can be a vital tool in criminal investigation for murder, rape and other serious crimes. In civil cases, it is crucial in correctly identifying the biological parents in a paternity dispute or an inheritance issue. It can also be used to confirm the identity of children given up for adoption abroad. Although the biological parents may no longer be alive, where there are siblings or close relations, DNA can help to make the connection and give the adopted person some information about their parentage.

A lot of the investigations involve surveillance, de-bugging, forensic accounting and analysis, handwriting analysis and even fingerprinting and palm print re-examination for the defence. While I had resident experts in these areas, as a long-standing member of the UK-based Forensic Science Association, I also had access to international experts, with a broad base of disciplines and facilities – some of which were not then available in Ireland. The area of forensics is one that has always held a fascination for me.

Attending lectures, training and conferences at places like Strathclyde University in Scotland or other locations was not only a source of ongoing education in the area of forensic developments, it also afforded an opportunity to develop these contacts to the benefit of my clients. I recall one conference held in Dublin hosted by the Forensic Science Laboratory under the auspices of the Department of Justice in Garda HQ, Dublin. International forensic scientists had gathered from all over the world to hear experts speak about their areas of expertise. The title of the conference was "*Dead Men DO Tell Tales*".

One of the speakers was Dr John Harbison, the then state pathologist in Ireland and well know for his wit. I sat next to him at the dinner that evening as he regaled us with the story of how the best Dublin Bay prawns he had ever seen were in a body he had just done a post-mortem on. When the starter was served, lo and behold – it was Dublin Bay prawns. The kitchen staff couldn't figure out why so many of the starters were returned untouched – obviously by non-forensic scientists, or at least those not dealing in death. They didn't have the stomach for the starter, following Dr Harbison's vivid but funny description.

It's not unusual to find a black sense of humour in certain professions – soldiers, medics, private investigators, scene of crime investigators (SOCOs) and of course pathologists. They deal with some very tough and harrowing situations from time to time and the black humour is an outlet, with no disrespect intended.

One unusual case involving DNA was that of a client who sent me a package for examination. It contained her husband's underwear, which she wanted forensically examined. She had seen it on an American TV show, so she "knew" it could be done. She was certain her husband was having an affair. It was not the usual means of establishing an affair and it certainly wouldn't identify who the lady was, unless she could provide some additional samples from the lady in her sights. Nonetheless, she was adamant that she wanted it checked out. She said it was the only "proof" she needed. The lab are used to seeing all sorts of things, so it didn't phase them and they got on with the job. When the report arrived, it seemed that the lady was right on the money – but perhaps it wasn't quite the result she was expecting. There was definite evidence of semen on the clothes . . . but with two different DNAs, which indicated that the affair had been with another man. The lady was right, as the forensic maxim that "every contact leaves a trace" proved.

In the Nick of Time

A young man in his late twenties came to me with a sorry tale. He'd been brought up in a dysfunctional family where *he* became the "adult" while only a young teenager himself. His parents split up, with the father heading for sunnier climes and the "good life", leaving him in the "care" of their elderly grandmother, who was more in need of care herself.

After a few years, the father turned up with a new girlfriend and moved back into the little house they all shared. It wasn't long before the young man realised that his father had picked up some new "habits" while he was abroad. Over the next few years the teenager was left to deal with his father's drug habit, which went from bad to worse; he was unemployable and his health was deteriorating. His son watched over and worried about him, while all the time trying to do well at school, so that he could get out of the hell he was living through. More than once the father was hospitalised, only to go back to his old ways, while all the time the grandmother refused to believe anything bad about her only son – her blue-eyed boy could do no wrong.

Things came to a head when, one day, coming home from school, the teenager saw a man running from the house. As he rushed in, he found his father lying in bed, his arm, with the syringe still intact, dangling on the floor and the evidence, the tell-tale scorched tinfoil lying around. The boy thought he was dead and called an ambulance. All the while his grandmother told him to "leave your father alone, he's just sleeping" – a serious case of blind love. She was so angry at her grandson's suggestion that his father had overdosed on drugs, she threw him out of the house.

Contact with their mother had been erratic – she too had her own life but she agreed to take him in for a few days. Life wasn't much easier there, as she wasn't exactly the motherly type. In a heated row, she told her son that his "father" wasn't his father anyway. The young man was shocked on several fronts, realising that if what she said was true, he'd spent his life caring for a stranger. He wondered if his "real" father would have been any better.

Reluctantly, she gave him a name – a one-night stand, she said – but refused to tell him any other information. It was a name he'd known since his childhood, a "family friend". She had no proof, of course, only her word. He didn't know if his other "father" knew about it and he wasn't exactly a reliable source of information given his situation, but there were other factors that made it add up.

Years later, an article in the paper sent him my way. He was now a successful young man with qualifications and a good job, but his mother's words still gnawed away at him. He needed to know who his "real" father was. Was it the man he'd looked after or the family friend? Given his harrowing story, I agreed to help.

From information he recalled from his childhood, I had the man's name and his age group and where he'd lived at the time. Checking back, I found that the man had married when my client was three or four. It was in a relatively small community area and, in the hope that some family members were still living there, I made enquiries and came up with an address for the man. Living in the south-west of Ireland, he was happily married with his own business. His children were away at university. Their lives were everything that my client's wasn't.

I met with my client and told him that while I'd tracked down the man there was still nothing to prove his mother's allegations. He was anxious to know the truth but, unselfishly, he was adamant that he didn't want the man's family to know. He knew what things like this could do to a family; they were happy and he wanted it to stay that way.

It was a tough call, as DNA was the only real way to prove his mother's allegations. I called on the man away from his family environment. What did I have to lose? The worst he could do was deny it. To my surprise, he was a lovely guy. When I asked if he knew the client's "parents", he said he did but that he had lost touch with them years before. I told him the background to the case and asked him, straight out, if he could possibly be the father – expecting him to throw me out of his office. He was shocked but, to my surprise, he said, "That was all a long time ago. If my wife ever found out, she'd kill me."

It was all I needed to know. I told him my client had no intention of intruding on him or his family, nor was he looking for a share in the man's wealth. He was a decent young man who just needed to know the truth. If he knew he wasn't the son of a junkie, he could finally "let go" and stop feeling responsible for the "parent" he'd looked after since childhood.

The man was very understanding, saying he'd been adopted himself and always wondered who his real parents were but never had the courage to find out. I asked him if he was prepared to take a DNA test. Surprised, he thought about it for a few minutes before finally agreeing. Luckily, I had come equipped with a "test kit" just in case, and got to work before he changed his mind. I took saliva swabs and samples of hair roots. Usually six to eight samples from the head or eyebrows are best, as thicker hairs carry more DNA, but it's important to collect the full hair, including the "root", which carries the identifying cells, which can be compared to the "child". Within two weeks the results came back and there was no doubt about "Who's the Daddy".

The client was delighted – at last he knew he didn't have his "father's" genes, as he'd always been worried that the addiction was genetic.

It would be nice to say that they all lived happily ever after, but unfortunately that wasn't the case. One of the main reasons the businessman readily agreed to have the DNA test done was that he knew time was running out. Though outwardly appearing healthy, he had a terminal condition, with just weeks to live. My client never got to meet his father again – he died before the results came back. But he passed on the gift of a "new life" to the son he never knew.

26

The Silver Fox and the Antwerp Diamond Deal with a Beit

An American company, long-standing clients, contacted me about an internal problem with one of their European subsidiaries. Mr A, a former employee recently made redundant, got a phone call from someone offering him a job. It seemed like a bit of good luck, under the circumstances, but he didn't know the guy and wondered how he knew he'd lost his job. When he asked where he got his number, the man said he was told he was looking for work. He seemed to know a lot about Mr A, including the positions he'd held and how much he'd earned. No detail was too small for the caller to impart, as he added, "You must be pissed off with them for dumping you".

Something was up; he didn't know what, but he was suspicious and he didn't like it. He felt uncomfortable that a complete stranger knew so much about him. The caller said his name was "John Ryan". He asked Mr A to meet him in the Gresham Hotel in Dublin three days later. Mr A didn't turn up for the meeting, but he phoned the hotel and had "Ryan" paged. He told him he wasn't interested in the job offer. Ryan was annoyed, but went on to offer Mr A £1,000 expenses to travel with him to Brussels, saying he would introduce him to people who would offer him a very lucrative job. Mr A asked Ryan if he was some kind of recruitment agent and Ryan laughed, saying, "You could say that, I suppose." Ryan said he would personally guarantee the job, adding that it would carry "considerable bonuses of tens of thousands of dollars". It sounded too good to be true. All Mr A had to do was "operate the business from home". They would "supply a phone and fax machine and do the rest". What exactly "the rest" was, was not explained. Mr A said he'd think about it and Ryan gave him a phone number to contact him when he'd decided.

Instead, Mr A contacted his former employer, a multi-faceted world-wide company with a high level of security awareness. When he told them what had happened, they too smelt a rat, which is when I was called in. Ryan could only have known the detailed information if he had a mole in the organisation. The company operated a stringent security policy, one of the best I've seen in recent years, which made them all the more concerned. They wanted to find out what was going on.

Investigations established that Mr A wasn't the only one to have been approached, as a number of employees, all specialists in their field, had been systematically approached one by one by Ryan. It was obvious that whoever was behind the approaches had inside information but, despite their own internal checks, they were unable to find out who it was or why.

As part of my investigation, Mr A agreed to play ball and go along with things, feigning interest in the job offer if he was contacted again. Meanwhile, the contact number for Ryan was checked out and identified as an unlisted number, which we tracked down to a well-known criminal, Paul Ryan. Originally from the inner city, he was then living in a council estate on the northside of Dublin. Paul Ryan had a long list of convictions, from brothel-keeping to forgery and receiving stolen goods, which included a major haul of jewellery and diamonds. The gangster often used the name of his brother, John, another career criminal, and this time was no different. John Ryan was well known to the Gardaí but had committed suicide in Mountjoy Prison a short time earlier. Such was Paul (aka John) Ryan's notoriety that he changed his name by deed poll to Paul Christopher Murphy, but what he couldn't change was his well-known face (short of plastic surgery) and MO (modus operandi). If Ryan aka Murphy was involved, it was bound to be something serious.

While Mr A was away on family business, an unidentified man called to his house asking for him. Described as tall, middle-aged with white hair and a Dublin accent, he carried himself with a military stature and gave the impression of being an ex-policeman, saying he had a "full file" on all the men who had left the company in recent months. He left a message for Mr A, saying, "Some people are very anxious to meet up with him", and that he was to be at an address in Clontarf at ten o'clock the next day. He left a contact number for Mr A to call him.

Mrs A was worried and felt uneasy about the cloak-and-dagger situation. She contacted her husband, who told her to phone and say he couldn't make it. When she did, she recognised the voice as the man who'd called to her house. When she told him her husband wouldn't be there, he got very annoyed. She asked what exactly the job was and he said, "It's a hush-hush business, but I have to talk to him before Friday. I need him to fly to Brussels on Tuesday on the 7.30 a.m. flight but he'll be back that evening. I'm prepared to give him £1,000 into his hand to go to Brussels for the day. Explain that to him and I'll ring back." He refused to tell her what the job was, but said he needed a team of six. The contact number turned out to be one used by a Niall Mulvihill.

Mulvihill was described as a tall silver-haired man with a Dublin accent. On the surface, he matched the description of the caller to Mr A's house but it could have fitted a lot of people. Mulvihill was kept under surveillance and was videoed and photographed at various locations throughout Dublin. Mrs A readily identified Mulvihill from our photographs as the man who'd called to her house with the "job offer".

On the face of things, he had a number of legitimate business operations, including a pub in the Sheriff Street area, which had had an unfortunate fire, resulting in a large insurance pay-out. It wasn't Mulvihill's last unfortunate accident, as a fire also occurred at another of his business premises, but by the time the fire brigade were notified, it had burned to the ground. Luckily he was fully insured.

A striking man in appearance, he was agile and youthful-looking and carried his six-foot-three frame with a military-style gait. A smart dresser, with his distinguished looks and silver hair, he was known as the "Silver Fox" and looked every inch the successful businessman, he held directorships in several companies.

Regarded as "the big fish" in the gang, an armchair general who masterminded many of the operations, his business interests included a furniture business on the Dublin Road in Sutton – yet another premises hit by an unfortunate fire which destroyed the entire contents – a carpet company known as Executive Carpets Limited and a company called L&M Productions. Operating from the premises in Sutton, L&M Productions claimed to supply "facilities" to the "film and video" industry. The carpet business operated from a shop with a secluded rear access, which also housed a large windowless and padlocked "bunker" believed to be connected with L&M Productions.

Mulvihill's business interests and his extra-curricular activities allowed him to drive a top-of-the-range Mercedes and a Red BMW, despite the fact that he had several convictions under the Road Traffic Act and was driving on a false licence. He'd moved from a modest house in a working-class area to an exclusive property in Shrewsbury Park in Ballsbridge, moving in diverse social, business and political circles, being at one time George Colley's election agent. Investigations quickly established that many of his "friends" and "business associates" were well known to the police. His "Who's Who" friends and of associates in the criminal world included well-known criminals and paramilitary terrorists such as Michael Weldon and Tommy Savage, a former INLA member involved in international drug trafficking; the Hutch brothers, Derek, Eddie and, most famous of all, Gerry (the Monk) Hutch; and John (the Coach) Traynor, who was later to deny allegations that he "set up" Veronica Guerin for a hit. Traynor was a known associate of "The General", the late Martin Cahill, who was murdered in 1994, and Cahill himself was a well-known criminal associate of Mulvihill.

Meanwhile, another former employee was contacted by a third man, his phone number once again unlisted. It was traced to the home of a man employed by the client company as a cleaner and janitor. It was the first direct link to the clients. While he'd had no direct contact with any of the former employees, his job, which he'd held for several years, gave him "access all areas". It was the usual story.

The janitor was kept under twenty-four-hour surveillance, his every move watched over the following weeks. It wasn't long before he was seen meeting a number of well-known hardened and dangerous criminals, being frequently seen in their company during the surveillance operation, which moved through back street garages, pubs and private houses. He was regularly seen in the company of Terry Brazil, the Hutch gang led by Gerry "the Monk" Hutch, and others. Mulvihill associated with these and other known criminals, including Lonan Hickey, who was charged with the theft of £1.5 million, part of the Marino Mart heist. Hickey later travelled to Newry and lodged large amounts of cash into bank accounts in the Monk's name. The janitor also hung around with other well-known characters believed to be involved in both criminal and subversive activities. Some of the gang's associates, while having no convictions, were well known to gardaí and described as hardened and ruthless individuals, involved in the sale and distribution of drugs. They were believed to be the main suspects for shootings in Cork city and Ballymun in Dublin, but witnesses "declined" to give evidence, fearing for their own safety and that of their families.

Our surveillance paid off, as all were found to have associations with and led back to one man, Niall Mulvihill, the man who had called to Mr A's house with the offer of a "very lucrative job". Investigations showed that Mulvihill tried to transfer US$975,000 from his account in the Bank of Ireland's Holloway Road branch in London to his Bank of Ireland account in Baggot Street, Dublin, but his request was refused. At the time, I worked closely with the main banks in fraud and related areas and Pat Coyne, head of BOI security, was particularly sharp and advised against the transfer. It is understood that the money was believed to have been paid to Mulvihill by two brothers, part of a European crime syndicate he had been doing business with, who were already under investigation by CAB and the bank at the time.

The Irish criminals had been importing flawed or poor quality diamonds from abroad, flogging them as the real deal in Ireland and the UK to unsuspecting punters through a company they called Giltex Marketing Limited, a "company" that was never registered in the Companies Office either as a limited company or as a business name. They thought they'd found an easier source for their market – hence the cloak-and-dagger attempt to recruit new "staff". What they hadn't reckoned on was the fact that the people they approached were honest and honourable people who, despite their redundancy, remained loyal to their former employer.

Mulvihill was in the business of selling diamonds stolen from a Dublin business to these brothers. With the connection made, he later set up the major deal with the brothers to buy the Beit paintings, stolen by Martin (The General) Cahill in May 1986. The heist became the centre of major crime deals involving international criminals, loyalist paramilitaries, undercover cops – and, inadvertently, me.

Despite his best efforts, Cahill hadn't been able to get rid of all the paintings and Mulvihill persuaded him to give them to him, with the promise of a sale and a major financial gain for all concerned. As a gesture of goodwill, he gave Cahill around £200,000 as a down-payment, with a promise of much more when the deal was done. Cahill was confident Mulvihill would come through for him. Anything less and Mulvihill was a dead man and he knew it.

With no luck in moving the funds from the Bank of Ireland, Mulvihill attempted to open a TSB account, explaining that he needed to transfer large amounts of cash in relation to his business dealings abroad. He was, after all, a legitimate businessman, dealing in carpets, furniture and other goods. But this attempt also failed.

Following covert surveillance, we discovered that Mulvihill and two other men were due to travel to Antwerp – the diamond centre of Belgium – on the 7.30 a.m. flight which Mulvihill had mentioned to Mrs A. We decided to keep them company. The trip over was without any drama and the "boys" were not met by anyone. Instead they rented a car and drove away from the airport.

Following close on their heels, I grabbed a taxi and said the immortal words for the first time in my life – "Follow that cab!" The taxi driver came back with a quick retort and, in perfect English, said, "I've waited all my life for someone to say that to me!" With a grin, he took off after them like a bat out of hell. He needn't have hurried – he didn't have far to go, as Mulvihill and his buddies pulled in to a secluded spot not far from the airport. Mulvihill and his companions got out of the car and approached a man sitting in a parked car nearby. Obviously it was a pre-arranged meeting. The man got out of his car and opened the boot and the Irish guys seemed to be checking out something inside – what exactly was not clear from our position. What happened next was astonishing as Belgian police suddenly appeared and surrounded the men at gunpoint. They were arrested and taken into custody. Whatever was going on, our job was finished. No point keeping them under surveillance in a police cell!

Enquiries from contacts revealed that they'd been arrested in a planned "sting" operation. Garda HQ had had a tip-off and alerted Interpol and the Belgian police. What was being examined in the boot of the car were some of the proceeds of Martin Cahill's multi-million-pound robbery of the Beit art collection at Russborough House in Wicklow seven years previously; at the time it was said to be one of the most important art thefts since the Second World War. It later emerged that the three Irishmen and a Yugoslav were involved in a deal on missing paintings, including Vermeer's *Lady Writing a Letter with her Maid* and Goya's *Portrait of Doña Antonia Zarate*. Police also found six other paintings, two from the Russborough raid, three drawings by Picasso and a painting by Degas. All but four of the stolen paintings were eventually recovered in Britain, Belgium and, more recently, in Turkey in 2002.

The men were released on bail in November 1993, pending their trial. The Belgian court eventually ruled that as the masterpieces had been stolen in another legal jurisdiction, Ireland, the men could not be committed for trial in Belgium. After three months waiting for the case to be heard, they were free to go. The three amigos didn't hang around and flew back to Dublin that evening. The Public Prosecutor's Office in Antwerp were bitterly disappointed and said: "We tried hard to bring the case to trial." An appeal to overturn the ruling of the court was not proceeded with, as it was believed the issue of jurisdiction would stand.

Mulvihill resumed his relationship with his associates and continued developing his "business interests", but The General was gunning for him and openly accused Mulvihill of having ripped him off. An attempt was made on his life, which was attributed to Martin Cahill, but circumstances and a Provo hit man saved Mulvihill. The "hit" was still out it was just a matter of time before the "Silver Fox" met his maker, but Cahill got there before him, being assassinated himself just months later.

Mulvihill continued to run the rackets and launder money. Like many of his associates, he applied for and got a taxi licence, touting for business around town – although what kind of business is another story, as by then he was associated with every major gangland figure. The Silver Fox was back in the big time, moving large amounts of money into bank accounts in the UK. CAB were right behind him. Mulvihill was slapped with a tax demand for around €1 million from the proceeds of crime and was being actively pursued to hand over the cash when he ran into another turn of bad luck.

On the night of 23 January 2003, he arranged to meet his associates at Spencer Dock Bridge in the docklands area, close to the International Financial Services Centre. Before he could get out of his car, he was shot five times at close range. Despite his wounds, the major deal-maker drove away from the scene and headed towards the Mater Hospital, on Dublin's Northside. Driving along Dorset Street, he was losing blood fast. Unable to remain conscious, he crashed into several cars before finally coming to a halt. He was found, slumped over the wheel, dead. The Silver Fox had finally been caught.

His execution was a major hit and caused panic in gangland circles. Fifty-seven-year-old Mulvihill was considered the mastermind behind many of the big deals and was an international fixer, setting up transactions to dispose of hot property and import other currencies, not always money. Speculation was rife amongst the crime lords and the police as to who had ordered the hit. There were several potential suspects, including a former commander of the IRA in Dublin who'd been removed from his position weeks previously, when his Provo bosses discovered he was skimming money from their multi-million-pound rackets.

The criminal world reckoned the hit had been ordered by a gangland boss who'd been involved in several deals with Mulvihill over the years. This notorious criminal, well known to police both in Ireland and abroad, was suspected of being one of Martin Cahill's accomplices in the Beit art robbery. He was also known to have had extensive dealings with Mulvihill, including a 1993 deal designed to swap the Beit paintings stolen by Martin Cahill and his gang for a consignment of drugs. Mulvihill set up the deal and got £500,000 sterling from Belgian criminals, as a down-payment on the deal – which is where I came in. He tried to move part of these monies to the Bank of Ireland before his efforts were stymied.

They say crime doesn't pay – but with the high stakes involved, there are many who think they can beat the odds, getting fabulously wealthy along the way. But at what price? Mulvihill died in a hail of bullets. Even his lieutenant, Paul Ryan, who called himself John Ryan, came to a sticky end – shot in the back of the head and dumped at the side of a country road – while his brother John committed suicide.

The rest, if not already dead, are on the run – always watching their backs. If it's not the cops, it's their former associates or harder criminals they've double-crossed. A big price to pay, whichever way you cut it.

27

Truth Will Out!

Over the years, I have dealt with numerous cases of people looking for their biological mother or father. Whether they had been adopted into good or bad families, or had spent their lives in orphanages or children's homes . . . it doesn't really matter – at the end of the day, they all want to know the same thing: *Who am I?*

On rarer occasions I have been contacted by a parent – a mother, father or sometimes both – wanting to find the child they had given away years before. Guilt-ridden, they have never forgotten their first-born and in these changing times want to make amends for situations and circumstances that did not allow them to keep their baby.

These cases are the true stories behind what might have been. They are a mixture of sadness, happiness and wonder, when adult children finally meet their birth mother or find they have a family they never knew of. The need to know who you are is universal. Speaking to investigators world-wide, they all report the same thing. Perhaps here in Ireland it is even more prevalent, given the religious domination of past years. Having a child outside wedlock was seen as shameful and the church was anxious to lock the mothers, and even the children, behind doors closed to the outside world, in places like the Magdalene Laundries, where religious held unmarried mothers virtual prisoners and treated them as unpaid slaves, working in the kitchens or the laundry. Many of these girls were forced to hand over their babies and regretted it in later years.

Never a month went by without our getting four or five cases of adopted children looking for their biological mothers. Cases came from Ireland, the UK, Australia and America, from children brought up in orphanages or placed into "good Catholic homes" by the clergy. Sometimes the mothers had gone to England and elsewhere to have their children, seeking the comfort of the anonymity of a foreign country. Leaving the children behind, they returned to Ireland and resumed their "normal" lives. "Private" adoptions were not unknown, as a family would arrange for their daughter's child to go to a "good home" – preferably outside of Ireland, where it was hoped the child wouldn't show up in later years to "embarrass" the family. For some reason we got a few of these from Malta.

In all the years, I only once came across an adopted child who didn't want to know who his biological mother was and that was a friend of mine, for whom the task would have been easy and free. Even when he got married and had to get his papers for the priest, he had an opportunity of finding out and turned it down – without any explanation. I suppose he had his reasons but if he ever changes his mind, it may be too late.

Some were lucky, brought up by kind, loving adoptive parents – yet they longed to knew "who" they really were.

When a parent and child were happily reunited, it was a wonderful sight as the years rolled away and they tried to make up for lost time. There is a great sense of satisfaction when a family is successfully reunited.

There is not always a happy ending. Sometimes the child has waited too long, left it too late, and the person they so wanted to get to know is dead.

For some, finding their parent was a doubly unhappy experience – adopted into cold or indifferent families who took a child "for appearances' sake" or to secure the relationship, leaving everyone involved miserable. And whether their adoptive family were loving or not, for some, finding their mother was not the "holy grail" they'd believed it would be and the void remained. For example, there was the occasional case where a mother was traced on behalf of an adult child but didn't want to know. For various reasons, she would have virtually eradicated the event from her mind. Sometimes she had married and had a family who knew nothing of her past. Even then, after all those years, she was ashamed and couldn't bring herself to do it.

On some occasions, they just appeared to be heartless women, some having had more than one child adopted, then rejecting their "child" for a second time when we eventually located them. They appeared to have no interest in knowing what kind of life their child had or have any desire to get to know them. Some would even refuse to tell them anything about their background, their father's name or even the smallest detail that would mean so much to the "child", now an adult. For many, the second rejection is often harder to take than the first.

There was little I could do about the outcome. I'd done my job in finding them; the rest was up to them.

Lost and Found

One case in particular sticks in my mind. John was in his early forties and had been adopted in America through a Catholic agency in Ireland. His mother had given him up for adoption when he was just two weeks old. She'd had a long-term boyfriend and her family knew about her pregnancy, but they didn't want anything to do with her, saying she had brought shame on the family.

John was one of the lucky ones. He was happy with his adoptive parents, he did very well in life and wanted for nothing, being loved and adored by his American family, who were very open and honest with him. From the beginning, they had told him that he had been adopted from Ireland. He was a very happy, well-adjusted man – except for one thing. All his life he'd wanted to know who his real parents were.

Not wanting to hurt his adoptive parents, whom he loved very much, he waited until after their deaths before he set out on his quest. He contacted me from New York and, with the few details he had, I set the investigation in train. It seemed that the wealthy but childless American family had had everything they could wish for but a child. They were a good Catholic family and were generous donors to the church. Their local parish priest knew of their longing for a child and offered to help. So it was that a baby boy given up for adoption by an eighteen-year-old Tipperary girl was shipped to America and a new life – just another export.

After several weeks, I managed to track down John's mother, who had long since married and had a large family of ten children. On John's instructions, no direct approach was made to his mother, as he wanted to come to Ireland to visit her. He was anxious to see for himself how his mother lived – what were her circumstances, was she poor or happy, how had her life been? He had *so* many questions.

When the day arrived, I met John at Dublin Airport and we travelled to the area where his mother lived with her husband and large family. Making sure her husband wasn't home, John knocked on the door and, rather hesitantly, he introduced himself, unsure of the welcome he might receive. The woman, who was alone in the house, was obviously very shocked, but she asked us in and mother and son spoke for a while about the circumstances surrounding his adoption. She never knew who had adopted him or that he had been sent to America and it seemed that she hadn't made any effort to find out. She asked lots of questions about his life, his adoptive family and whether they had any other children. He told her he'd been an only child.

He wanted to ask her about his father, whom he presumed to be long gone from her life. Although he was longing to ask, he felt he should wait a while, in case he embarrassed her or frightened her off. She'd probably never told her husband she'd had a baby and given him up for adoption. He understood how delicate and difficult her situation was and decided to leave the questions about his father for now. That part of his life could wait a little while longer, now that he'd found his birth mother. She told him more about her life and her large family and when John said he'd like to meet them sometime, to his surprise, she seemed pleased and said she'd get them together and he could meet them all.

At this point, the woman's husband returned from working on the family farm, and she introduced John to him, saying, "This is my husband." His mother didn't seem embarrassed or uneasy as to what her husband's reaction might be – perhaps he already knew about her past, John thought, as he later told me. He wasn't ready for what came next, as his mother added, "John, this is your father."

The young man was speechless. The woman casually went on to tell him that they had married shortly after John had been adopted, much to her parents' disapproval. They'd moved to another part of the country to get away from the small-town gossip and had settled down in their new home.

They admitted they'd made no attempt to find John or to try to get him back. Within a year, they'd had another child – a replacement for the baby boy they'd given away. Shockingly, they'd called *him* John too. They never told anyone about their first child. They simply wiped him from their memory. They thought it was "for the best", they said. They got on with their lives.

John was speechless; he couldn't believe what he was hearing. All he kept asking was, why? "Why, when you got married, could you not have tried to find me?" They made no attempt to offer an explanation. They just sat there, looking at him, saying nothing.

Shocked to his core, John walked out and went back to his hotel without ever looking back. Two days later, he contacted his brothers and sisters and invited them to join him in a meal at his hotel. His parents were not invited. The siblings got to know a little about each other's lives and they told him what it was like to have grown up in such a large family. They too were shocked when they found out they had another, older brother. In all the years, there had never even been a mention of him, not even a pretence that they had "lost" a child. It was as if he had never existed.

John loved meeting his "new" brothers and sisters and he was surprised at how much he resembled them. He wondered what life would have been like growing up with them. He was wealthy, his adoptive parents adored him and he wanted for nothing, but he had always longed to be part of a big family.

To find out that he could have been was almost too much to take.

They parted company that night, with promises to stay in touch and to visit him in New York. Before he left, he gave each and every one of them a cheque for £10,000, to do with as they pleased. To his parents, he gave nothing.

I don't know if the family did stay in touch. All I know is that John told me he would never again have anything to do with his natural parents. He couldn't accept that they'd made no effort to find him after they had married. He, on the other hand, had spent half his life looking for them. When he finally found them, he wished he'd never bothered.

Closer to Home Than You Think

I recall another case, this time of a professional couple who gave away their baby for adoption. They were students at the time but had later married and had a large family. Their children had grown up and they decided they wanted to find their first-born, a little girl. The child's siblings were in the medical profession, as were the parents. I don't know if the parents ever told their other children they had an older sister, but the parents were anxious to know that their first-born had had a good home and a college education.

It turned out that their daughter had been adopted by a prominent Irish political family. She was one of several children and she had been loved and well looked-after by this closely knit family and had been to college. She appeared well adjusted and happy. I don't know if they told her she had been adopted, but I imagine they did. I never found out if her biological family made contact with her or merely kept an eye on her progress from afar.

28

Has Anyone Seen my Missing Jumbo?

I was in regular contact with major legal firms on behalf of clients, so we got to know each other quite well. Sometimes they'd shoot the breeze or have a bit of crack on the phone before getting down to business. So when I got a call one day from a lawyer whose opening words were, "I want you to find a missing Jumbo," I laughed and replied, "No problem! Now what do you really want?" The caller said, "I'm not joking. We really *do* need you to find a plane – in fact, two planes." He went on to say that they were looking for a Jumbo Jet – a Boeing 747 – and a Boeing 737 aircraft, both of which had been leased to a company that had gone bust and the company appeared to have no assets.

With very little information available, where do you begin to look for a "missing" plane, especially a Boeing, used by virtually every airline in the world? The client had no information on the original registration of the aircraft, which, like car registrations, can help in locating the current owner or operator. The difference with an aircraft is that, when they are sold to owners in different countries, they can be re-registered. The client's top priority was to find the aircraft, who was operating them and whether their new "owner" had mortgaged them.

As Mrs Beeton almost said, "First, catch your Jumbo." The start of the search was anything but exciting. It involved hours of painstaking investigation just to establish which airlines operated 737s and 747s, what routes they flew and where their bases were. Many large airlines have numerous bases around the world. I had to find out who had leased Boeing aircraft to airlines or organisations and whether they had "wet- or dry-leased" (in other words, with or without crew and services) their own aircraft during their slack season, as often happens. It was torturous and complicated, a slow but crucial part of the investigation before the real hunt could move on. I had to find the haystack before I could even begin to look for the needle.

Can you imagine being asked to find a Mercedes or a Honda car, "somewhere in the world" knowing nothing more than the fact that it was a Mercedes 250 or a Honda Civic, especially before the internet was available? But if it was easy, they wouldn't have needed me. The first job was to establish how many Jumbos and 737s had been manufactured by Boeing, from the time the Jumbo first went into production, and their serial numbers. Boeing had already produced more than a thousand Jumbos alone. I eliminated the ones registered to airlines known as "primary users" such as Cathay Pacific, Korean Air, Japan Airlines and British Airways, as most of these airlines' fleets were made up of Boeing aircraft. Having ruled out these possibilities, the trail moved to smaller airlines, including Aer Lingus, Delta, American Airlines and others, which were also ruled out, significantly reducing the possibilities.

Commercial aircraft are subject to stringent rules and regulations, both by the Aviation Authority in their country of operation and under the strict maintenance requirements as stipulated by the manufacturer. Without compliance in these crucial areas, an aircraft will not get a "C of A" (Certificate of Airworthiness) or insurance cover, two essential documents without which they can't operate for "hire and reward" – in other words, they can't fly fare-paying passengers. The hunt therefore moved to find out which maintenance companies were licensed to service 737s and 747s. Having eliminated dozens of possibilities from America to Australia and virtually all places in between, the trail moved closer to home when I found a company in Stansted, but they had no record of having worked on any aircraft fitting the bill. Meantime, as the trawl through aircraft serial numbers went on – mind-numbing but important work – I was becoming a fully fledged member of the "anorak club". Better than train-spotting, I suppose!

Finally, the breakthrough came. I found two aircraft operated by a small West African airline that seemed to fit the bill. They had a 737 and a Jumbo operating to various African destinations, with one or two longer-haul flights. With no PIs in the country it was a long way to go on a hunch. The nearest WAD agent was in Lagos, Nigeria, almost 2,000 kilometres away. Efforts to make enquiries there met with the response that they had no records "available" in relation to either aircraft and were not willing to help.

I tracked back the serial numbers, which confirmed that the 737 was based in the country but there was no trace of the government-owned company having a Jumbo. It wasn't listed with the Civil Aviation Authority or the International Flight Register. ICAO, the International Civil Aviation

Organisation, issues a flight number to every aircraft – much like the flight number you would see on a boarding card. This flight number is used to track the aircraft's path as it flies over various countries and a bill is then sent to the holder of the flight number, to cover the costs of the air traffic control services in each country the plane flies over. Checks on this still failed to identify the aircraft.

Another line of investigation was through international aviation insurers and I found that the 737 was insured by a London-based company. Now at least I had the aircraft registration, proving it was registered to the government-owned African airline. I still needed to know who did the servicing, as it would have been virtually impossible to track and recover the aircraft while it was flying within Africa – we would have had to get an internationally enforceable court order with the assistance of the local police force and provide pilots to fly it back to Ireland. Given local African politics, we knew we'd get no assistance there.

As sometimes happens, I got a lucky break when I discovered that the 737 aircraft had a maintenance contract with an Aer Lingus subsidiary at Dublin Airport. It was a matter of checking when their next compulsory maintenance was due and "snatching" them on foot of a court order. Incredibly, it turned out that both the 737 and the Jumbo were in Dublin at that very moment – but for how long? The trouble was, the maintenance was finished and they were getting ready to leave. I checked with Air Traffic Control and found that, up to then, no flight plans had been lodged for either aircraft, which would be compulsory for all aircraft.

As flight plans have to be "in" at least an hour before take-off, I reckoned we probably had a couple of hours, at best. I called the clients and they mobilised staff to enforce the court order, while I raced to find out more about the crew – who were they, where were they staying – any information to buy us more time. With the huge numbers of aircraft-leasing companies, flight crews and contractors world-wide, the crew could have been from anywhere, most likely local African pilots.

In just one of a series of incredible coincidences I found that the crew had been supplied by Parc Aviation, an Irish company, then part of Aer Lingus, which supplies crews and services to the industry world-wide. Parc, a highly respected international company, had of course no knowledge of any wrongdoing or legal difficulties surrounding the aircraft and acted at all times in good faith. It was now up to the lawyers to notify the various parties of the court order and to recover both aircraft for their clients.

My job was done. What had appeared to be the proverbial needle in a haystack that could have led us anywhere in the world had, ironically, ended up in my own back yard. Who could have predicted that?

The story caught the media imagination and BBC Northern Ireland made a documentary called *Has Anyone Seen My Jumbo?* Hence the title of this story!

29

A Case of the Bizarre

Something Fishy Going On!

One amusing case involved a large amount of expensive musical equipment which had been stolen. I was contacted by a musician friend on behalf of a company that had rented out expensive Bose equipment. They had leased a large amount of high-tech equipment to a band that had subsequently split up. No payments were made and the gear had gone missing. It had been reported to the police but, frankly, it wasn't a high priority for them, especially as there had been a legal agreement involved. It was really more of a commercial problem than a police matter. Normally, I didn't do those types of cases – bad debts or missing cats – but as a favour to a friend I agreed to help out.

Investigations into the background of the band indicated that their manager had a history of dodgy dealings. In this case he'd divided up the gear between "mates" who'd been asked to "mind it" for a while. The rest was sold to willing buyers. I managed to trace most of it to a rural spot in the west of Ireland and notified the local gardaí as to its whereabouts. It was probably the most exciting case they'd had for some time. They obligingly took it into protective custody and kept it in a cell in the small station until I could collect it. Case solved – but there was a twist.

Accompanied by my musician friend, who came along to identify the goodies, I headed to the west. We were warmly greeted by the local garda sergeant, who "entertained" us to a wonderful spread of afternoon tea at his house. Having been royally treated, we "accompanied him to the station" to "release" the stolen gear and thanked him for his assistance. He helped us pack up my car with our booty and insisted on sending us on our way with a "gift" of several confiscated salmon, which he'd recovered from local poachers caught fishing out of season. The salmon had been "doing time" in the sergeant's freezer. To wash down the salmon, he handed me a Lucozade bottle full of poitín, which he'd confiscated from some hardened criminals. The bottle was still intact, with the Garda seizure evidence label, giving details of the name address and car registration of the culprits, together with the case number and court date.

As we drove back to Dublin, laughing, I wondered aloud to my friend how the hell I would explain my "cargo" if I was stopped at a Garda checkpoint! Between the stolen musical gear, the illegal salmon and poitín that still had a Garda seizure label on it, they'd never believe my story.

I still remember that garda sergeant's wonderful welcome, the tea, sandwiches and cream cakes he produced for us, and the "gifts" of illegal hooch and stolen fish. Now that's what I call local policing! I still have that bottle of poitín, untouched, for posterity.

The Spy Who Came In from the Cold

During the 1990s I commissioned a high-tech surveillance van, which to all intents and purposes looked like an average delivery van. This, however, wasn't an average van; inside it were concealed cameras and video equipment that could film remotely from virtually anywhere. It had highly sensitive microphones to pick up conversations and was equipped with telephones, fax and computer equipment, as well as full office facilities and a refreshment station. A bank of CCTV cameras could be trained on any target and everything was automatically recorded, to be produced later as evidence in court. The van could be left parked or driven around, communication with the driver being by way of internal intercom, directing them wherever was required.

When I subsequently left the business, I no longer needed such a high-tech vehicle. Being busy, I stored it at a friend's business premises, with the intention of doing something about it. By then the tax and insurance had expired but, as it wasn't in use and not on a public road, there was no problem – that is, until recently. A guy known as Pete the Yank – an American pilot who worked for a company based there asked if he could borrow a van. No problem, he was told, so he went to pick out a van. Being a trucking yard, there were many to choose from. Unknown to me, he picked my van, which was automatically covered by the business's insurance and carried yard plates but, as I said, had no road tax. Without looking in the back, he took the van. Driving back to his place in the freezing cold to pick up his things, he was stopped at a routine police checkpoint. They noticed the lack of a tax or insurance disc on the windscreen and asked him for his identification and driving licence. The only ID he had on him at the time was a Samoan driving licence.

They asked him to step out of the van and open it up. To their surprise and his horror, they found the artillery of surveillance equipment on board. They asked him if he was CIA; with his American accent and driving a covert surveillance vehicle, you can see why – although they surely didn't expect him to admit it, if he had been! Still in a state of shock, he tried to explain that he knew nothing about it. He was promptly arrested and taken to the police station. He was held for questioning until the early hours of the morning before being released without charge.

At the time of writing, I haven't heard what happened to my van – maybe the cops kept it for on-the-job training! For his part, Pete left Ireland and headed to the safety of somewhere nice and quiet like Guam. But at least he'll have a story to tell his grandchildren about his time as a CIA agent in Ireland!

The Wild West

Not all PI cases are serious; sometimes you can get a laugh from the most unexpected of quarters. I got a case involving a relatively straightforward insurance claim. The only problem was that it was situated in a remote village in the west of Ireland. When I got there, it was like something out of *The Quiet Man*, with small cottages and piles of turf everywhere. It was one of those places where everyone knew everyone else's business – not exactly somewhere you could maintain a surveillance operation. The village population – about twenty people – stopped and stared as I arrived in town, like a lone gunslinger looking for trouble.

It was a weird feeling and I felt I was stepping back in time. I'd been given the name of the man making the claim and the address of the village – nothing else. I soon found out why. The cottages had no numbers and virtually the whole village were related to each other. Most had the same surname. With no clue as to who was who, it wasn't going to be easy to pin down the right man without drawing even more attention, if that was possible.

I needn't have worried. In one of those quirky incidents, before I got a chance to work out how to tackle the problem, I was approached by an elderly woman who invited me into her home. I couldn't believe my luck. Perhaps she just wanted to be friendly or wanted company, in what must have been a claustrophobic environment. It was a chance to make conversation and find out more about the place.

It didn't quite work out that way, as I found out why she was so friendly and hospitable to me. Having made tea, she produced a selection of home-made cakes, insisting I "eat up", saying I was far too thin. She began talking about her family and showed me photos going back years. Eventually she showed me a coloured photo, sent to her from America, as she pointed out her distant relations in New York. She had never met them, but claimed she "knew me" straight away the minute she saw me. I was, she said, the image of "Katie", with my red hair.

I hated to disillusion the old lady, especially when she insisted on taking me to meet my "other relations" – one of whom was the man at the centre of the accident claim. We all had our photos taken together in front of the stacks of turf and I spent the rest of the day in the village – about the only place in Ireland without either a pub or a shop – getting to know "my relations".

Thankfully, the claimant *was* genuine. After the warm welcome and wonderful hospitality, it would have been unfortunate if he'd been a fraud. In fact, that day, I was the fraud – though it wasn't planned that way. I wonder if they ever sent on those photos to the "family" in America and, if so, what their reaction was to their new-found family member. At least it gave them something to talk about for a while!

Riding High

While working as an apprentice in my father's business, a staff member, "Andy", a uniformed security guard, expressed an interest in becoming a private investigator. He was a sharp guy, very good at his job, and he seemed to have the aptitude for PI work, so my Dad agreed to give him a shot. For several weeks he was teamed up with an experienced investigator who knew his stuff. Reports were good and it looked like the guy had the makings of a PI.

Finally, after a few months, Andy was given a chance to go "solo" on a very easy job – following a delivery van and checking its drop-off points. An experienced motorcyclist, he tailed the van on a motorbike to ensure he wasn't caught up in city traffic. All he had to do was make a note of where and when the driver made a delivery. No photographs or specifics were required. It couldn't have been an easier introduction to his first "case".

Halfway through the morning, a red-faced Andy came back to the office. Asked how the job had gone, he sheepishly admitted, "Not too well." My father wondered what could possibly have gone wrong on such an simple job – did he lose him or have an accident?

Andy explained that, anxious to make a good impression, he was afraid he'd lose the guy, so he stuck close by – too close. When the van pulled up at the next stop, the driver got out and walked back in Andy's direction. Andy ignored him, pretending to be having trouble with his bike. The man stopped right beside him and said, "I'm going to Bray tomorrow if you want to bring your lunch." It was time to pack up and go home.

Andy was mortified, as we all laughed at his baptism of fire. It was just a case of over-enthusiasm. With experience, he'd have made a very good PI, but his confidence was sorely dented and he decided it was not for him. He stayed "within the law", however, joining the Department of Justice where he worked in the courts service.

Happy in His Work

Another funny incident, while not directly involving me, still makes me smile when I think of it now, many years later. While working on an investigation in the Arklow area, I was chatting to some gardaí I knew. They were "out in force", down from Dublin on a drug case. They had swooped on a local farm where 15,000 cannabis plants had been drying in the midday sun. At the time, it was not illegal to grow the plants but it was to harvest them and the gardaí had been waiting for the harvest before they could make their move.

It was a beautiful summer day and most of the gardaí were happy to be out in the countryside enjoying the weather. But there's always one. Known to be less than a happy camper at any time, this individual was even grumpier than usual, moaning about the task in hand. As the cannabis was gathered up, ready to burn, he was posted to keep the road clear of traffic and curious onlookers. Unfortunately, it just so happened that the post he was sent to man was downwind of the fire. The burning cannabis fumes wafted over him. By the time they had burnt out and his job was finished, he was mellow, delighted to be out in the countryside. He just couldn't understand why he hadn't realised it before. I suppose you could call it "on the job" training!

30

Lamb to the Slaughter: The Murder of Little Blue Eyes

I was asked to investigate the true background to the murder of Little Tommy H, which was to be the subject of a film called *Lamb*. Based on real events, the film was from a book of the same name by Bernard MacLaverty. I became involved when the filmmakers' insurance company contacted me, anxious to ensure that all the facts of the case were true for "Errors and Omissions" Insurance. That was how I came to investigate the murder of a little angel, eight-year-old Tommy H. Some details in the book differ in a number of areas, for various reasons. In the book, the child is called Owen Keegan and is older than Tommy. This is the real story.

Tommy, from Dublin's inner city, had a tough life from the moment he was born. Taken from his mother for "neglect", he was put into care at the age of four and sent to Madonna House, along with his two younger brothers. While he was there, a new member of staff was taken on in somewhat unusual circumstances. "Mr Z" called to Madonna House looking for a teaching job. They hadn't advertised for one, but nonetheless, he said he was "very interested in children" and was taken on by Sister Xavier who was in charge of Madonna House for over thirty years. Z, although only twenty-five, was a former member of the De La Salle Christian Brothers and Sister Xavier gave him a job as a "housefather" cum social worker at Madonna House. Staff recalled that Z was kind to all the children.

Shortly after Z's arrival at Madonna House, young Tommy was transferred to St Kyran's in Rathdrum, County Wicklow – away from his younger brothers. Completely distraught at leaving them, the only real family he'd known, he ran away from St Kyran's on a number of occasions. Z, who was described as a soft, caring young man, was particularly worried about little Tommy, who hadn't even been in his class.

After a while, he handed in his notice and left Madonna House, without giving his reasons. He sold his car for £2,000 at a local garage, taking a cheque by way of payment, and made his way to St Kyran's to visit young Tommy. During the visit, he abducted the child, although Tommy was apparently more than happy to go with him, having at one time asked Z to "adopt" him. They spent their first night in a Dublin hotel, booking in as father and son. By then, the police had been alerted and there was an APB (all points bulletin) our for any sightings of Tommy and Mr Z.

Gardaí gave details of Z's car registration number and asked for the public's assistance in finding the missing pair. A garage owner came forward, having recognised the car as one he'd bought from a man fitting Z's description days before. He had given him a cheque, which Z had already cashed.

With the hunt still on, Z, fearing they'd be picked up, took the ferry to England, where they stayed in small London hotels, moving every few days. He replaced Tommy's rags with new clothes and shoes, bought him toys and "fed him up" – his scrawny body was just skin and bone. They spent several days wandering around London sightseeing. Z let the child have some fun in toy shops, amusement arcades and the cinema and treated him to ice-cream and sweets – simple things young Tommy had never had and he was enjoying every minute of it.

But Z began to worry when he heard a news bulletin about a young Dublin boy who'd been "kidnapped". The description fitted them exactly – it was only a matter of time before they were caught, and Z was afraid young Tommy would be sent back to a life "in care". Having worked there, he knew what it was like and he wanted to save young Tommy from that existence.

His initial plan had been for them to run away and he would look after the child and bring him up as his own, to save him from a life in care. But at just twenty-five, he had little or no life experience outside of the Order and with the money running out, he didn't know what to do. Z wanted the best for the boy and, from investigations, there was no suggestion that he had ulterior motives. His situation was well described in a review of the book in the *Observer* newspaper, which praised Bernard MacLaverty, who had managed "to deal convincingly with innocence and the impossibility of innocence, without being falsely naïve". But it was true. Z was without an agenda, he had no designs on the child, he really just wanted him to have a better life.

Rather than let the authorities take young Tommy back to a life in care and all that went with it, Z came up with a drastic solution. He took the child out for one last day of fun and enjoyment, before taking him back to their hotel. He mixed some sleeping tablets into his food and then ran a hot bath for the little boy. When the child became drowsy, he pushed the sleepy child beneath the warm bath water and, in an act of desperation, drowned him. He apparently saw it as the only way of "saving" the lad from a life of certain misery. He dried the dead child, dressed him into his pyjamas, put him to bed, sitting with him all night, holding his hand, praying there really was a heaven.

When I investigated the full background to this true story, I understood just how bad little Tommy's life had really been. Tommy's mother Catherine had married young. By the time she was twenty-three, she was pregnant with her third child. Three weeks after the birth, her husband died of cancer. Unable to look after the children on her widow's pension and the children's allowance, Catherine went "out to work". Neighbours in the close-knit community were worried about the children, concerned how Catherine was making a living. It wasn't long before all three children were taken into care as allegations of neglect and cruelty abounded.

Catherine maintained that she had handed over her children as she was homeless and destitute. The children were sent to Madonna House in Blackrock, Dublin – later to become well known for all the wrong reasons, as investigations revealed details of the horrific cruelty meted out by some of the staff to the very children they were supposed to be protecting. Madonna House was run by the Sisters of Mercy, who were paid on a per capita basis for each child by the Health Board.

Within a year, Tommy's mother Catherine had another baby, this time a girl, and her then boyfriend was believed to be the father. At the time Tommy went missing from St

Kyran's, his mother Catherine was expecting twins and was squatting with her boyfriend and her two-year-old daughter in a derelict flat due for demolition, in Gardiner Street in Dublin's inner city. They had refused to leave and had been served with an eviction notice by Dublin Corporation. Her little girl was later also taken into care, while Catherine went on to have four more children, three boys and another girl. These children remained with their mother and her partner, who was believed to be the children's father.

During the course of the investigation, I tracked them down to their council house on the north side of Dublin and called to see them. The house was in a very run-down area and was in an appalling condition, far worse than any of the neighbouring houses. I was shocked at the conditions they were living in – apparently of their own making. All the floors were bare, the rooms had dirty rags for curtains and the living-room furniture was comprised of a scruffy, broken two-seater couch, a dilapidated chair and a child's cot. The kitchen, if you could call it that, resembled something out of another era, with a filthy trough-like sink, no presses, a small breakfast ring-cooker, bed-sit style, and nothing else. No fridge, table, chairs, nor even food of any description. The three bedrooms were no better. The main bedroom had a double bed, two single beds and a cot, while the second bedroom had two single beds, and the third room had just a single bed, all dirty and worn and with little or no bedclothes. There was evidence of the remains of heavy drinking sessions, with beer cans and cigarette butts strewn everywhere; the stench of stale beer and cigarettes hung like a pall over everything. With the exception of one small wardrobe, there were no other furnishings in the house, which was more like a "squat" than a home.

At that time the family were living on the partner's unemployment benefit of £89, the single man's allowance at the time, and Catherine had the princely sum of £36 children's allowance, as she was still repaying the Department of Social Welfare for monies "overpaid" some time previously. It was the equivalent of less than €200 to feed, clothe and provide for six people – but from what I saw, most of this "budget" went on drink. Catherine's family, her mother and a sister lived close by and helped her out with food for the kids, although their own circumstances were not good. When I spoke to Catherine's mother, she said her daughter's partner was a heavy drinker and was often found lying drunk in the street or the garden. Of her daughter, she said, "She had a choice of staying with him or keeping her children; she chose him."

It was into this environment that the poor blue-eyed blond little boy, Tommy, and his siblings were born. Better off in care, you might think, but obviously not in those days – which is apparently what Mr Z, who had witnessed it at first hand, had thought, whether his actions were right or wrong. Tommy and his two brothers had been taken into care because of neglect. His neglect at the hands of the State and his "carers" in Madonna House and St Kyran's went unheeded. The little boy ended up dead.

31

United Nations, Divided Love: The Thai Hooker and the Diplomat

One intriguing case which crossed international borders started out as a simple "domestic" investigation. A prominent employee of the United Nations, based in New York, contacted me with a little problem. While on a business trip to Germany, he met a former colleague who was based in Frankfurt and they had dinner together. The man invited him to a party his wife was holding at their penthouse apartment. Though not much of a socialiser, he decided to go – it was better than hanging around a hotel room on his own.

By the time he arrived, the party was already in full swing, with champagne and beautiful people everywhere. He'd never met his colleague's wife before but she was very attentive and introduced him to everyone, making him feel at ease. During the course of the evening, he met a young Thai woman who said she worked with his colleague's wife. They talked the night away and, despite his lack of sophistication in women's company, he felt completely comfortable with her. After the party, he headed back to his hotel alone and flew back to New York but he couldn't get her out of his head and a month later, he went back to Frankfurt and looked up his friend, who invited him back to his apartment.

His colleague led an active social life and hosted monthly parties at his home. My client was delighted to see his Thai "friend" at the party and they resumed their conversation where they'd left off. This time, he didn't return alone to his hotel and over the following days they became very close. When he went back to New York, he kept in contact with her and visited her whenever he got the chance.

In his own words, he "became besotted with her". Over the following weeks he visited Frankfurt as often as possible. On one occasion, wanting to surprise her, he arrived unexpectedly at her apartment but found she was not home. A neighbour told him she was at work and gave him the address. He called there, only to find it was a nightclub and that the girl was, in fact, a hostess there. She explained she was working two jobs – her secretarial position by day and the club at night. She said she had been too embarrassed to tell him, because of his high position, saying she had a daughter back in Thailand and was working to send money back for her upbringing. By now he was, according to himself, "hopelessly in love" with her and overlooked her omission.

A few weeks later, she said she had to go to Thailand to see her daughter and her elderly parents who were looking after the girl. He offered to go with her but she refused, saying it would bring shame on her parents if the villagers knew she was with a white man. He gave her money for the child and paid for her flight, anxious to have her back as soon as possible. A month later, he met her at the airport on her return.

Things were going really well between them and he regularly gave her money to send home for her child. A few months later, she again said she had to return home. He insisted on going with her, but again she refused. This time he wasn't taking no for an answer. By then he had decided to marry her, though he hadn't asked her yet, and he wanted to meet her family, especially her little daughter. Reluctantly, she agreed to let him go with her but said he would have to stay in a hotel until she had spoken to her family and explained the situation. If everything went well, she would bring him to her father's village and introduce him to everyone. A few days after they arrived in Thailand, she went to her village alone, returning two or three days later. She said she had told her family about him and had arranged for him to meet them.

The next day, they set out on the long journey to her village, where he was introduced to her elderly parents. They had no English but they welcomed him, bowing and offering to share their food with him. There was no sign of her daughter. She explained that they had sent her to her aunt, as they wanted to meet him alone. The meeting went well, as he seemed to have been accepted by her father. The couple returned home, she to Frankfurt and he to his job in the UN.

They continued to see each other and they were making plans to marry when, for some inexplicable reason, he contacted me. He gave me the background to the situation and asked me to check things out for him. Obviously, something was bothering him. Perhaps he hadn't told me the whole story.

The investigation started in Frankfurt and was interesting, to say the least. The girl was in Germany illegally and had never worked as a secretary. She was a hooker and had worked in a number of clubs in Hamburg, Berlin and other cities, moving from place to place before arriving in Frankfurt, where she was recruited by a "society madam", the wife of the UN man's former colleague. The lady held regular parties for "clients" at which she provided a number of international high-class escorts – in other words, expensive call girls – who got a small percentage of her extortionate fee. He hadn't been charged, as it was usual to "hook" the men in with a few "freebies" first.

The "madam" provided anonymity and the front of a respectable soiree to high-flying diplomats, businessmen and politicians, who were secure in the knowledge that it was a strictly "private" party, as they weren't too keen to be found in a common brothel. Armed with this information, the investigation moved on to Thailand, where I enlisted the help of a Thai colleague from the World Association of Detectives, Sanong Ratanavichai. His investigators visited the remote village where my client had met his future "in-laws" and they spoke to the locals, who had no English, reporting back to me what had actually happened.

The Thai "girlfriend" had brought him to a poor and remote village, where she had introduced him to the local "elders" as a big foreign investor, who wanted to spend a lot of money in the area and give them work. Naturally, they were delighted to meet him and they made him most welcome. They had never met the woman before – she was from a different part of Thailand and they never saw or heard from her or the "foreign investor" again.

Investigations proved that she had no child, either in Thailand or elsewhere. She was a very successful prostitute who'd worked around Europe and amassed a small fortune. She returned to Thailand on a regular basis, buying up land. She had already built several hotels in various beach resorts.

She was making plans to build another hotel close to the village of her imaginary "parents". My client wasn't her only "boyfriend", as she particularly encouraged western businessmen of a certain calibre to "befriend" her. Inevitably, they all eventually unknowingly "invested" in her hotel plans, giving her money to send home to "support her family".

When I gave my client the report, he was genuinely upset – despite the fact that he obviously had his own suspicions. He confessed that he was married with a family but had believed he'd met the "love of his life" and was ready to give up everything for her. He was devastated to find out the extent of her duplicity. Just one more guy she'd caught in a "honey-trap". He left my office literally in tears. I doubt if he ever saw the Thai girl again or confronted her with what he now knew. I can only assume he returned to his wife and family, though he'd never actually left them and they weren't aware he was considering it. Hopefully, he realised he already had what he thought he was looking for, closer to home.

32

Private Eyes and Nosy Newshounds – What's the Difference?

After many years as a private investigator, I decided to change career and become a journalist. Having done a masters in journalism at DCU, I was lucky enough to be immediately employed, writing about everything from travel to legal matters, business stories, medical pieces and, of course, political issues – always high on the Irish agenda. It is very similar to private investigation, the difference being that now I can write openly about everything, including the political scandals, whereas as a PI, I often investigated these issues, politicians included, for international clients and only disclosed the outcome to the clients or in a court of law. Often, years later, I would read about these issues, such as the Traynor/Haughey/Ansbacher "revelations", one of the issues I was asked to investigate by an international organisation, years before the Tribunals were a twinkle in the government's eye. Everything comes full circle – eventually.

I suppose it was an obvious transition from private investigator to investigative journalist. The job, for the most part, is very similar. A journalist investigates a story, establishes the facts beyond doubt and writes it up. A private investigator takes on a case, investigates the problem, establishes the facts of the situation and writes a report, often followed up by a court case at which the evidence is presented in either the civil or criminal courts. The divide was very slim.

Having worked for numerous media organisations in radio, television and print journalism over the years, investigating stories they were working on, I was already familiar with investigative journalism. In some cases I would provide the background information for television investigative programmes and, on occasion, take part in the broadcast. Funnily, a lot of these media cases related to political figures, prostitutes, pariahs and paramilitary characters, where a newspaper would publish an article and later be threatened with legal action, which they then referred to their legal advisors. The lawyers in turn would pass the case on to me and ask for a detailed investigation into the matter, to enable them to rebut the complaint and prove that the original story was truthful, correct and justified, or at least fair comment.

Usually the journalist had already done a good job but perhaps had not dug deep enough to withstand a legal challenge, time not always being on their side. With tight deadlines, the story needs to get out there when it's hot before a rival publication gets the scoop. The problem is that when a case goes before a jury, human nature being involved, anything is possible. If the person claiming to have been libelled is a well-known or popular character, the results can sometimes be surprising, with substantial damages being awarded for what was "fair comment", resulting in an appeal by the media outlet.

Other cases can be awarded token damages, such as in the case taken by former Taoiseach Albert Reynolds, when he sued an English newspaper and was awarded damages of one penny – a pyrrhic victory, given the costs involved. More recently, a ground-breaking €900,000 in damages was awarded against the *Sunday World* to a convicted criminal and tax dodger for libel. The article had also referred to the man as a drug dealer and loan shark. The criterion is usually that the person's good name has been damaged by the article. In this case, while the jury found that although he *was* a tax dodger and a convicted criminal, he had not been convicted of drug dealing or money lending, and accordingly awarded him record damages. The paper appealed the decision and the award.

On occasion, therefore, a litigant has just cause for taking a libel case and, while the financial award will not necessarily restore their good name, at least justice is being seen to be done.

Smoking Gun: The One that Got Away

They say there is no smoke without fire, which brings to mind an incident I was personally involved in as a journalist, involving a fire and a hell of a lot of smoke – not to mention the late Liam Lawlor.

I called to Lawlor's house on the spur of the moment. I had written a piece about his involvement in an investment deal known as the Irish Consortium. Looking back at it now, it might read like an Irish version of a Len Deighton novel. The setting was Prague, which was then the brave new world of eastern promise after the fall of the iron curtain, and investment opportunities were rife. The characters included the usual cast: some very high-profile businessmen and a politician – Liam Lawlor. The plot, which spanned over six years, was still unfolding but was coming under the scrutiny of the Flood Tribunal. Lawlor had connections with the Czech Minister for Trade and Industry, who later resigned in a corruption scandal. Some Irish investors were "uncomfortable" when I started asking questions and "referred" me to others involved, which made me all the more curious.

During my investigations it emerged that, five years previously, one of the investors, Michael Kenny, a Dublin architect, had become "uncomfortable" about the scheme. He personally invested £50,000, but within months he began to worry when he discovered that such an office operated by the Irish Consortium already existed.

Kenny was so concerned about his investment that he contacted the Fraud Squad to report his fears. He told me that neither he nor other investors were aware of Lawlor's involvement in either the Irish Consortium or Longwater Investments and he said, "If I'd known Liam Lawlor was involved I'd never have put my money in, I can guarantee you that." His "investment" had been due to mature in 1998-99, but at the time I spoke to him in 2000, some six years after he'd made the 1994 investment, he still had not seen a penny.

Kenny discovered that the company he'd invested in had failed to file returns for five years and was dissolved, as were two other associated companies. Michael Kenny said that Liam Lawlor was a regular visitor, and named big builders and their PR people who were frequently seen together in the company boardroom.

It was time to pay Lawlor a visit. On the spur of the moment, on 16 January 2001, I called out to Lawlor unannounced, parking at the end of the long avenue outside his front door, intending to "doorstep" him. Despite repeated knocking, there was no answer. However, while I was standing there, I noticed smoke coming from the garden area at the front of the house, which was partly shielded by hedging. I walked towards the smoke and saw a man burning papers in an old metal drum. I didn't approach him, as I didn't want to alert him to my presence. Lawlor was the man I wanted to talk to, without giving him an opportunity to avoid me.

I walked around the back, to where there was a large building which Lawlor used as an office. To my amazement, there was a huge industrial skip, filled to the top with files and documents. It was getting ready to leave, as a couple of guys were standing on top flattening down the mountain of files. I immediately rang the newspaper I was working for and asked them to get a photographer out quickly. They said they'd call me back. When they did, they said they'd spoken to another journalist and the *Sunday World* to know if they had heard anything, as "they always have an ear to the ground". I was shocked on two fronts. I couldn't imagine why anyone would ring another paper, however well you knew the guys, to ask such a question, given the "scoop" that was under our noses. Secondly, why the hesitation?

Even if I was wrong (and I wasn't), they had nothing to lose. They called me back to say, "No, nothing happening. No photographer, come back to the office." I couldn't believe it. Here was the evidence the Tribunal and everyone else was looking for. I still regret not just following my instinct, regardless of what anyone had said, and sticking with it. Had I simply followed the truck to wherever they dumped that incriminating cargo, who knows what would have been uncovered?

If I was mad at myself then, I was even more so that Sunday, when I opened the *Sunday World*, which had front-page coverage of charred documents "found" in the vicinity of Lawlor's house, obviously from the remnants of the oil drum fire close to the front of the house. It was only half the story – if they had known what they'd missed. Lawlor accused the journalists of trespassing but, by that time, the wind had blown away the embers from the fire, which could be seen on the laneway at the back of his house.

I had always followed my instinct as a PI but as an "employee" I had followed instructions and lost a great story. I should have known better. I had enough experience to know when something was up. There's no substitute for experience and instinct and, by ignoring it, that story was the one that got away.

Cop On!

Before the Donegal garda corruption scandal became front-page news, I was sent by Harry McGee, then Editor of *Magill* magazine, to chase up rumours of "foul play" by the forces of the State. What I found shocked me to the core. While I had come across many cases of individual or small groups of corrupt gardaí during my time as a PI, I had never encountered a systematic onslaught of corrupt cops, who appeared to be operating a private fiefdom in parts of Donegal. However, during that first foray into incompetence and corruption, I met many serving and retired gardaí who had nothing but disdain for their corrupt colleagues. One former "member" told me that he would never cross the station door again, he was so disgusted at the openly known actions of some members.

The general public have become very familiar with the name McBrearty, but they were only one of several families targeted by these cops. The Gallaghers, a highly respected local family, were also targeted. Their home was raided by armed men and the family were held virtual hostages in their own home for three days and nights. The men sat in darkness, shining torches in the elderly couple's faces. It later emerged that these "armed men" were gardaí, who didn't identify themselves at first. The Gallaghers' house and farm was torn asunder, searched by a combined force of two hundred soldiers and forty gardaí, and helicopters supposedly looking for "a bomb factory". They uprooted hundreds of young trees and their pregnant ewes ran terrified into barbed wire, aborting their lambs. Alfie Gallagher, who was recovering from a heart by-pass operation, had a machine-gun stuck in his ribs. Nothing was found. It later emerged that the gardaí were acting on allegations made by a local informer, William Doherty, a well-known criminal with a long list of convictions for larceny, assault and using an offensive weapon. Doherty had done time in Mountjoy and the Gardaí's own "official" description of him is "of violent disposition".

When I first spoke to the Gallaghers they were very embarrassed, concerned that their neighbours would think them guilty. Annie Gallagher, a retired teacher, was very upset and reluctant to talk to me, ashamed of what had happened. She said, "My father was the local garda sergeant, we're law-abiding citizens. They treated us very badly on the word of a criminal."

When I broke the Gallagher story in *Magill* magazine, they realised they were not alone – others who had met with similar fates at the hands of certain Donegal gardaí contacted them in support. They thanked me for exposing the truth as they would never have had the courage to take it further, afraid of what else might happen. The State recently agreed a compensation settlement with the Gallaghers.

After investigating the McBrearty story, I managed to get hold of and published documentation that showed the goings-on in Donegal at the time. Some little-known aspects of the case added fuel to the fire of possible corruption. I discovered the case of Edward Moss, who came across the situation literally by accident. Moss, from Strabane, had gone to Frankie's nightclub in Raphoe, run by the McBreartys. Ejected from the club, he tripped on the way out and injured his ankle. He contacted a solicitor in Strabane and sued for damages, getting an out-of-court settlement of £10,000. There the matter apparently ended – that is, until the gardaí got wind of it.

They immediately contacted Moss and urged him to also press charges for assault against the McBreartys. He wasn't interested but they continued to call on him at work in Donegal, making life difficult for him with his boss. Moss claimed he was put under inordinate pressure to make a statement and eventually gave in, saying the McBreartys offered him £15,000 not to go to court. He refused to go to court to give evidence and claimed that the gardaí told him he'd never work in Donegal again if he didn't. His solicitor, John Fahy from Strabane, said he'd written to the gardaí putting them on notice that if they persisted in contacting Moss, he would take court proceedings to have them restrained.

Fahy, a partner in a large practice, told me he had stopped taking cases in the Donegal courts because of the difficulties he'd encountered. He said, "I found that some gardaí were intimidatory even towards me as an extension of the client. I accepted that situation prevailed in the North but I had expected more from the gardaí in the South. Unfortunately that is not the case. I'd rather take my chances in a Northern court."

During the course of my lengthy investigation, I wrote another article in *Magill* and published documents which included a letter marked "confidential" from the then Chief

Superintendent's Office in Letterkenny, entitled "*Re:* Campaign to discredit Gardaí in Donegal Division" which said that McBrearty was financing a campaign to discredit the force and all gardaí involved should be notified and report any incidents or unusual contact that may occur with McBrearty's extended family and other parties. In itself this was not unusual. What *was* "unusual" was that when the McBreartys' legal team applied for a copy of this document, on at least six occasions, gardaí denied on oath that it existed.

Superintendent Kevin Lennon, the author of the document, also denied its existence. I knew it did, because I had a copy and I published it. With the findings of the Tribunal, most if not all of the real story is emerging, but the consequences are that, at a time when the Gardaí need public support in fighting crime, the public trust in them has been severely dented. No-one suggests that all Gardaí are untrustworthy, but a major PR campaign is needed to restore them to the revered state they once enjoyed by honest citizens.

The Prostitute and the Paper

When a Sunday newspaper ran an expose on the sex industry in Ireland, it led to a complaint from a woman who claimed that she had been "named and shamed" in the article, which said that she was "on the game". Through her solicitors, the woman sought a retraction, an immediate apology and a substantial payment for her trauma as a result of the libel. If the newspaper didn't pay up a very substantial amount immediately, she threatened to take her case to the High Court. If she won, the paper would be at the mercy of the jury and it could turn out to be a virtual lotto win for the woman, not to mention the substantial legal costs they'd have to pay. Most journalists are very careful to check that their facts are correct before printing such allegations and newspaper lawyers are even more cautious in their effort to protect their clients. So, with this in mind the newspaper, through their legal advisors, asked me to take a look at the case. I was still a PI at the time.

The woman claimed she was Mrs O, a respectable married woman, who was "outraged and embarrassed" at the allegations made against her. She arrived at her solicitors looking well groomed and immaculately dressed in a new suit. Her make-up, hair and expensive jewellery suggested that she was genuine and convinced her legal team that they had a solid case in hand. Damages would be substantial.

I began an investigation on behalf of the newspaper to check her background and to establish the accuracy or otherwise of the article. Observation and surveillance is an essential part of the job. I needed to check out where she went, the people she met and what she did. We monitored her movements closely and soon a picture began to emerge. The outraged woman was not the respectable Mrs O she was claiming to be. She was, in fact, a Miss Y, a lady of the night, who plied her trade on a regular basis in the Benburb Street area, an old part of Dublin close to Heuston Station and a regular stomping ground for prostitutes. She had been living with her pimp, an unemployed and well-known criminal on Dublin's northside. For the purposes of taking the case, she had moved from their flat to a more respectable area under an assumed name – the name she used to take the case against the newspaper.

In spite of the pending court case, after a few weeks she became careless or short of money or both, and returned to her "pitch" at Benburb Street where she worked from two o'clock until seven every afternoon, returning again later in the evening, when she continued picking up punters until the early hours of the morning.

Investigations revealed that she was well known to the Gardaí and had numerous convictions for soliciting under her real name. In defence of their case, the newspaper said they were prepared to go to court to fight the case and had supporting evidence. The woman's solicitors were told their client's real identity and background, which was established beyond doubt, supported by video evidence. The woman, not surprisingly, dropped the case and moved back to her rather unhappy pimp. The clients were delighted, not alone in that it saved them a lot of money but it vindicated the professionalism of their journalist in getting their facts right in the first place.